CAMPAIGN 261

PYLOS AND SPHACTERIA 425 BC

Sparta's island of disaster

WILLIAM SHEPHERD   ILLUSTRATED BY PETER DENNIS
                             Series editor Marcus Cowper

First published in Great Britain in 2013 by Osprey Publishing,
PO Box 883, Oxford, OX1 9PL, UK
PO Box 3985, New York, NY 10185-3985, USA
E-mail: info@ospreypublishing.com

© 2013 Osprey Publishing Ltd

OSPREY PUBLISHING IS PART OF THE OSPREY GROUP.

A CIP catalogue record for this book is available from the British Library.

ISBN: 978 1 78200 271 0
E-book ISBN: 978 1 78200 272 7
E-pub ISBN: 978 1 78200 273 4

Editorial by Ilios Publishing Ltd, Oxford, UK (www.iliospublishing.com)
Index by Zoe Ross
Typeset in Myriad Pro and Sabon
Maps by Bounford.com
3D bird's-eye view by The Black Spot
Battlescene illustrations by Peter Dennis
Originated by PDQ Media, Bungay, UK
Printed in China through Worldprint Ltd.

14 15 16 17 18   10 9 8 7 6 5 4 3 2 1

AUTHOR'S NOTE

Text references are given for translated extracts from Thucydides and other
ancient sources in the normal fashion. The translations are my own. I have
also given references where my narrative paraphrases or summarises
substantial passages of Thucydides. I have used the more comfortable
latinised spellings of Greek names, in *Oxford Classical Dictionary* style.
The photographs are my own other than images whose sources are
acknowledged in the captions.
My thanks to Paul Cartledge and Jeremy Mynott for reading and
commenting on parts of the text at various stages, and to others who have
generously shared insight and expertise, especially Boris Rankov and Hans
van Wees; also to Peter Dennis for, yet again, time-travelling with me so
brilliantly, and to Marcus Cowper for his patient support.
This book is dedicated to Netta, my wife, and to my children, Chrissie, Jess,
Henry and Flo.

ARTIST'S NOTE

Readers may care to note that the original paintings from which the color
plates in this book were prepared are available for private sale. The
Publishers retain all reproduction copyright whatsoever. All enquiries
should be addressed to:

Peter Dennis, Fieldhead, The Park, Manselfield, Notts, NG18 2AT, UK
magie.h@ntlworld.com

The Publishers regret that they can enter into no correspondence upon this
matter.

THE WOODLAND TRUST
Osprey Publishing are supporting the Woodland Trust, the UK's leading
woodland conservation charity, by funding the dedication of trees.

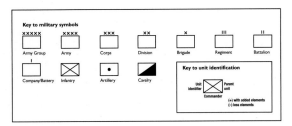

CONTENTS

Theatre of war (excluding Sicily) to 432 BC

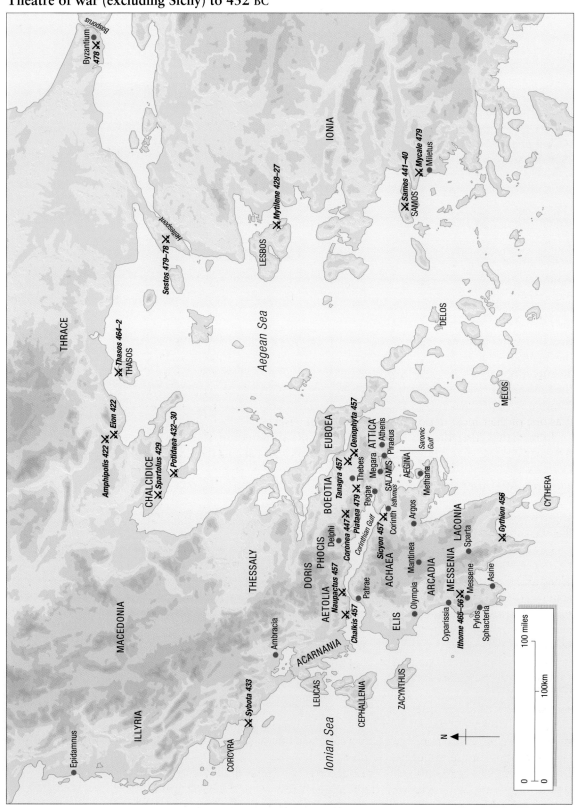

ORIGINS OF THE CAMPAIGN

479–460 BC

In 479 BC, immediately after the victories of Hellas (the ideal, never actually achieved, of a united nation of all the Greeks) over the Persians at Plataea and Mycale, the Athenians persuaded those who had fought at Mycale to bring the liberated Greeks of Ionia into the Hellenic Alliance for their long-term protection. This was against the wishes of the Spartans, who had argued that they should be repatriated from Asia. The Hellenic fleet then sailed to the Hellespont to destroy Xerxes' bridges of boats, which had actually already been dismantled in 480 BC. Considering their mission accomplished, the Peloponnesian contingent went home. However, the Athenians, led by Xanthippus, the father of Pericles, stayed on and captured Sestos, establishing it as one of their most important overseas naval bases.

Immediately after the battle of Plataea and the surrender of Thebes, the Athenians had set about rebuilding their city and its walls against the strongly expressed wishes of the Spartans, who were nervous of Athens' recently acquired strength, so powerfully demonstrated in the war against the Persians. According to Thucydides, 'the Spartans did not make any show of anger with the Athenians … but were privately angered at failing to achieve their purpose.'

In 478 BC, Pausanias, the Spartan regent who had led the Greeks to victory at Plataea, took a Hellenic fleet to Cyprus, conquered most of the island and then sailed north and took the city of Byzantium from the Persians, gaining control of the Bosporus. However, at this point, the rest of the Greeks rejected Spartan leadership on the grounds that Pausanias was now 'acting more like a tyrant than a general' (Thucydides I.95: all subsequent Thucydides references are given with book and paragraph numbers only). They placed themselves under the Athenians, who almost immediately started to raise contributions from allies to support the collective effort of defending Hellas from Persia. These funds were to be administered by Athens but held on the sacred island of Delos, and the voluntary alliance known as the Delian League had come into being. In not much more than a year the first roots were put down of the conflict that would, from 459 BC, so violently split Hellas for most of the rest of the century.

The League was successful in its purpose of protecting Hellas from Persia. By the time of its great victory on the Eurymedon River on the north shore of the eastern Mediterranean in 466 BC, it controlled the whole of the eastern

Portrait of Thucydides (c.455–395 BC) back-to-back with Herodotus (c.485–425 BC) in a Roman copy of a Greek double bust. Herodotus' account of the Persian War stands as a massive evolutionary stepping stone between the archaic oral tradition of narrative of the past and the recognizably 'modern' history-writing of Thucydides. Thucydides' superb account of the Peloponnesian War is regarded as a foundational text in Western political thought. It is also an excellent source for the military historian because Thucydides lived through this war and served Athens, at least competently, as a general in it. He deals with the Pylos campaign in the first third of Book IV of the eight books of his unfinished history, which takes the conflict to 411 BC, seven years before Sparta's final victory. Sicily 415–413 BC is the only campaign covered at greater length. Naples Museum.

Aegean and the western coastal strip of Asia. Sparta played no part in the Eurymedon campaign. A year or so later the important island of Thasos seceded and it was to take an Athenian expeditionary force two years to bring about its return to the League. The Thasians appealed to the Spartans for support, which suggests there was some expectation that it might be given.

However, that year Sparta was struck by a massive earthquake, which killed tens of thousands and flattened most of their buildings, and also by a rebellion of their Helot subjects in Messenia, their third since the Spartans conquered them in the 7th century BC. By 462 BC the Spartans had the Messenians contained in Ithome, their mountain stronghold, but were making no further progress. They had little expertise in siege warfare, most probably because they had no taste for it.

They called on the Athenians, still formally their allies, for help and they sent a large force under Cimon. He was son of Miltiades, the victor of Marathon, and had led the Greeks to victory at Eurymedon. But, in Thucydides' words, 'the first open difference between the Spartans and the Athenians came about because of this campaign'. The siege dragged on. The Spartans became increasingly nervous that the Athenians, with their more liberal attitudes, might become dangerously sympathetic with the enemy, so they told them they were no longer needed. The Athenians took offence, breaking off the alliance that had been formally in place since the Persian invasion and entered new ones with Sparta's old enemy, Argos, and with Thessaly, threatening Sparta's friends in Boeotia. Finally, they began work on the long walls that would connect the city securely with Piraeus and the sea. The roots of conflict had spread wider and deeper.

THE FIRST PELOPONNESIAN WAR 459–446 BC

In 459 BC the Athenians made a landing on the Peloponnese at Halieis. It is not known if this was intended as an act of war or if the purpose was simply to beach for the night and obtain food and water by reasonably peaceable means, but a force from Corinth confronted the Athenians and defeated them. Their ship-borne hoplites were probably outnumbered and the much larger throng of light-armed rowers and seamen who also landed would have been quite easily overwhelmed. Immediately after this the Athenian fleet defeated a Peloponnesian fleet off the island of Cecryphalia west of Aegina. These were the opening clashes in the 13 years of conflict known as the First Peloponnesian War, and immediately fitted the general strategic pattern of Peloponnesian superiority on land and Athenian superiority at sea.

Then the Athenians went to war with Aegina, an enemy in the past and historically aligned with the Peloponnese, to force the island into the Delian League. Around this time Megara voluntarily joined the League, pulling out of the Peloponnesian Alliance because of border disputes with Corinth. This city was strategically placed on the main route between the Peloponnese and Attica and Boeotia, and controlled the ports of Pegae on the Corinthian Gulf and Nisaea on the Saronic Gulf.

Greece was still at war with Persia and the Athenians had diverted a large force from operations against Persian interests in Cyprus to support a revolt against Persian rule in Egypt. Artaxerxes, the Great King, tried without success to use Persian gold to persuade the Spartans to invade Attica to make the Athenians withdraw from Egypt. The Corinthians saw the Athenians' heavy commitment on two fronts, Aegina and Egypt, as an opportunity to take Megara back. However, the Athenians mobilized their reserves, 'the old and the young' above and below campaigning age, marched the 50km into the Megarid and fought the Corinthians to a draw in a closely contested battle. Both sides claimed victory but a second battle a few days later ended decisively in the Athenians' favour.

No details of the fighting survive except for Thucydides' brief description of an incident during the Corinthian retreat. A large element lost its way and became trapped in a piece of land surrounded by a deep ditch. Athenian hoplites blocked the entrance and their light-armed troops, *psiloi*, surrounded the Corinthians and pelted them with stones 'causing them great loss' (I.106). The two battles outside Megara may have been predominantly between massed hoplites, but less conventional engagements similar to that described here were to become much more the norm.

In 457 BC Phocis invaded neighbouring Doris. Honouring ancient ties with the Dorians, the Spartans sent 11,500 hoplites, 1,500 Spartans and 10,000 allies, to their aid and ejected the Phocians. Then the Spartans received information that the Athenians were planning to block their return to the Peloponnese. They delayed in friendly Boeotia, positioning themselves to exploit the outcome of a conspiracy to overturn democracy in Athens that they knew of. The Athenians marched against them with all 14,000 of their hoplites of fighting age, 1,000 from Argos and other allied contingents.

At Tanagra the two leading powers of Hellas faced each other in battle for the first time. The Spartans and their allies won a bloody victory and returned home unopposed. The conspiracy in Athens came to nothing and, two months later, with characteristic resilience, the Athenians returned and defeated the Boeotians at Oenophyta, not far from Tanagra. This victory gave them control of Boeotia and Phocis, and at about this time, Aegina surrendered. Also, an Athenian fleet sailed round the Peloponnese and raided and burned Sparta's naval base at Gythion. It went on to capture the seaport of Chalkis, a Corinthian possession at the west end of the Corinthian Gulf, and mounted a successful attack on Sicyon, a neighbour of Corinth at the east end.

At this time, the Athenians took possession of Naupactus, a seaport that commanded the narrowest point at the west end of the Corinthian Gulf. The Messenians in Ithome had finally surrendered in 456 BC and the terms agreed allowed the defenders to go into exile outside the Peloponnese. In another act of hostility to the Spartans, the Athenians settled them in Naupactus; both the city and its new inhabitants were to prove valuable assets in the years ahead. The only bad news was the failure in 454 BC of the intervention in Egypt and the total loss of the expeditionary force.

Themistocles (*c.*524–459 BC): his leadership at Salamis and strategic vision of Athens as dominant naval power in the Aegean saved Hellas from Persia. After the war he supervised the refortification of the city and took charge of negotiations with the Spartans, playing for time until this was completed. In 478 BC the Athenians went on to fortify the port of Piraeus under his direction, 'laying the foundations of empire'. Ostia Museum, Rome.

In that year the Athenians moved the treasury of the Delian League to Athens, arguing that after this setback it would be safer from the Persians there. League members now began to be referred to officially as the cities that Athens ruled and were often treated as such. The Spartans' concern at the growth of Athens' power had been well justified. Thucydides explains why they did so little about it. 'The Spartans could see this but did not attempt to hinder it except in minor ways and remained inactive for most of the time. Historically they had been slow to go to war except when it was absolutely necessary and, in any case, they were constrained by conflict close to home.' (I.118) The disastrous effects of the great earthquake of 464 BC must also have been a significant factor.

Around 454 BC the Athenians tried unsuccessfully to extend their influence into Thessaly. They also carried out operations at the eastern end of the Corinthian Gulf, using Pegae, Megara's western port, as their base; Pericles, now a force in Athenian government and a driver of the city's expansionist policies, was in command. They won a battle against the Sicyonians and brought Achaea over to their side. However an uneasy truce was agreed between the Athenians and the Peloponnesians and hostilities were resumed with the Persian Empire in Cyprus and Egypt. These seem to have come to an end by 450 BC.

There is uncertainty as to whether a formal treaty with Persia (the so-called Peace of Callias) was actually agreed, but it was no longer easy to justify the Delian League as the defensive alliance originally formed. In 447 BC Boeotians who had been sent into exile after the Athenian victory at Oenophyta ten years before had returned and regained power in some of the cities. They defeated an Athenian force sent to remove them at Coronea and negotiated independence in exchange for the hoplites they had taken prisoner.

Then, in 446 BC Euboea rebelled against Athens. Pericles took an Athenian army over and, while there, heard that Megara had decided to realign with the Peloponnesians and that a Peloponnesian army was about to invade Attica. Somehow this crisis was defused. Thucydides deals with it in a few, matter-of-fact words: 'Pericles quickly brought the army back from Euboea. The Peloponnesians under Pleistoanax, the Spartan king, invaded Attica as far as Eleusis and Thria, destroyed the crops and advanced no further and

The heavy hoplite spear, *doru*, and shield were lethally effective in combat with the more lightly armed Asian troops, especially in Spartan hands. They were the offensive and defensive armament that continued to define the hoplite through the second half of the 5th century BC when body armour and closed helmets were no longer standard equipment. Metropolitan Museum of Art, New York.

The Hellenic Navy's *Olympias*, a full-size, fully functioning reconstruction of the elegant and agile warship used by both sides in the Peloponnesian War. *Doru* was used as a poetic term for the trireme and, as a weapon in the hands of the Greeks, especially the Athenians, it played as important a part in the victory over the Persians as the hoplite spear. Masts were unstepped for battle because the trireme was much more manoeuvrable under oar power. All sailing gear was generally left on shore to reduce weight. Photograph Hellenic Navy.

then marched home. The Athenians then went back over to Euboea under Pericles' command and subdued the whole island.' (I.114). Plutarch in his *Life of Pericles* expands on this a little:

> He did not venture to join battle with hoplites who were so many, so brave, and so eager to fight. But, he saw that Pleistoanax was very young, and that out of all his advisers he depended most on Cleandridas, whom the *ephors* [senior elected magistrates] had sent along to be a guardian and an assistant to him because of his youth. He secretly tested this man's integrity, speedily corrupting him with bribes, and persuaded him to lead the Peloponnesians back out of Attica. (Plutarch *Pericles* 22)

Avoidance of a full hoplite confrontation with the Spartans and their allies was actually a major strategic priority for Pericles, because he knew the Athenians and their allies would be the losers. However, the terms of the peace treaty that was then agreed to run for 30 years suggest that no individual needed bribing. The Athenians were to give up all the places they held in the Peloponnese, and also Nisaea and Pegae in the Megarid. So, without striking a blow, the Peloponnese had been secured. But, on the other hand, the treaty placed no restriction on Athenian activities throughout the rest of the Greek world. In 447 BC work began on the construction of the Parthenon and the rest of the great public building programme which continued through the 430s BC. This was financed by what could now only be described as imperial tribute from many cities and states that had formerly been allies in the Delian League.

445–432 BC

The rest of the decade was peaceful, and during this time Athens grew in power and wealth. However, in 440 BC Samos went to war with Miletus and the Athenians intervened at Miletus' request. They imposed democracy on Samos as part of their resolution of the conflict, but after they had returned home, Samian exiles, with Persian support, overturned the new government and declared independence. Athens reacted quickly and laid siege to Samos: after nine months, the Samians surrendered. At about the same time Byzantium rebelled but was not allowed independence for long. Three years later, in another demonstration of imperial power and ambition, Athens colonised the strategically and economically important Thracian city of Amphipolis.

In 435 BC Corcyra, a significant naval power and an important staging post for trade with Italy, Sicily and the west coast of northern Greece, went to war with Corinth over the seaport city of Epidamnus, a colony on the coast of Illyria which historically they shared. Corcyra won a decisive victory over the Corinthian fleet but, after a year of intensive shipbuilding, the Corinthians

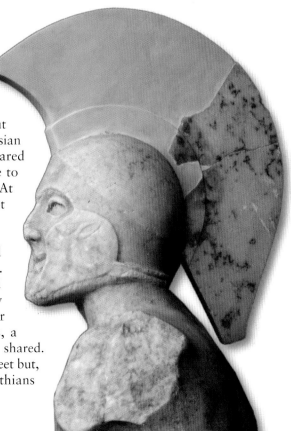

Sometimes labelled as a portrait of Leonidas, this imposing hero-figure was probably part of a group decorating a temple pediment. It was sculpted earlier in the 5th century BC than the battle of Thermopylae and at a time when portraits were not made of living individuals. However the serene and unflinchingly resolute expression is an excellent reflection of the unique Spartan military spirit. Sparta Museum.

Athena, the complex patron goddess of Athens, equally and appropriately associated with military prowess and the more civilized qualities of craft skill and wisdom. This statuette is a miniature, 3rd-century copy in marble of the massive figure made by Phidias and erected in the Parthenon on its completion and dedication in 438 BC. It was faced with ivory and gold; the gold was stripped off in the 420s BC to help fund the Athenian war effort. National Archaeological Museum, Athens.

launched a new campaign. Corcyra, not aligned with either Athens or Sparta, now needed support and persuaded Athens to agree to an alliance. It was to be a defensive alliance out of public respect for the Thirty Years Peace.

But by now fresh conflict seemed inevitable and it made sense to keep the substantial Corcyrean navy out of the hands of the Peloponnesians. Ten Athenian triremes joined a 110-strong Corcyrean fleet facing 149 Corinthians and allies between Sybota on the mainland and the southern tip of Corcyra. At first they stood off, but when the Corinthians began to get the upper hand, they became fully involved. Their intervention did not prevent the Corinthians routing the Corcyreans, inflicting heavy losses and driving them back to shore. But the Corinthians then withdrew in the face of Athenian reinforcements and were unable to exploit their crushing victory.

This was the first clear breach of the treaty between the Athenians and the Peloponnesians, but war was not yet formally declared. Then in 432 BC, Potidaea, a commercially and strategically important seaport in Chalcidice, broke away from Athenian rule, provoked by an increase in tribute and by measures to cut off their historic links with Corinth. This threatened to destabilize the whole region. Both Athens and Corinth sent fleets and strong hoplite forces and, after winning a battle nearby, the Athenians laid siege to the city. In the diplomatic exchanges that followed Sparta demanded that the siege of Potidaea be abandoned. Closer to home, they stipulated that Aegina be granted independence and that crippling trade sanctions, recently imposed by Athens on Megara, be removed. A final embassy delivered a laconic, overarching message. 'The Spartans want peace to continue. It will if you grant the Hellenes independence.' (I.139) In the Athenian Assembly Pericles spoke powerfully and decisively in favour of rejecting all Sparta's demands, arguing that war was both necessary and inevitable, and that Athens' naval expertise and power, financial and manpower resources, and extensive possessions would guarantee ultimate victory. His only concession was that Athens would not start the fighting.

THE ARCHIDAMIAN WAR TO 426 BC

Early in the summer of 431 BC, Thebes, Sparta's most powerful Boeotian ally, attempted a surprise attack on their neighbour Plataea, a staunch ally of Athens in the Persian War. Although more parochial an affair than Sybota and Potidaea, it finally triggered open preparations for war between the two power blocs. Athens sent a small force to strengthen the garrison and assisted in the evacuation of non-combatants in preparation for the siege that was to follow, which lasted for four years.

Archidamus, the Spartan king after whom this decade of war is named, led a massive Peloponnesian army into Attica and the population took shelter behind the walls of Athens. The corn was now ripe and Archidamus' troops lived off the land and wrecked the crops in time-honoured fashion. The invasion was intended to provoke a full-scale battle to bring the war to a quick and decisive end. However, the Athenians could bring in ample food supplies by sea and their direct response was limited to cavalry sorties. These served to contain the invading force to some extent, and supported morale inside the walls by protecting the land closest to them.

At the same time a large fleet of more than 150 triremes was sent to cruise round the Peloponnese. It raided a number of coastal strongholds and settlements, including Methone in the south-west, and had an uncomfortable encounter with Brasidas, one of the war's most capable commanders, making his first appearance in Thucydides' history (II.25). Sailing up to the north-west coast the fleet linked up with Messenians from Naupactus to occupy Pheia for a period. Later in the summer they carried out successful operations against Corinthian interests in Acarnania and also brought the island of Cephallenia into the empire.

Soon after this fleet had sailed, Archidamus, with provisions now in short supply, marched his army home across the Isthmus taking it north and west through Boeotia before turning south. This was not to keep it out of reach of the Athenians but because Attica and the plain of Eleusis had already been stripped of food.

A smaller Athenian fleet was sent to patrol the west coast of Euboea and attack places in Opuntian Locris, Boeotia's coastal neighbour. It also established a fortified outpost on the island of Atalanta to police these waters and serve as a base for harassing operations on the mainland.

Additional naval force was used to neutralize Aegina as a threat in the centre of the Saronic Gulf. Its entire population was uprooted and replaced with colonists from Athens. The refugees were given asylum by Sparta and most of them settled in Thyrea on the east coast of the Peloponnese, which the Athenians took and burned eight years later. Finally, towards the end of the summer, Pericles led a large force into the Megarid. This was to become almost an annual event, like the Spartan invasions of Attica.

The first year of the war had gone well for Athens. It is unlikely that the invading army had done any lasting damage to the relatively small area of Attica's extensive farmland it had laid waste, and Archidamus had little to show for his massive expenditure of resources. Any shortfall in food supplies in Athens had been easily covered from overseas and the Athenian fleet had carried out its missions without any naval opposition and with considerable success in enemy territory.

Archidamus invaded Attica again in the early summer of 430 BC and achieved little more than in 431 BC. This was to be the longest of the five

LEFT
The Parthenon on the Athenian Acropolis, showing the progress of the ongoing restoration in May 2010. The original building was begun in 447 BC and replaced the slightly less grand temple begun after Marathon but unfinished when the invading Persians destroyed it in 480 BC. It powerfully symbolizes the 5th-century flowering of Athenian culture and also the imperial power of the Periclean state. Like the other great public works of this period it was funded by tribute money.

RIGHT
In contrast with Athens, the city of Sparta was an unwalled cluster of large villages in the valley of the river Eurotas, sheltered by the massive Taygetus mountain range. Modern Sparta, seen from the late Byzantine city of Mystras, covers much of the same area as the ancient city.

occupations, lasting about 40 days and penetrating furthest, as far as Laurium; strangely there is no record of any damage done to Athens' silver mines in this area, which would have had much more impact than the destruction of a year's harvest in the surrounding fields, vineyards and orchards. However, plague, possibly a virulent mutation of typhus or typhoid, broke out within the walls. This first epidemic was to last for the best part of two years and would kill a far greater number of Athenians, Pericles amongst them, than enemy action.

The Athenians' tactical response at home was the same as in 431 BC. Overseas operations were less extensive, limited to Chalcidice and the continuation of the siege of Potidaea, now in its third year of resistance and finally starved into surrender that winter. The Spartans attempted to take the island of Zacynthus without success. According to Thucydides, and not surprisingly, 'with their land laid waste a second time and plague and war weighing heavily on them, the Athenian people's mood had changed. They blamed Pericles for making them go to war and for the misfortune they were now suffering, and were eager to agree terms with the Spartans. They even sent an embassy but it achieved nothing.' (II.59) Pericles successfully persuaded the people to continue on the course he had set, reminding them above all of their invincible sea power. They made him pay a heavy fine 'but soon afterwards, as is the way with the mass of the people, they elected him general again and placed their trust in him completely' (II.65). When he took office again in the summer of 429 BC, Pericles was already sick with the plague.

Pericles (c.495–429 BC), a 2nd-century AD Roman copy of a Greek original, which was probably made in the 420s BC. However, unlike the Ostia bust of Themistocles, this is not thought to have been a life portrait but an idealized image of the supreme citizen. British Museum.

That year Archidamus did not invade Attica but took his army to Plataea. His main purpose was to bind Thebes into the Peloponnesian alliance, but he may also have hoped to provoke the Athenians into confronting him there. The Athenians did not react, clearly feeling they had fully met their obligations to their faithful ally. Although Potidaea had been secured, Chalcidice was still out of control. A force of 2,000 hoplites, 200 cavalry and supporting *psiloi* were sent out to subdue it and were badly mauled at Spartolus. Although the Athenians won the initial hoplite engagement, they were then overwhelmed by superior non-hoplite numbers, including peltasts. First they routed the Athenian light-armed troops and cavalry, then 'whenever the Athenians charged, they fell back and, when the Athenians withdrew, they closed with them and threw javelins at them' (II.79). The Chalcidian cavalry completed the rout.

Spartan hoplites had a similar encounter with missile troops in the same year, in an unsuccessful invasion of Acarnania. The Peloponnesians wanted to control this area, not least because the beaches and harbours could serve the Athenians as bases from which to mount attacks on the northern and western shores of the Peloponnese. Advancing on the city of Stratus the Spartan hoplites were pinned down and forced to withdraw. 'The Stratians did not engage with them at close quarters … but shot at them with slings from a distance and made things very difficult for them because they could not make a move without the protection of armour' (II.81).

Support for the Spartans in Acarnania had been on the way. A fleet of 47 triremes and some smaller ships was sailing west along the Corinthian Gulf with 1,500–2,000 hoplites on board, but was intercepted by a squadron of 20 Athenian triremes out of Naupactus. Phormio, the general in command, launched his attack in the more open water of the Gulf of Patrae to exploit to the full the 'better sailing' qualities of his ships (better construction, speed and manoeuvrability, better steersmen and crews, better rowers); the Peloponnesian triremes were at even more of a disadvantage because they were being used as troop-carriers. Phormio literally ran rings around them and captured or disabled at least 12. (II.83–4) The Spartans put this defeat down to incompetent leadership rather than their fleet's general lack of battle experience and inferior quality, and sent three senior commanders, one of them Brasidas, to oversee operations.

Both sides anticipated further action and called up reinforcements. Twenty triremes were immediately sent from Athens, but were unhelpfully given a mission to carry out in Crete first and arrived too late. The Peloponnesian fleet, reinforced and now better drilled in battle-manoeuvres, sailed from its temporary base in Cyllene on the west coast of the Peloponnese to Panormus on the south side of the Gulf to link up with the Peloponnesian land force that had arrived to support it. Phormio was now facing 77 enemy ships and the Gulf was about a kilometre across across at this point. He was unwilling to give battle in this tight space, whilst the Peloponnesians would not risk another engagement in more open water.

After a week of inaction the Peloponnesians moved eastward along their side of the Gulf in column of four to threaten Naupactus. Phormio took his ships along the northern shore in single file with his own hoplite support, Messenians from Naupactus, keeping pace with them on land. When both sides had covered about 4,000m, the Peloponnesians suddenly swung from column into line and bore down on the Athenians in an attempt to cut off the whole squadron. It is tempting to give Brasidas the credit for this well-rehearsed tactical move and it was initially half-successful, trapping nine ships against the shore.

However, some of these were recaptured by Messenians dashing into the sea and boarding them. Ten of the 11 that got away reached Naupactus well ahead of their pursuers and formed up in close order to defend the harbour. A Leucadian ship that had pulled ahead of the rest of the Peloponnesians was gaining on the 11th. But the Athenian trireme made a tight turn around an anchored merchant ship and rammed the Leucadian from the side, putting it out of action. The Peloponnesians following were so shocked by this that they dug in their oars and came to a halt. Not knowing the area, some ran onto shoals and the remainder drifted out of formation and within easy striking distance of the Athenians. The 11 Athenians immediately darted out and drove them off, capturing six and recovering the ships they had lost initially.

This was an extraordinary victory for the outnumbered Athenians and a humiliating defeat for the Peloponnesians; Thucydides records that one of the three Spartans sent out to get a grip on the campaign happened to be on the unfortunate Leucadian trireme and killed himself for shame. With the summer coming to an end, the elements of the Peloponnesian fleet that had been supplied by Corinth, Megara and Sicyon sailed back to the eastern end of the Gulf and the rest dispersed.

The commanders of the Peloponnesian fleet decided to launch an attack on Piraeus; Brasidas may have been influential in the planning of this operation, which, in conception at least, stood out from the Spartans' rather pedestrian conduct of the war to date. They were encouraged to do this by the Megarians, who offered them the use of 40 ships from their eastern seaport, Nisaea. 8,000–9,000 men, including 6,800 rowers, walked across the Isthmus and launched this fleet under cover of darkness. Losing their nerve, or held back by adverse weather conditions (the two explanations Thucydides offers), they only made the short crossing to the west end of the island of Salamis. They captured three triremes and the small fort there and went on to plunder and lay waste most of the island. This caused great panic in Athens and Piraeus.

The Athenians immediately mobilized to defend the port and prepared ships to cross to Salamis at dawn. The Peloponnesians rapidly withdrew with their plunder and prisoners. Thucydides thought they could easily have mounted an attack on Piraeus 'if they had had the will and had not shied away from it; a bit of wind would not have stopped them' (II.94). However, he reveals a little later that the Megarian ships had been out of the water for a long time and so were leaky. Even if they had managed the longer crossing to Piraeus, they would have been slowed up by the water taken in and no match for the Athenians.

During the winter Phormio took some of his fleet to Acarnania and marched inland with 800 hoplites to reinforce support for Athens. Pericles died of plague that September. The strategy which he had set and held to, while successful in defensive terms, had shown no sign of persuading the Spartans to abandon the war inside the anticipated maximum of four years, and the exceptional financial resources which had made the strategy possible were now dangerously depleted. No alternative strategy had emerged.

In 428 BC, 'just as the corn was ripening', Archidamus led his Peloponnesian army into Attica for the third time and the Athenians stayed behind their walls as before, avoiding a full hoplite confrontation. 'Their cavalry, as usual, mounted attacks whenever they could and prevented the mass of *psiloi* leaving the protection of the hoplites to lay waste the land close to the city, following the established pattern. The Peloponnesians stayed as long as their provisions allowed, then withdrew and dispersed to their cities.' (III.1) There were operations again in the north-eastern Aegean and on the west coast of central Greece, and Plataea continued to hold out.

In spite of the continuing plague epidemic the Athenians were planning to send 40 triremes on the customary retaliatory cruise round the Peloponnese. Instead they sent them to blockade and lay siege to Mytilene, the leading city on Lesbos, to prevent this important source of revenue and naval assets going over to the Peloponnesians. A smaller fleet of 30 ships was sent round the Peloponnese to raid Laconia and afterwards to sail north and attack Peloponnesian allies on the southern borders of Acarnania. Failing to capture Oeniadae, its main objective in Acarnania, the fleet sailed on and made a landing on the island of Leucas; this operation ended in defeat.

The Spartans, reckoning that Athens was now dangerously overstretched, decided to attack Attica and Athens again, this time by sea as well as by land. They summoned their allies to assemble at the Isthmus in force. 'The Spartans arrived first and prepared to drag their ships on rollers over from Corinth to the shore on the Athens side so that they could attack simultaneously by land and sea. They set about this energetically, but their allies were slow to muster because they it was harvest time and they were weary of campaigning.' (III.15)

The Athenians countered by manning 100 ships, drawing on the entire citizen body, only excluding the very rich, and also on the resident-alien section of the population, and sending them to cruise down the Isthmus and raid the north-eastern shores of the Peloponnese. This unexpected show of strength and the non-appearance of their allies left the Spartans with no option but to withdraw. The Athenians were then able to send reinforcements to Lesbos under the command of the general Paches but, exceptionally, each of the 1,000 hoplites had to take an oar in the ships they sailed in. Thucydides notes that Athens, with her naval strength at its peak, had 250 triremes, their complements totalling around 50,000, on active service that summer; he also comments on the unsustainable level of expenditure that this and the Lesbos expedition entailed. Despite all the activity, there still seemed to be no prospect of either side bringing the war to a conclusion.

During the winter, with food running low and no prospect of relief, half the tiny garrison of Plataea made a daring escape over the encircling wall. So the war continued into 427 BC. Once again the Spartans invaded Attica, doing more damage to the countryside than in any year except 430 BC, but as usual they failed to provoke the Athenians into marching out against them and withdrew when their supplies ran out. The Spartans also sent a fleet of 42 ships to support the Mytileneans but its ineffectual commander, Alcidas, took the crossing of the Aegean very slowly and was only halfway there when he received news that the city had fallen. He continued east to the coast of Ionia where he could have seriously threatened Athenian interests, but took no action and was soon chased back west by Paches.

The Greek word for a light-armed soldier was *psilos*, literally 'bare' or 'naked'. This one is using a cloak as a shield and his weapon is a cudgel. Athenians from the lowest citizen class and non-citizens served as troops of this kind, as well as serving as rowers in the fleet. They took on both roles in the Athenian navy's frequent raiding missions around the coast of the Peloponnese. British Museum.

On this gravestone two Athenians bid each other farewell in the presence of a priest. The heavy shield and spear (the top and bottom of that carried by the middle figure would have been painted on) define them as hoplites. The open *pilos*-style helmet had generally superseded the classic Corinthian helmet decades before, and body armour and other more closed styles of helmet were much less frequently worn. Antikensammlung, Berlin.

The Athenian Assembly famously and just in time reversed its decision to execute the entire adult male population of Mytilene, a reprisal forcefully advocated by the popular leader, Cleon. However, over 1,000 prisoners from the anti-democratic faction judged to be most responsible for the rebellion were killed. When Plataea finally gave in to starvation and surrendered, the Spartans had the surviving 200 Plataean and 25 Athenian defenders executed after a show trial. The war had grown more vicious.

Next, Athens and Sparta became involved on opposite sides in civil war in Corcyra. A small Athenian fleet, 12 ships carrying 500 Messenian hoplites from Naupactus arrived first to support the governing democrats against the oligarchic faction that had attempted to take over. The situation was contained but a few days later the Peloponnesian fleet arrived. It had been stationed in Cyllene since the Ionian fiasco. Alcidas was still in command (strangely, the Spartans were much more forgiving of failure than the Athenians) but Brasidas was also on board in the same advisory and supervisory capacity as in the Gulf of Corinth the previous summer.

The Corcyreans hastily launched 60 ships and sent them out piecemeal to face the Peloponnesians, ignoring Athenian offers to take the lead. The Peloponnesians left 20 of their ships to face the Corcyreans' shambolic attack and the remaining 33 bore down on the 12 Athenians. The Athenians not only avoided envelopment but also attacked one wing of the enemy formation. With one ship rammed and disabled the Peloponnesians lost their nerve and formed a defensive circle. The Athenians adopted the same tactic as off Naupactus the previous year and circled around them threateningly, with the aim of disrupting their formation. The rest of the Peloponnesians, perhaps led by Brasidas, saw the danger and broke away from the Corcyreans to take on the Athenians.

Acknowledging that odds greater than four-to-one were too much, even for 12 of the finest warships and crews in the world (including Athens' very best, the state triremes *Salaminia* and *Paralus*), the Athenians decided on a tactical withdrawal. Thucydides, who had commanded triremes during his time as a general, concludes his account of the battle, 'They backed off with their prows always pointing at the enemy, going at a leisurely pace to ensure that the Corcyreans could pull clear while the Peloponnesians were formed up to face them' (III.78). The Athenian squadron suffered no loss but the Peloponnesians were able to tow away 13 Corcyrean ships. The city was in a state of panic after this defeat.

Brasidas tried to persuade Alcidas to exploit the situation but all he did was order a landing on the opposite end of the island to lay waste some farmland. Then the Peloponnesians learned by beacon signals of the approach of a larger Athenian fleet. Earlier the Athenians had managed to prevent the democrats massacring their oligarch enemies but now they could no longer restrain them, or they simply stood back and let it happen because, of course, the elimination of local opposition was in their interest. Late that summer, for the first time Athens committed troops and ships to a campaign in Sicily, supporting Leontini in its conflict with Syracuse, but with the longer-term objectives of denying the Peloponnese Sicilian corn and bringing the whole island into the empire. This was the first move towards a more aggressive and proactive war plan.

426 BC

Over the winter, plague flared up again in Athens. The population of Athens and Attica in 431 BC has been estimated to total 300,000, and a quarter to a third may have died of the disease. In 426 BC the region was also hit by earthquakes, and because of this, the Peloponnesian force assembled for the annual invasion turned back at the Isthmus. The Spartans attempted one strategic initiative, planting a colony at Heraclea near Thermopylae. Their aim was to establish a secure staging post on the land route to Thrace and a base from which to raid Euboea. This was unsuccessful, due in part to Thessalian resistance to a potentially powerful new presence in the region, in part to Spartan mismanagement.

The Athenians had some successes through the year in Sicily and one defeat at the hands of the Syracusans. An expedition under the command of Nicias made an unsuccessful attempt on the island of Melos, which was neutral but with Spartan sympathies. However, before returning home Nicias sailed north, linking up with a force that marched from Athens to Tanagra in Boeotia, and won a local battle there, avoiding facing the Thebans in full force.

Maintaining strategic focus on the north-western theatre, Demosthenes, one of the ten generals for the year 427/6 BC, was given command of 30 ships to campaign against Sparta's allies along the west coast north of the Corinthian Gulf. Gathering reinforcements from Athenian allies in the region, he initially attacked the island of Leucas, advancing on the main city with enthusiastic support from the Acarnanians, the Leucadians' mainland enemies. However, the Messenians that had joined him from Naupactus persuaded Demosthenes to put the forces now at his disposal to better strategic use by invading their enemy, Aetolia. They assured him that the scattered, backward Aetolian tribes lived in 'unwalled villages' (so did the Spartans!) and could be easily defeated. Though tough and warlike, 'they used light weapons' and were disunited. By subduing the Aetolians, he would remove a constant threat hanging over Naupactus and secure new alliances in this part of north-west Greece.

Demosthenes was particularly attracted by the prospect of then being in a position to attack Sparta's powerful Boeotian allies from the west. He therefore abandoned operations on Leucas and, ignoring the objections of the Acarnanians, moved on to the port of Oeneon on the western borders of Aetolia. The several hundred hoplites and approximately 120 archers from his ships and a body of Messenian hoplites formed the nucleus of his force:

Peloponnese, Attica, Boeotia and Corinthian Gulf, 431–427 BC

MELOS ✗ 426

EUBOEA

Chalcis

Heraclea

✗ Delium 424

Decelea 413 ✗

ATTICA

✗ 431–425

Laurium

Athens

Piraeus

Eleusis

AEGINA ✗ 431

Saronic Gulf

Aegean Sea

Atalanta 431 ✗

OPUNTIAN LOCRIS

BOEOTIA

Thebes

Plataea 431–27 ✗

Megara 431 ✗

Nisaea 431 ✗

429 ✗

SALAMIS

Methana

Troizen 430 ✗

Hermione 430 ✗

DORIS

PHOCIS

Delphi

Pegae

Isthmus

Corinth

Epidaurus 430 ✗

Halieis 30 ✗

Corinthian Gulf

Solygia 425 ✗

CYTHERA

Aegitium 426 ✗

AETOLIA

OZOLIAN LOCRIS

Oeneon

Naupactus

Panormus

429 ✗

Patrae

429 ✗

Chalkis

Argos

Thyrea 424 ✗

Prasiae 430 ✗

LACONIA

Mantinea 418 ✗

ARCADIA

Sparta

Taygetus Mt

Gythion

✗ Stratus 429

ACARNANIA

Oeniadae

ELIS

Olympia

Cyparissia

Aegaleon Mt

Messene

MESSENIA

Asine

Pylos

Sphacteria

Methone 431 ✗

Cyllene

Pheia 431 ✗

CEPHALLENIA

ZACYNTHUS

N

25 miles

25 km

0

0

the Acarnanians refused to be part of it. The Locrians were to follow and link up with him in Aetolia, bringing 'knowledge of the country and local ways of fighting'. The operation went well for the first three days with the easy capture of three towns. However, the Aetolian tribes, against expectations, were now beginning to unite to oppose him in force.

Encouraged by his initial success and urged on by the Messenians, Demosthenes pressed on towards a fourth centre of population, Aegitium, without waiting for the Locrians to join him and remedy his dangerous lack of light missile troops. If, as is likely, his force also included rowers and other crew from his ship as *psiloi*, they were not the specialists he needed. Aegitium was easily taken. Then the large army that had now been assembled from the various tribes attacked, charging down on Demosthenes' force from all sides and showering it with javelins and other missiles. The Aetolains fell back whenever the Athenians counterattacked and came on again when they fell back. The Athenians were soon struggling, but managed to hold out until the archers ran out of arrows. Before long the now exhausted hoplites and any light-armed support that was left broke and ran. Their Messenian guide had been killed so many became lost and separated in the forest paths and dried-up stream beds, and were hunted down by the more mobile Aetolians with their javelins.

To add to this nightmare, some of Demosthenes' men became trapped in dense forest, which the enemy then set on fire. The casualties included the exceptionally heavy loss of up to 40 per cent of the Athenian hoplite contingent, Demosthenes' fellow general and many of the allied troops. Demosthenes and the other survivors retreated with difficulty to the coast. He sent his ships back to Athens but stayed behind himself, fearful of his fellow-citizens' reaction and the real prospect of exile or even worse. (III.94–98)

Athenian cavalry played an important role harassing the invading Spartan armies and supporting morale inside the city walls by protecting countryside nearby. The Spartans were slow to realize that cavalry might be of use protecting their coastline from Athenian raiders. This relief is from a public memorial to the Athenian war-dead in the early 4th century BC. Cavalry was ineffective against hoplites in close formation but lethal if this was broken. National Archaeological Museum, Athens.

Within a few weeks of their victory at Aegitium, the Aetolians persuaded the Spartans to support a counterattack on Naupactus, sending 3,000 allied hoplites under the command of a Spartiate, Eurylochus. However, he did not go directly for Naupactus, which was weakly defended and this gave Demosthenes time to make his peace with the Acarnanians and raise a force of 1,000 hoplites to reinforce the Messenian garrison. This was enough to persuade Eurylochus that the city could not be taken and, with winter coming on, he turned his attention to the north-west where the Ambraciots had invited him to attack Athens' allies, including Amphilochia and Acarnania, from the north. The opposing armies faced each other near Olpae. Demosthenes joined his allies with 200 Messenian hoplites and 60 Athenian archers, the latter possibly from a squadron of 20 triremes that had arrived in the Gulf of Ambracia. Demosthenes was voted commander of this quite significantly outnumbered force.

The Athenian corps of archers, an asset unmatched by any other Greek city, was made up of mercenaries from Crete and Scythia, and some citizens, resident aliens and, probably, slaves. They served in both navy and army and also as police. As here, they were usually depicted in exotic Asian dress and were looked down upon as an inferior kind of warrior by the hoplite elite, especially the Spartans. British Museum.

After five days of inaction the two sides formed up in phalanxes in the conventional way to give battle. Demosthenes made it easy for Eurylochus to outflank his right, which he personally commanded, comprising his Messenian contingent and a few Athenian hoplites. However, he had concealed a 400-strong mixed force of hoplites and *psiloi* along an overgrown sunken road that ran roughly parallel to the battle lines and behind Eurylochus' position. When the two phalanxes came together and the Athenians and Messenians were about to be enveloped, the ambush force charged into Eurylochus' left from behind and routed it. His centre then also collapsed. His right, made up of Ambraciots, was initially more successful and put Demosthenes' left to flight but was then demolished by the Acarnanians from his centre. Demosthenes then learned that a larger Ambraciot force approaching, unaware that the battle had been fought. He dealt with this decisively by making a night march and attacking at dawn 'when they were still in their beds'. Any Ambraciots that got away were mopped up easily by the Amphilochians, positioned to cover all escape routes and 'well acquainted with their own country and *psiloi* fighting against hoplites'. (III.100–112)

Demosthenes could return to Athens with his reputation repaired and enhanced, and having acquired battle-experience that would be critical to success in his next campaign.

The already lengthy and global conflict, in terms of the Greek world, between the Athenians and the Spartans had brought warfare a long way from the simple model of the conventional hoplite confrontation 'on the clearest and most level piece of ground' (Herodotus VII.9), as ridiculed by Mardonius when arguing the case for the Persian invasion of Greece in 480 BC.

CHRONOLOGY

(All dates BC)

479	Battle of Plataea: Persians driven out of Greece.
	Walls of Athens rebuilt.
478	Piraeus fortified.
478–77	Hellenic Alliance formed under Athenian leadership.
466	Battle of Eurymedon River.
464	Earthquake at Sparta; Messenian War begins.
462	Athenian assistance at Ithome rejected by Sparta.
	Athens breaks off historic alliance with Sparta.
461	Long Walls joining Athens and Piraeus begun.

First Peloponnesian War 457–446

457	Battles of Tanagra and Oinophyta.
456	Messenian War ends.
c.455	Thucydides born.
454	Delian League treasury moved from Delos to Athens.

451	Five-year truce between Athens and Sparta.
c.450	Treaty between Athens and Persia, Peace of Callias.
447	Parthenon begun.
446	Treaty between Athens and Sparta, Thirty Years Peace.
438	Parthenon completed and dedicated.
435	War between Corcyra and Corinth begins.
433	Alliance between Athens and Corcyra.
	Battle of Sybota.

Archidamian War 431–421

431	Spring: Thebans attack Plataea.
	Spartans invade Attica.
	Summer: Athenian fleet raids Peloponnese.
	Athenians attack Megara.
430	Spring: Spartans invade Attica.
	Plague in Athens, epidemic for two years.

429	Summer: Athenian operations in Chalcidice; Spartolus.	426	Summer: Athenian victories in Sicily.
	Spartan operations in Acarnania.		Battle of Aegitium.
	Athenian naval victories off Patrae and Naupactus.		Winter: Athenian operations in Sicily; defeat and victory.
	Death of Pericles.		Battle of Olpae.
	Winter: Spartans raid Salamis.	425	Spring: Spartans invade Attica.
428	Spring: Spartans invade Attica.		Peloponnesian fleet sent to Corcyra.
	Summer: Athenians raid Laconian coast.		Athenian expedition to Corcyra and Sicily.
427	Spring: Spartans invade Attica.		Summer: **Pylos and Sphacteria.**
	Summer: Plataea surrenders.	424	Summer: Athenians occupy Cythera.
	Civil war in Corcyra; Athenian and Peloponnesian intervention.		Winter: Battle of Delium.
	First Athenian expedition to Sicily.	423	One-year truce.
	Winter: Plague in Athens, epidemic for one year.	422	Athenians defeated at Amphipolis.
		421	Peace of Nicias.
		418	Battle of Mantinea.
		417–15	Athenian disaster in Sicily.

OPPOSING COMMANDERS

ATHENIAN COMMANDERS

Demosthenes is generally considered to have been one of the best Athenian generals to serve in the Archidamian War. He was the architect in every sense of the Athenian occupation of Pylos and in command there for the entire summer. For the last few days, he nominally shared command with the politician Cleon.

Demosthenes' first recorded campaign, in Aetolia the previous year, had ended in disaster. It is likely that he already had some experience as a commander and had acquired a good reputation. It seems he was appointed general on merit, because there is no indication that he had any affiliation to help him follow the political route to this important public office. However, what he specifically experienced on campaign in 426–425 BC, in defeat and in victory, undoubtedly shaped the tactical thinking that led to his triumph in the late summer of 425 BC. Thucydides' account of Demosthenes' campaigning in 426 BC builds a portrait of an accomplished tactician and strategist with strong leadership qualities that he could exercise as effectively over allies as over fellow-Athenians. He overreached himself in Aetolia but the fault may not have been entirely his. His good friends the Messenians gave him poor intelligence and the Locrians may simply have let him down.

In any case he redeemed himself spectacularly at Olpae months later. In 424 BC Demosthenes, as one of the two generals in command of an attempt to bring Megara back to the Athenian side, led a force of light-armed troops in a successful surprise attack on its eastern seaport, Nisaea. Megara was not taken because of the intervention of Brasidas, but Nisaea was held for the next 15 years. Demosthenes then led a thrust from the west in an ambitious pincer operation against Boeotia but his part of the plan ended in failure and the bloody Athenian defeat at Delium that winter was a consequence. Thucydides names Demosthenes as one of the 17 who 'took the oath for the Athenians' in 422–421 BC, in the treaty that ended the Archidamian War, but otherwise does not mention him again until he was sent as a general with Eurymedon on the doomed mission to reinforce Nicias in Sicily in 414 BC.

Eurymedon and **Sophocles** were the two generals in command of the fleet that took Demosthenes to Pylos. Eurymedon had commanded a larger fleet in 427 BC, sent to Corcyra to support the democratic faction in the vicious civil war that finally aligned the island with Athens. He was probably a veteran of previous campaigns, with experience of senior command, and his name, after the great victory over the Persians in 466 BC, suggests a family tradition of distinguished military service. He was in joint command of the army that marched from Athens to link up with Nicias' seaborne force in eastern Boeotia in 426 BC.

In 425 BC Eurymedon and Sophocles failed to intercept the Peloponnesian fleet, leaving Demosthenes with his small garrison and handful of ships at Pylos with no naval protection for a couple of days. But they soon remedied that lapse, comprehensively demonstrating the superiority of Athenian seamanship. At the end of the Pylos campaign Eurymedon and Sophocles resumed their mission and finally reached Corcyra. Reinforcing the Corcyrean democrats, they attacked and defeated the oligarchic insurgents in their mountain stronghold. They stood back (a second time for Eurymedon) as the prisoners, who were supposed to be under their protection to be shipped to Athens for trial, were horribly massacred.

Then they took the fleet on to Sicily and wintered there. The following year the warring Sicilians made peace so they returned to Athens. They were charged with taking bribes to abandon Sicily rather than attempt to establish a foothold there as ordered, which would probably have been impossible without an alliance with one of the major Sicilian powers. Sophocles was exiled (the fate Thucydides was to suffer) and Eurymedon was heavily fined. Eurymedon died in battle in the Grand Harbour of Syracuse shortly before Demosthenes and Nicias were executed after the Athenian surrender.

Nicias was a competent but cautious general, regularly one of the board of ten, and a leading politician from the wealthy, propertied class. He was opposed to the aggressive imperialism and radical politics of Cleon and his lower-class faction, and his goal was to bring about peace with Sparta as soon as possible on reasonable terms. Thucydides mourns his death in Sicily in 413 BC as the cruel and undeserved fate of a man 'whose whole life had been governed by virtue (*arete*)' (VII.86.5), words that identify him as a paragon of the old-fashioned values that, in Thucydides' view, Cleon did not reflect.

The historian introduces **Cleon** as the 'the most aggressive of all the citizens' (III.36) and later describes him as 'a popular leader (*demagogos*) with great influence over the mass of the people' (IV.21). He was a powerful orator and the first of a new breed of politicians who pursued their agendas in the Assembly and the law courts rather than through service in positions of responsibility. He became a general in 425 BC by accident. Much of the credit for the Athenians' success in the Pylos and Sphacteria campaign belonged to

This Athenian red-figure pottery cup, dated to 420 BC, is unusual for the period because from 450 BC onwards painters seem to have depicted scenes of combat very rarely. On the rim, the style is anachronistically heroic with the hoplites nude and fighting over a fallen comrade. The double-grip system that made the heavy hoplite shield manageable is clearly shown. The helmets are of a form that lies between the closed Corinthian type and the *pilos* that was most commonly worn in the second half of the 5th century BC. British Museum. (British Museum)

Demosthenes, but it was Cleon who secured the Assembly's support in principle for action to end the stalemate, and their authorization to take the specialist troops that Demosthenes' plan called for. He served as general again in 422 BC and campaigned in Chalcidice with initial success. However, he was comprehensively defeated by Brasidas in front of Amphipolis and killed by a peltast in the rout. Ironically, Brasidas also died in this battle.

SPARTAN COMMANDERS

Thucydides names only three of the Spartan commanders in the Pylos campaign, Thrasymelidas, Brasidas and Epitadas. All three were Spartiates, members of the warrior elite.

Thrasymelidas is only mentioned once, as admiral (*nauarchos*) in command of the triremes that made the attack on Pylos at the beginning of the campaign. He may not have been the only admiral, and whoever did have overall responsibility for the disastrous action in the Harbour two days later is not named.

Epitadas was in command of the 420 Spartans on Sphacteria and nothing else is known of him; he was probably at least of *lochagos* rank, a *lochos* having a 'paper' strength of 512.

Brasidas commanded a Spartan trireme in the abortive seaborne assault on Pylos, and according to Thucydides, displayed strong leadership. He may

The inside image is contemporary rather than anachronistic. It is too damaged for a definitive interpretation but a conventional farewell scene would be less energetic and the two figures are clearly not fighting each other. They seem to be two comrades going into battle, both carrying spears. The figure on the right appears to have a shield but is bare-headed. The figure on the left wears a *pilos*, but it could be the universally worn felt hat that the bronze helmet was modelled on. If they are each holding their spears in their left hand (as shown in the Berlin relief in the case of the man on the right) they could be clasping right hands in a manly fashion. An intriguing possibility is that the figure on the left is a light-armed attendant. British Museum. (British Museum)

have had command responsibility for part of the fleet, applying experience acquired in the Corinthian Gulf earlier in the war. If he had not been wounded in the first action of the campaign, his continued involvement could not have prevented defeat in the Harbour but the engagement might have been less one-sided. Had he survived this, Brasidas would probably have injected some much-needed energy and tactical imagination into the Spartans' not very proactive response to the situation which they were to face for the next ten weeks. From 424 BC until his death in 422 BC he rapidly built a reputation as a dashing and innovative commander and also as a highly effective negotiator and diplomat. His successful campaigning in northern Greece and Thrace took a number of important cities out of the Athenian alliance, including Amphipolis, the biggest prize strategically. Thucydides, a general in 424–423 BC, was punished with exile for failing to save Amphipolis from Brasidas (though he did manage to hold the nearby seaport of Eion, another attractive target) but admired the man greatly. Brasidas met his death successfully beating off Cleon's attempt to recover Amphipolis for Athens. His successes left Sparta in a significantly stronger bargaining position than in late 425 BC for the peace negotiations that soon followed.

King Agis was in command of the Spartan army that occupied Attica briefly before withdrawing to deal with the occupation of Pylos, and it is likely he was at its head throughout that campaign. However, Thucydides mentions no one higher up the chain of command than Epitadas. The ultimate disaster caused the Spartans great distress and embarrassment and it may be that the historian is here paying a modest price for the goodwill of important sources. Agis' greatest achievement was to lead his army to victory seven years later at Mantinea, the largest land battle of the conflict and, as it happened, one of the few classic hoplite engagements. He was also in command in 413 BC when the Spartans fortified and permanently occupied Decelea, a village (*deme*) in Attica, a base planted in enemy territory with exactly the same purpose as Demosthenes' fort at Pylos. But this was only 24km from Athens and actually in sight of the city, so had significantly more tactical and strategic impact.

OPPOSING FORCES

The Peloponnesian War was contested between very similar forces. Both sides could muster substantial numbers of heavy-armed hoplite infantry, uniformly equipped and following the same basic tactical rules. But in this historic form of warfare, the supreme expertise and unique military ethos of the Spartans and the high quality of the troops supplied by the *perioikoi* (Laconian neighbours, with some political rights but lacking full Spartan citizenship) and by some of their allies, gave the Peloponnesians a significant edge.

However, through the six years of formal hostilities up to 425 BC, much of the fighting had been between mixed forces and was characterized by an absence of the symmetry generally seen in traditional phalanx warfare. More fluid and less formalized ways of fighting had developed, with learning generally slower on the Spartan side. Non-hoplite troops had taken on a much more significant role and were clearly more highly valued, though still excluded from the historians' body-counts. These less heavily armed troops ranged from specialists such as archers, peltast javelin-fighters, and slingers, to the much larger masses of *psiloi*, in literal translation 'bare men', so termed because they wore no armour.

Cavalry played an important role on occasion but was not used in the Pylos campaign. Sieges had all been long drawn-out affairs with little or no use of the technology or tactics of scaling or breaking through fortifications.

Adapting to the realities of a war of greater mobility, it seems that hoplites generally went into battle more lightly and less elaborately equipped than their forefathers. Body armour, if not dispensed with completely, was perhaps only worn in particular circumstances, which might have included guard duty or wall-defence or one of the quite rare, classic phalanx clashes. More specifically, the reference to armour in Thucydides' account of the Spartans' painful encounter with the Stratian slingers can be read as implying that in an operation of that nature they would not normally have worn armour. The iconic closed and semi-closed helmets of the heroic past were superseded by the open *pilos*, trading comprehensive protection for better vision and hearing, and greater comfort. However, the heavy shield and thrusting spear continued to be the defining defensive and offensive armament.

So on the battlefields of the second half of the 5th century BC, it was often not the absence of body armour that distinguished *psiloi* from hoplites, but the latter's different and lighter offensive and defensive weapons. A few *psiloi* had shields but they would have been made of wicker or hide, not heavy wood and bronze; more improvised with cloaks or hides wrapped around their left arms. Some carried hunting weapons or swords or knives, but probably more wielded farm implements or crude cudgels, and many simply fought with whatever they could lay their hands on, usually sticks and stones. *Psiloi* were originally used in an unsophisticated way as skirmishers, engaging out in front of their hoplite superiors before the opposing formations came together and the real battle began. In the Peloponnesian War, light-armed tactics had become more organized and effective. Thucydides records several instances in which light-armed units, in support of hoplites or on their own, carried out ambushes, flank attacks or assaults on positions, and actually defeated

LEFT
This fine Corinthian helmet from the first half of the 5th century BC was dedicated as a war trophy by the Messenians, Demosthenes' brothers-in-arms. Olympia Museum.

RIGHT
A more open, Illyrian-style helmet from the second half of the 6th century BC, showing that the Corinthian helmet's disadvantages of restricted vision and hearing and poor ventilation were being addressed by armourers ahead of the development of the bronze *pilos*. The decorative horses on the moveable cheek-pieces and the lions on the brow are done in silver. The double ridge held a crest in place. Olympia Museum.

hoplites. In these engagements smaller numbers of specialist archers, peltasts, or slingers often played an important part alongside the 'mass' of *psiloi*.

The navies of both sides went into battle in triremes, but the Athenian navy was significantly superior. The Athenians were better at building and operating triremes than any of the rest of the Greeks and, in the Archidamian War, also had many more at their disposal and the necessary capital and income to keep them at sea for long periods. At sea, the Athenians had so far been consistently successful in using their naval supremacy to project power and carry on the war outside Attica. Thucydides mentions the Spartans' unrealistic demand that their allies build 500 new ships between them as part of their preparations for war in 431 BC (II.7). Persian gold finally bought them the sea power that assured ultimate victory in 404 BC.

A fully fitted-out and manned trireme weighed 40–50 tonnes. It was approximately 6m wide, including the outriggers (*parexeiresia*) for the top tier of oars, and approximately 40m long. It measured about 4m from deck to keel, which was a little less than 1m below the waterline. The deck superstructure accounted for about a third of the height above the waterline. The trireme was as light and durable, and as streamlined as materials, craftsmanship and techniques would permit. These qualities gave it the speed and manoeuvrability required for combat, and a working life that could exceed 20 years. Its shallow draft made it easy to beach and launch, and suited it to the enclosed or inshore waters on which it fought. But it was a fair-weather ship. In waves larger than a little over 1m from crest to trough it risked taking in water through oar-ports and springing planks as a result of sagging in the middle as bow and stern were lifted.

The hull was built as a shell from the keel up, with the planks flush, and mortised and tenoned together at the edges. Decking ran from bow to stern, forming a protective canopy over the oarsmen and providing a fighting platform. On fast triremes this was a light structure, limiting the number of troops that could be carried on board. A companionway ran up the centre line of the ship below deck level. This gave access to the rowing positions and allowed movement and communication between the crew stations at each end. Also, importantly, commands and encouragement were relayed along it from the helmsman to the oarsmen.

A trireme snugly accommodated 170 oarsmen in three tiers. The rowers, like the *psiloi*, were recruited mainly from citizens in the lowest property class but Athens also drew on her wider population of resident aliens and privately and state-owned slaves. Manual labour would have given the majority of these recruits the stamina and upper-body strength necessary to pull an oar effectively for hours at a time, and the *Olympias* experiment revealed that a complete beginner could master the necessary basic rowing skill surprisingly quickly. Oarsmen were paid a daily wage and required to supply nothing except, perhaps, for the sheepskin pad they sat on. Their personal kit probably consisted of a cloak and tunic and, for at least some, a personal weapon. There was not space to accommodate much more, and water in large skins and jars would have taken up most of what there was. On *Olympias* the rowers consumed it at the rate of more

The simple, open *pilos* helmet that was very widely used in the Peloponnesian War. National Archaeological Museum, Athens.

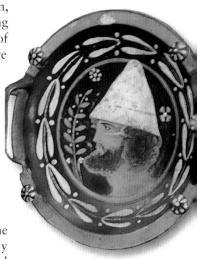

A 4th-century red-figure painting from Apulia of a young man wearing the felt *pilos* on which the bronze helmet was modelled. Louvre, Paris.

than a litre per hour so each trireme would have started the day with hundreds of litres on board, hence the importance on campaign of beaches with a good supply of fresh water.

In addition to the rowers, the late 5th-century trireme carried 16 officers and crewmen, and a standard fighting strength of ten hoplites and four archers. In the Athenian fleet's regular raids around the coast of the Peloponnese, rowers and sailors doubled as *psiloi*, and some would have had specialist skill with weapons.

On campaign, waiting for action or pausing on voyages for food and drink or rest, triremes were beached with their sterns ashore and their rams facing out to sea, and with ladders on each side of the stern for boarding and disembarking. It was found to be possible to embark or disembark the entire complement of *Olympias* in a matter of minutes. Some manpower was needed on the beach to push off, but with most of the oars immediately in action and the bows and the weight of the ram out to sea, the process would generally have been straightforward and quick. Anchoring offshore was a less desirable alternative. Boarding and disembarkation at sea was a laborious process and, on board, there was not enough space for whole crews to sleep, and almost no scope for catering. Normally crews camped on the shore close by their ships, and shared feeding arrangements. Barley porridge, perhaps spiced up with a little salt fish was regularly, if not permanently, on the menu. This would have been supplemented by whatever could be foraged, purchased, stolen or looted on shore.

Ancient evidence for the time taken over various voyages indicates that a Greek trireme could sustain a cruising speed of 6–7 knots over a period of several hours and the *Olympias* project confirmed 10 knots to be a reasonable estimate of its top speed, produced in very short bursts. (The British Olympic eight averaged 11.5 knots over 2,000m to win gold in 2004 and the modern eight is the fastest oared boat ever built.) With one side rowing and the other with oars out of the water, *Olympias* could make a 360-degree turn in a circle less than two ship-lengths in diameter. With both sides rowing, she could turn in a circle 3.4 lengths in diameter. A 90-degree change of direction could be made in seconds in half a length, and in less than a length under full oar power. *Olympias* could also zig-zag with precision and showed potential for sharp acceleration and deceleration. On this evidence the historic trireme with a good helmsman, rowing master and oarsmen could feint and weave and dart with even greater agility, essential capabilities for ramming.

The trireme was also an efficient sailing ship and the *Olympias* sea trials demonstrated that, in good sailing conditions, a cruising speed could be achieved as fast under sail as under oar. She performed best with the wind at around 15 knots and 30–40 degrees abaft her beam and, for a boat of such shallow draft, could sail surprisingly close to the wind. The sails were easily handled by a small number of deck hands and steering was straightforward. However, under sail, the trireme could never achieve the manoeuvrability necessary for battle.

The Athenian force that initially occupied Pylos, the combined complements of 40 triremes, was at least 8,000 strong including a minimum of 400 hoplites supported by 80 archers. If, as is likely for an expedition which could be expected to involve operations on both sea and land, the fleet included troop-carriers, each of these would have delivered up to 30 additional hoplites taking the probable strength above 1,000. Oarsmen and other crew-members, mustered as *psiloi*, a role in which many would already have been experienced from previous campaigns, gave the generals the potential to add several thousand, albeit of lesser combat-effectiveness, to this core. This element also gave them the manpower required for the construction of defence works. To counter the Athenian occupation the Spartans had a 60-strong fleet operating up at Corcyra a few days sailing away and the option of sending an overwhelmingly superior hoplite force overland, raised from Sparta itself, the *perioikoi* and Peloponnesian allies, and by withdrawing the annual invasion force from Attica. Unfortunately Thucydides gives no numbers here. However, even if past experience had not shown that 40 Athenian triremes would be more than a match for 60 Peloponnesians, the Athenians had many more triremes in reserve than they had. And Sparta's hoplite superiority could only be brought to bear in pitched battle. Small garrisons behind good fortifications could hold out for a very long time against much larger besieging forces, Plataea being the most telling example. Ten weeks stalemate followed the opening actions of the campaign in which the Athenians won total control at sea, and it would require a radical tactical initiative and an injection of specialist non-hoplite reinforcements to break this.

Olympias: the outrigger through which the top-tier rowers worked their oars can be clearly seen. Photograph Hellenic Navy.

OPPOSING PLANS

A hoplite goes into battle accompanied by a light-armed attendant wearing a *pilos* helmet and carrying two javelins. British Museum.

In spring 425 BC the war entered its seventh year. Pericles had died in 429 BC, Archidamus in 426 BC. Both sides had begun to explore new ways of breaking the costly stalemate that was all that had so far been achieved. The Spartans' aggressive colonization of Heraclea in central Greece had been sound in principle but weakly executed, producing little or no benefit in the short or longer term. The Athenians' attack on Melos was motivated by the need to add to their sources of tribute, but, though officially neutral, the island was originally a Spartan colony and was a potential source of financial support for the enemy. The Athenian strike into Boeotia was an aggressive response to the pressure the Athenians felt from Sparta's northern allies.

The first Sicilian expedition in 427 BC had opened a new front with significant new strategic objectives: denying the Spartans potential naval and financial support from their powerful connections on the island; securing important trade links, grain imports especially; and ultimately adding Sicily or as many of its cities as possible to the empire. Escalating efforts to achieve these particular objectives over the coming decade were, of course, to end in crippling disaster with Demosthenes, Eurymedon and Nicias amongst the 15,000–20,000 Athenian dead.

Finally, both sides were now taking a keen interest in Corcyra and other islands, and the mainland territories to the north-west of the Gulf of Corinth. They were potential sources of valuable assets and strategically important as bases from which to control the coastal waters of western Greece, the sea lanes to Sicily and Italy, and the land approaches to central Greece.

ATHENIAN PLANS

The Athenian occupation of Pylos in 425 BC came about as a side-mission in the continuation of operations in the north-western theatre. Early in 425 BC the Athenians agreed to their Sicilian allies' suggestion that they send more ships to help contain the Syracusans' growing naval power. A fleet of 40 triremes was prepared and manned and the generals Eurymedon and Sophocles were put in command. They had orders to put in at Corcyra on the way to support the pro-Athenian democrats against a group of oligarchic exiles who had returned to the island and were harassing them from a strong position in the mountains north of the city. The Corcyreans were weakened by famine and it was known that the exiles would soon have the support of the Peloponnesian fleet. Demosthenes, not currently in office as a general but elected to serve again for the 12 months from June, was on board when the fleet sailed. 'He had been authorized at his own request to make what use he wished of the ships as they rounded the Peloponnese' (IV.2).

A peltast charging, here with a thrusting spear and wearing a bronze helmet rather than a fox-skin cap. The *pelte* shields are often shown decorated with the 'evil eye' motif, as also seen on trireme prows and painted on drinking vessels. British Museum.

The two explicit assignments were of similar strategic value but the focus on Sicily was blurred by the Corcyra mission, the likelihood of meeting a larger, if inferior enemy fleet and the possibility of longer-term entanglement there. As when they sent Phormio's urgently needed reinforcements to the Corinthian Gulf via Crete in the previous year, the Athenian Assembly was exercising high command with unrealistic expectations of its generals, and it was in the habit of exacting severe penalties for perceived failure.

Demosthenes' vaguely defined personal authority and unofficial status must have been additionally undermining for Eurymedon and Sophocles. His instruction to them to put in at Pylos on the way up the west coast of the Peloponnese 'to do what needed to be done there' was not well received. Thucydides' account (IV.3) of the arguments Demosthenes then presented summarizes his plan well. He told them about the rocky bluff and its natural defences, and how these could be readily reinforced with local stone and timber, and pointed out that the region was currently unprotected, though not a great distance from Sparta. He also reminded them that the creation of a permanent base on Spartan soil was the special mission given to him by the Assembly. The generals scoffed that there were any number of deserted spots along the coast that he could occupy if he wanted to add to the cost of the war. But Pylos was different, Demosthenes argued. It was next to a superb natural harbour and in the Messenians' former homeland, so it could be exploited by both the Athenian navy and by Messenian exiles to do Sparta a great deal of damage. A Messenian garrison would be highly motivated as an occupation force and their kinship with the native Messenians who had stayed there as restless Spartan subjects would be a great advantage.

The blockade of Sphacteria, the island nearby, was not part of the original plan but a consequence of the Athenians' elimination of the Spartan fleet at the end of the initial actions in defence of Pylos. The final outcome, secured in an operation that demonstrated Demosthenes' tactical ability and the lessons he had learned in his campaigning over the previous year, was almost sufficient to break the stalemate and bring about a negotiated peace that would have been favourable to Athens and might have lasted, if the Athenians, as Thucydides observes on more than one occasion, had not been 'grasping for more'.

SPARTAN PLANS

In 425 BC the Spartans were no better equipped to deal with the regular Athenian seaborne raids on their coastline than at the beginning of the war. It took the permanent occupation of Pylos, and then of the offshore island

Athenian gravestone from the late 5th century BC showing spear, shield and *pilos* helmet. The baldric supporting his sword, the hoplite's secondary weapon, would have been painted on. National Archaeological Museum, Istanbul.

Cythera in 424 BC, to persuade them to raise forces of cavalry and archers. These could have provided the mobility and flexibility required for rapid response, but Thucydides also suggests the development was motivated by chronic homeland security considerations.

When the Spartan army and fleet finally arrived at Pylos, Demosthenes' small force was well prepared and well protected. The Spartan plan to attack simultaneously by sea and land had some appeal in the abstract, but failed to take account of the strength of the Athenians' natural and man-made defences or to predict the result of Demosthenes' effective tactical response. If there was a plan for opposing the Athenian fleet when it cruised into the Harbour two days after the assault on Pylos had been abandoned, it was not executed, and if any thought was given to alternative ways of dislodging the Athenians from their stronghold during the ten weeks of siege that followed, nothing appears to have been tried.

On Sphacteria the defensive plan was to divide up the small force stranded there to watch over different sectors whilst using the ample cover to conceal unit strengths and positions. This worked well until large areas of the scrub and trees were burnt off, and blockade-running under cover of darkness and bad weather kept the defenders from starving. Overall the Spartan plan was simple and passive, to hold out on Sphacteria for the rest of the summer until autumn weather conditions made it impossible for the Athenians to bring in supplies by sea and then the blockade would become unsustainable. This plan would have worked, but for Demosthenes' tactical vision and Cleon's political leverage and opportunism.

THE CAMPAIGN TO PYLOS

Eurymedon and Sophocles were not persuaded by Demosthenes' arguments, but, as they were passing that part of the coast, bad weather forced them to take the fleet into the Harbour, now known as Navarino Bay, to shelter behind the heights of Pylos and the north end of Sphacteria. Demosthenes was then unable to persuade the generals to give orders to build a stronghold, and he was equally unsuccessful with the *taxiarchoi*, the next level in the rather loose chain of command. But, when the bad weather had prevented them sailing for a few days, the soldiers and sailors set to work on their own initiative.

Demosthenes' leadership and the respect in which he was held may have been a factor, but self-interest probably played a major part: the Spartans were likely to arrive in force very soon and there were gaps in Pylos' natural defences and no protection from land attack for the beached ships. Thucydides describes some effective improvisation: 'They had no iron masonry tools so had to pick out stones and fit them together as best they could and, when they needed to use mortar, they had nothing to carry it in, so they bent double with it on their backs, clasping their hands behind them to keep it from slipping off' (IV.4). The main construction work was completed in six days and, with weather conditions now favourable, Eurymedon and Sophocles sailed on towards Corcyra leaving Demosthenes on Pylos with five ships and their complements, 1,000 men at least, including around 75 hoplites and 20–30 archers.

King Agis had led the Spartan army into Attica towards the end of April 'while the ears were still forming on the corn'. As in previous years, the

The southern end of Sphacteria, the Island, from the open sea to the north-west. The peak in the background is on the mainland.

Campaigning on the west coast of Central Greece and the Peloponnese, and in the Corinthian Gulf in 426–424 BC

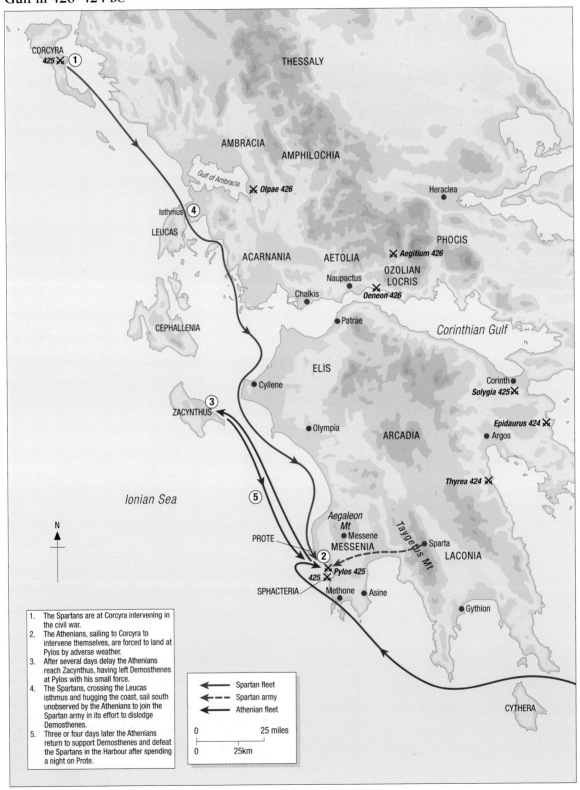

1. The Spartans are at Corcyra intervening in the civil war.
2. The Athenians, sailing to Corcyra to intervene themselves, are forced to land at Pylos by adverse weather.
3. After several days delay the Athenians reach Zacynthus, having left Demosthenes at Pylos with his small force.
4. The Spartans, crossing the Leucas isthmus and hugging the coast, sail south unobserved by the Athenians to join the Spartan army in its effort to dislodge Demosthenes.
5. Three or four days later the Athenians return to support Demosthenes and defeat the Spartans in the Harbour after spending a night on Prote.

Spartan fleet
Spartan army
Athenian fleet

0   25 miles
0   25km

Athenians would not be drawn out from behind their walls to give battle and the Spartans destroyed as much of their crops and buildings as they could. The weather was unusually stormy for the time of year, perhaps part of the same bad spell that detained the Athenian fleet at Pylos, so the invading army was suffering. The Spartans at home had not been much concerned by the news of this latest landing on their shores, confident that the Athenians would soon sail on in their usual fashion or if not, that they could be easily driven off. But Agis immediately decided to abandon the occupation of Attica and bring his army back. It was, at 15 days, the shortest of the five invasions to date.

As soon as Agis and his army had returned from Attica, a substantial force of Spartiates and *perioikoi* set off for Pylos. Additional contingents were called in from allies around the Peloponnese. A message was also sent to the 60-ship fleet up at Corcyra, which Eurymedon and Sophocles had sailed north to tackle. The Athenians had got as far as Zacynthus and may have been waiting there to catch the Spartan fleet in open water. However, the Spartans got past the Athenians by dragging their ships across the isthmus joining the island of Leucas to the mainland and then hugging the coast, possibly passing Zacynthus under cover of darkness. Both fleets would have sent out scout ships and at this point the Spartans' intelligence gathering may have been more effective, or they were just lucky.

They reached Pylos after three or four days, beaching their ships along the sandy northern shore of the Harbour under the protection of the army.

ABOVE
The whole of the Island and the Pylos bluff from inland to the north-east, the site of the extensive Mycenaean palace complex known as Nestor's Palace. The spit that separates the modern lagoon from Navarino Bay, the Harbour, swings round to the southern tip of Pylos and the narrow Sikia Channel that separates it from the Island.

LEFT
The wide southern entrance to Navarino Bay, the Harbour, and the southern end of the Island from Nestor's Palace. The area of the lagoon was dry land in the 5th century BC.

Looking north from the 16th-century Ottoman castle above the modern town of Pylos at the southern end of the bay. Across the water from left to right: the northern half of the Island; the heights of Old Pylos on the other side of the Sikia Channel; the dunes that made Homer call Nestor's kingdom 'sandy Pylos'; and the long beach sweeping round to the east. The site of Nestor's Palace is near the top of the lower ridge towards the right-hand edge of the picture.

Demosthenes' landing, as well as bringing about Agis' withdrawal from Attica, had gone some way towards achieving the Athenian fleet's first objective of securing Corcyra by drawing the Spartans away from the island. But the Spartans were now ready to attack the Athenian base in overwhelming force by land and sea.

Thucydides credits Demosthenes with anticipating the Spartan fleet's manoeuvre and Messenian friends probably brought him news of it. He had sent two of his five ships to let Eurymedon and Sophocles know of the threat and to call on them to sail back to join in the defence of Pylos. By sending two ships he improved the chance of getting the message through. It significantly reduced his numbers, but Demosthenes undoubtedly retained both ship's complements of hoplites and archers and probably some members of the deck crew. This would have lightened the triremes, enabling them to

The north end of Pylos, topped by remains of the substantial fort established by the Franks in the 13th century, added to by the Venetians in the 15th and further enlarged by the Ottoman Turks in the 16th. The Athenians' northern defences, the natural bastion reinforced where necessary with stone and timber, would have followed much the same line. The cave at the foot of the cliff is associated with Homer and Nestor, and extensive archaeological finds demonstrate the importance from Neolithic times onward of the place's natural harbours and citadels backed by rich agricultural land.

travel faster, whilst leaving him with 600–700 men, a larger force than the garrison that was able to hold the city of Plataea for four years.

Demosthenes continued with his preparations to hold off the imminent Spartan attack. He had abandoned the excellent beach that curved across the top of the Harbour because it was very vulnerable to attack from inland. The three remaining triremes were pulled up on to a small area of beach at the north-west corner of the Harbour. This triangular space and the Athenians' access to the sea were enclosed by walls, a palisade along the water's edge and the southern end of the Pylos outcrop.

A longer wall had also been built from the mid-point of the west side of Pylos where the shoreline is backed by quite gently sloping ground. It was less substantially constructed than the wall facing the mainland because the Athenians were counting on naval protection against attack from the open sea to the west. This wall connected with the short inner wall that ran to the edge of the Sikia channel across the lower ground at the base of the southern tip of the outcrop. The rest of the ridge, which was also occupied, was protected by mostly unclimbable cliffs ('no fortification needed there' Thucydides remarks), though guards would have to be posted at the few points where a scaling party might have been able to work its way up. The north end of the ridge required some fortification at its western corner.

The sailors and oarsmen took on the role of *psiloi*, which most would have been accustomed to from previous years' raiding of the Peloponnese or service in land operations. They carried whatever improvised or conventional weapons were available and some were issued with light shields. According to Thucydides these were made of wicker and provided by a group of Messenian privateers who had joined them in a 30-oared *triakonter* and a smaller cutter. The majority would have settled for the more basic protection of a cloak or hide. Thucydides says these Messenians just 'happened to turn up' but it is likely that Demosthenes had invited comrades from the previous year's campaigning to come along as the nucleus of his planned garrison and naval base. There cannot have been many more than 100 of them but this number included the valuable reinforcement of 40 hoplites, some of whom had probably doubled as rowers.

Sheltered from the open sea by the heights of Pylos and Sphacteria, the northern shore of the Harbour provided the Athenians with an ideal refuge where they could beach their fleet and establish a strategic foothold on the Peloponnesian mainland. This long perimeter was indefensible against the land forces Sparta could send against it, but in the fortnight before the Spartans got troops to the place, the opportunity was taken to construct a stronghold that proved impregnable for several years. When it finally fell to the Spartans in the winter of 409 BC, it was not taken by storm: the Messenian garrison was starved into surrender because, according to Diodorus (XIII.64.5), a long spell of bad weather prevented the Athenians sending supplies.

Looking south from the sand dunes on the south side of Voidokilia Bay along the eastern flank of Pylos and across the present-day lagoon. The section of beach walled in by the Athenians at the foot of the cliffs and the eastern end of the Sikia channel was directly below the highest point on the Island and the Spartans' stronghold.

The beach that was enclosed by the Athenians' eastern wall. Thucydides' brief description suggests there was also a short wall running straight down the ridge to the water's edge.

Demosthenes now had a force of 700–800, including over 100 hoplites, to face a much more numerous Spartan army, probably comprising several thousand hoplites and light-armed men. Demosthenes' three triremes and two smaller ships could have no impact on the 60-strong Spartan fleet and it was not possible for them even to put to sea in the absence of the rest of the Athenian fleet. Each Spartan trireme would have at least ten hoplites and four archers on board, adding significantly to the enemy's infantry strength. However, because much of his perimeter was very well protected by the cliffs and crags that it ran along, Demosthenes could concentrate most of his men behind the strong 100–150m of wall that faced the mainland, and along the south-western shoreline, the only sector open to attack from the sea. He took only 60 hoplites and a few archers to oppose the landing that he expected the Spartans would attempt there.

Thucydides states that the 60 hoplites were less than half of the Athenian heavy-infantry strength, which implies that Demosthenes had been left on Pylos with rather more than the regular marine complement of five triremes. Even allowing for an equal or larger number of light-armed support troops, this seems a very small number to set against the fighting complement of the

The eastern wall of the Athenians' fortified harbour probably ran from this outcrop down to the water's edge.

43 triremes (Thucydides' precise count) in the assault. This would have totalled at least 430 hoplites and 172 archers, and it is likely that larger numbers would have been put on board. However, Demosthenes knew that there were few points along the rocky shoreline at which a trireme could run in close enough for disembarkation, and that it was only possible for men to make their way down each ship's twin gangplanks in single file.

The Spartans were confident they could take the Athenian fort with little difficulty because it had been so hastily constructed and was defended by such a small force. Their army outnumbered the garrison by a significant factor and, for as long as the Athenian fleet was absent, they had complete control of the surrounding sea, within the bay and outside it. They planned a massive assault on the eastern side of the fort and, as anticipated by Demosthenes, a simultaneous seaborne attack from the open sea to the west. They also intended to keep the Athenian fleet out of the bay when it arrived. Very few ships would be required to block the Sikia channel, which narrowed to approximately 30m at its eastern end. However, the southern entrance to the bay was 1,250m wide and to block it effectively would require about twice as many ships in a single line as the Spartans had at their disposal.

Thucydides correctly states that the Sikia channel could accommodate only two triremes abreast at its narrowest, eastern exit, but his statement that the southern channel was only wide enough for eight is a gross underestimate. It cannot be established whether there is something wrong with the text here (IV.8) or an uncharacteristic factual error on Thucydides' part, which seems less likely. But the account may anyway reflect sloppy Spartan planning and poor intelligence, which is also suggested by the generals' overconfidence and, specifically, their evident failure to anticipate the need for heavy siege equipment.

However, the final element of their plan proved to be their biggest mistake. To complete the isolation of the garrison at Pylos, they considered it necessary to secure Sphacteria to prevent the Athenians using the island as a base if they were kept away from the sheltered water and beaches of the Harbour. In fact, the Island's western and eastern shorelines, unless they have changed greatly in character since 425 BC, offered little more space for beaching triremes than was now available to the Athenians at Pylos. On the same tactical logic that Demosthenes was applying, an agile and alert force of 420 hoplites with a similar number of Helots in support would probably have been sufficient to prevent landings. However, it would not be possible to support this garrison if the Spartan fleet lost control of the bay and it was a dangerous assumption that they could hold on to it in the face of the superior seamanship and fighting capability of the Athenians.

THE BATTLES

THE DEFENCE OF PYLOS

The speech Thucydides has Demosthenes making to his men as he forms them up to face the open sea sums up his tactics precisely:

> Don't let their superior numbers frighten you. They will have to fight in small groups because space for landing is so limited... You Athenians know from experience what it takes to fight your way ashore against firm opposition; you know that, if a man stands his ground and does not give way to terror at the beat of the oars and the looming hull that bears down on him, he can never be driven back. Now, stand firm and stop this attack here, right at the water's edge, and keep us and our position safe! (IV.10)

The perimeter wall behind them was long and not very substantial and could not be held by his small detachment if the Spartans established a beachhead. Over the last 2,500 years the whole Peloponnesian landmass has tilted, raising the sea level by up to 2m on this part of the coast. Erosion has

The south-west corner of Pylos where the Spartans attempted to land, seen from the heights at the north end of the Island.

Pylos, Sphacteria and the Harbour; the Spartans attack.

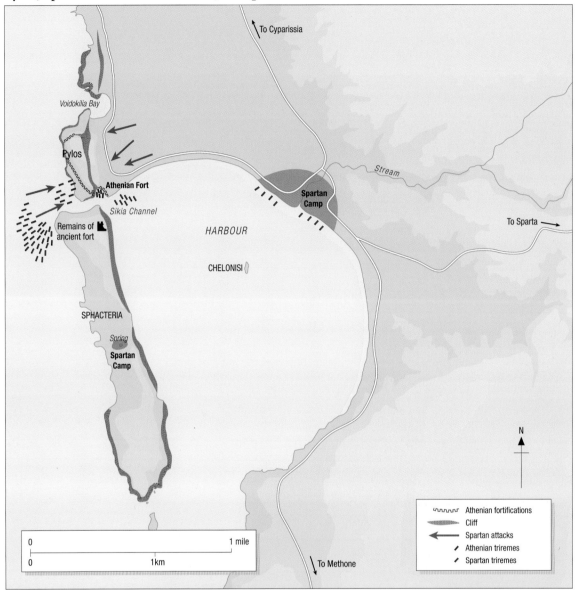

also had its effect, and there are now no points along the western or south-western shoreline of Pylos at which it would be possible to run a trireme up the beach. The edge falls away steeply and in places underwater rocks come close to the surface. The character of the shoreline was probably very similar in the 5th century BC, so it appears that the Spartans were faced with performing a docking manoeuvre at the most accessible points, bow or stern-first, rather than actually beaching their ships to disembark their troops. The process would normally be assisted by men on shore pulling on ropes, but this would not be possible in an opposed landing. In any case, Thucydides' narrative makes it clear that this was a difficult and risky, even hopeless, line of attack, so Demosthenes had good reason to be confident of driving it off.

The weight of the ram and the general structure of the prow made it difficult to beach triremes bows-first. Here the rowers are resting while *Olympias* makes good speed under sail. Photograph Hellenic Navy.

When they were ready, the Spartans launched their two attacks simultaneously, on land from the east and by sea from the west. Thrasymelidas, a Spartiate, was in command of their amphibious assault and he directed it exactly as Demosthenes had anticipated:

> The Spartans divided their fleet into small attack groups because there wasn't room for larger numbers to drive ashore. They rowed in and stood off in turn, urging each other on with great spirit to land and breach the fortifications. Brasidas, in command of one of the triremes, excelled above the rest. When he saw other Spartan commanders or helmsmen holding off to save their ships from damage because the approach was difficult but still offered a chance of making a landing, he shouted, 'There's no point looking after your ship's timbers while you allow our enemies to establish a fort on our land! Smash them up to get ashore!' His rallying cry for the allied commanders was 'Remember the good things that Sparta has done for you. Don't hold back payment for them with your ships at this critical moment: run them aground, get ashore any way you can and drive these men from their position!' [Brasidas' acknowledgment of the risk of running on to rocks rather than up a sloping beach strongly suggests the shoreline was as it is today.] Urging the rest on with these words, Brasidas ordered his own helmsman to run his ship in and charged down the gangplank. But as he attempted to get on to the shore he was seriously wounded and thrown backwards. He passed out and, as he fell into the outrigger, his shield slipped off his arm into the sea and was washed ashore. The Athenians picked it up and later used it in the trophy they set up to mark this successful action. (IV.11)

Brasidas was probably an early casualty and certainly a costly one, but Thrasymelidas continued to try to get men ashore.

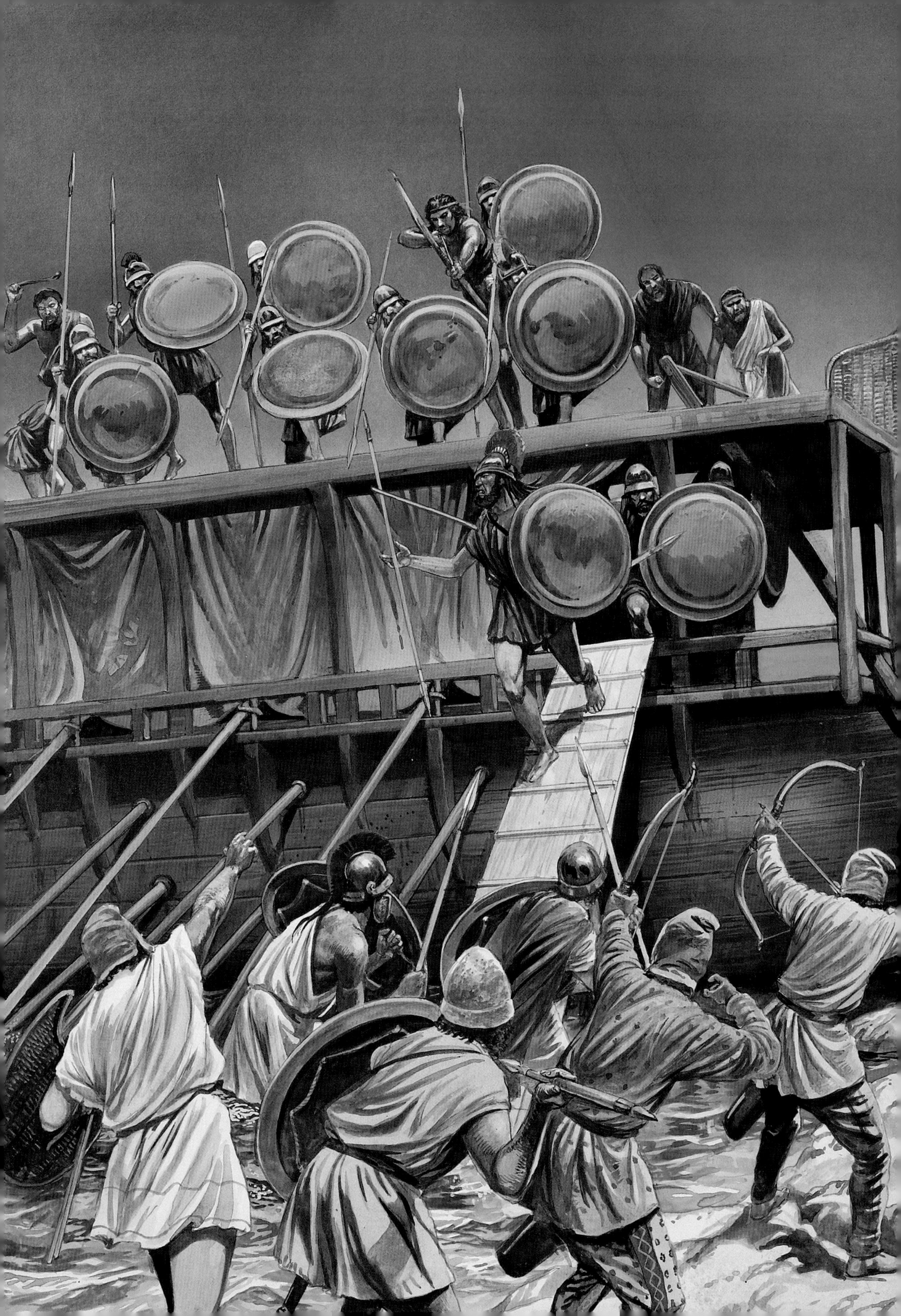

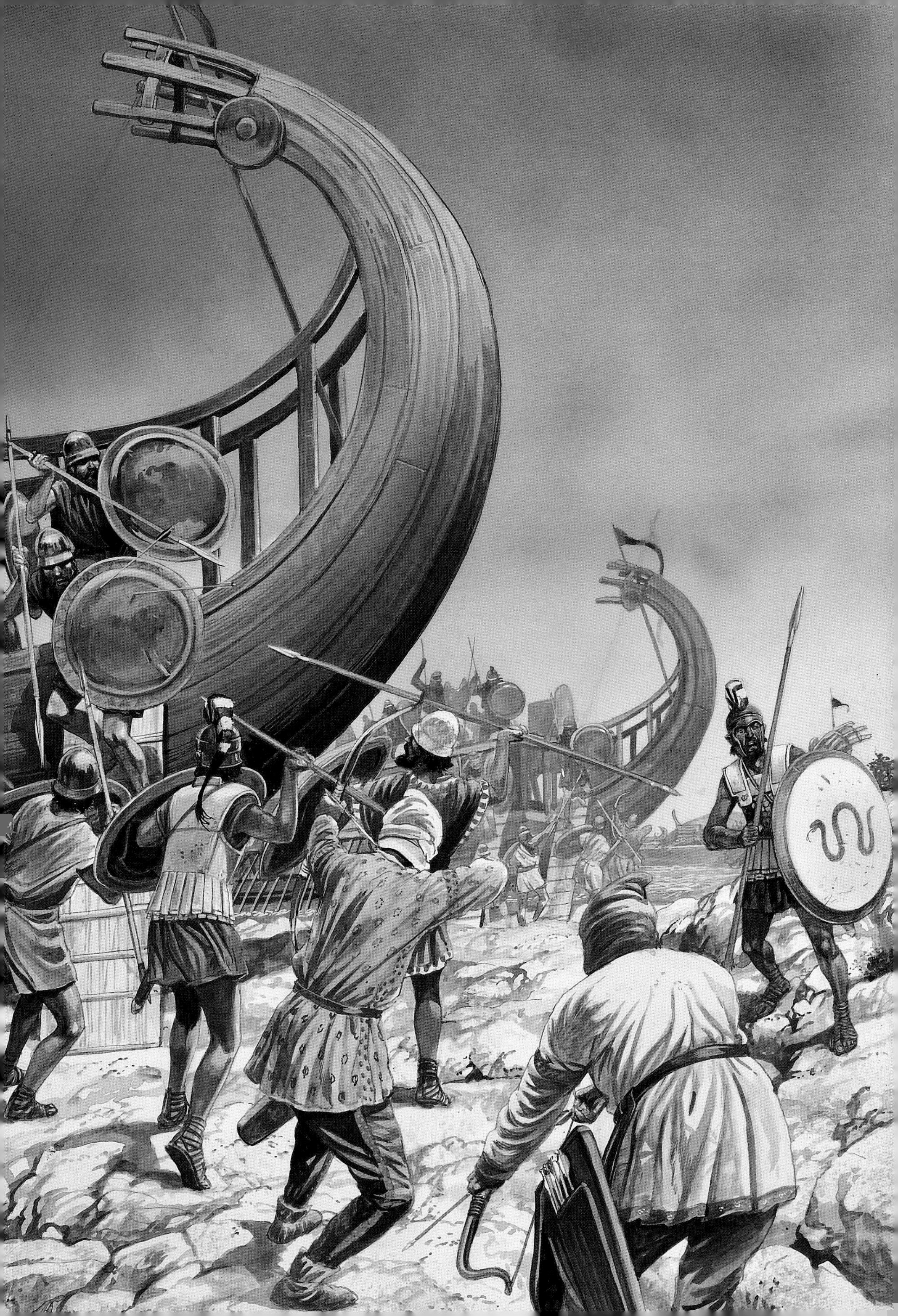

THE SPARTANS ATTACK FROM THE SEA (PP.46–47)

Triremes were generally beached stern-first. The shape of the prow and the weight of the ram meant that much more effort was needed to pull the hull any distance out of the water bows-first. The structure of the stern section also made disembarkation easier than from the bows or sides, and it was found in the sea-trials that with rowers in reversed position *Olympias* handled almost as well going astern as forward. However, the failure of this operation demonstrates the inadequacies of a trireme as an assault landing craft!

Brasidas' ship has been brought ashore obliquely so that both of its two gangplanks can be lowered on the same side. The rudder (1) is raised to clear the shore and the rowers, protected on the top tier by leather or canvas screens (2), are pulling on their oars to hold the ship against it. The helmsman is crouching to the side of the commander's chair (3). Demosthenes' plan is working. Brasidas (4), leading the attack, has taken a javelin in the shoulder as he steps out on to the gangplank. The Spartan on the second gangplank is about to be met by three Athenian spears and his comrade behind him can give no support. Other are lining up behind but the Athenians will not allow them to set foot on the rocks, let alone form up in numbers. Other ships are being equally unsuccessful.

Demosthenes (5) and one of his hoplites, perhaps also higher-ranking, are wearing body armour and crested helmets. The rest of the Athenian hoplites are more lightly clad in the style that had been generally adopted in the second half of the century. With one exception they wear *pilos* headgear, either bronze or felt. The long-haired and bearded Spartans, on the other hand, are uniformly kitted out in scarlet tunics and bronze *piloi*. At some point in the late 5th century Sparta adopted the *lambda* (inverted V) shield-blazon, 'L' for Lacedaemon, but plain polished bronze is shown here. The transverse crest on Brasidas' *pilos* indicates his rank. Thucydides only mentions hoplites and archers, but Demosthenes is likely to have included the pick of the light-armed missile troops from his mixed garrison in the detachment he took down to the south-western shore. The *psilos* (6) who has just hit Brasidas with the first of his two javelins carries a light peltast-style shield, made of wicker and possibly supplied by Demosthenes' Messenian allies. The Athenian archers wear their traditional trousers and soft Scythian caps. A sailor with a sling (7) supports the archers on the Spartan ship.

Thucydides gives no details of the fighting on the land side, but it is clear that no serious impression was made on the Athenian defences. The Spartans would have used ladders in repeated attempts to scale the wall but groups of hoplites supported by *psiloi* would have met them at every point. The hoplites fought with spear and shield. The *psiloi* fought at close quarters with spears, boathooks, axes or cudgels, whatever was available to them, or, with the archers, harassed the attackers from either side with missiles of all kinds, arrows, javelins, slingshots, but mainly rocks and stones. The fighting on both fronts went on for the whole of that day and was resumed for some of the next, but then the Spartans withdrew.

The following day they sent some of their ships down to Asine to collect the heavy timber they would need to construct *mechanai*, siege machinery. The type is not specified but they would probably have constructed battering rams and siege towers and larger and more substantial scaling ladders than could be built from the local timber. A Persian army would have arrived with a siege train ready-prepared, but the Greek way was generally to starve the enemy out, which took time, or to rely on betrayal from within. With the Athenian fleet on its way, time was not on the Spartans' side, as Brasidas clearly understood; and there was no prospect of betrayal. Thucydides implies that the Spartans abandoned the land attack and the sea attack at the same time, although it would have been better to sustain the pressure on the land side.

THE BATTLE IN THE HARBOUR

On the same day as the Spartan ships were despatched to Asine or a little later, the Athenian fleet returned from Zacynthus. Some reinforcements had joined and it was now nearer 50 ships strong. The generals observed that there was nowhere they could beach the fleet without fighting their way to the shore and on to it. Also, their ships were not battle-ready after the 100km passage from Zacynthus. So they took them back north a little way to the island of Prote, beached or moored there and camped for the night. Early next morning the Athenians prepared their ships for action, taking down their masts and probably leaving them on shore with the rest of the sailing gear and anything else not needed for battle that might weigh them down. Then they rowed down to Pylos and Sphacteria again.

They were ready to fight the Spartans either in the open sea or inside the bay, forcing their way in if necessary. It would not have been a surprise that the Spartans did not come out to meet them in the open sea. It is likely that the Athenian trireme was a better sea-boat than any other Greek warship it faced, and the fleet's superior speed and manoeuvrability, and the experience and expertise of its helmsmen and crews, would have combined to overwhelming advantage in the open sea. The smoother water of the bay made things relatively easier for the Spartans and it would be a positive benefit for them to fight with a friendly, occupied shore at their backs. However, the Athenian generals must have been pleasantly surprised to be allowed to enter the bay unopposed through both channels, especially the very defensible northern one, and then amazed to see the Spartan fleet still in the process of putting to sea.

By the time the Athenians had crossed the bay, which would have taken 15–20 minutes from the southern entrance, a good number of Spartan ships had formed into line offshore but the Athenians swept into them, immediately damaging several and capturing five, and drove the rest back. With only part of the Spartan fleet deployed, the Athenians could use their superior numbers to outflank it. Spartan efforts to counter this would open gaps in their line, which was not very well ordered in the first place. This gave Athenian

In their seaborne attack the Spartans were faced by this shelved and rocky shoreline, rather than gently inclined sand or shingle. Bows-first it would have been difficult to get in close enough to reach the shore with a gangplank but the overhang of the stern structure would have made this considerably easier.

Pylos and Sphacteria: the battle in the Harbour

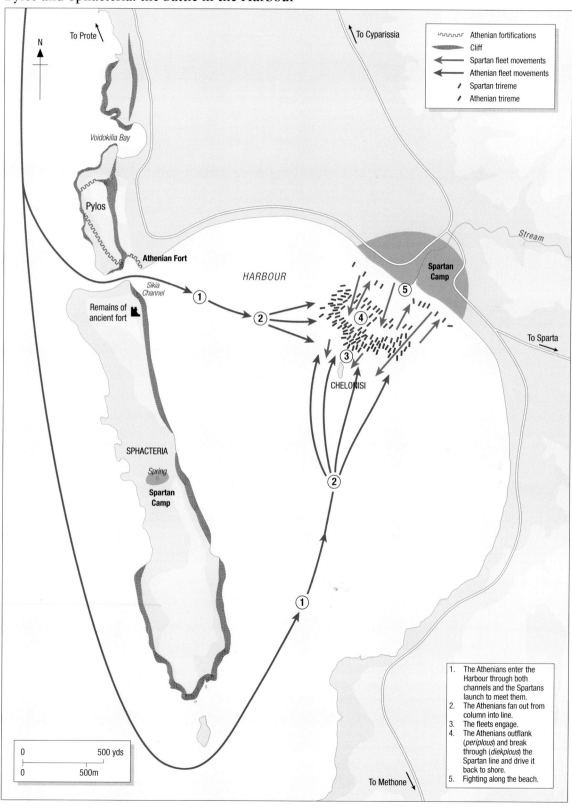

Legend:
- ~~~~ Athenian fortifications
- Cliff
- Spartan fleet movements
- Athenian fleet movements
- Spartan trireme
- Athenian trireme

1. The Athenians enter the Harbour through both channels and the Spartans launch to meet them.
2. The Athenians fan out from column into line.
3. The fleets engage.
4. The Athenians outflank (*periplous*) and break through (*diekplous*) the Spartan line and drive it back to shore.
5. Fighting along the beach.

The western shoreline that Demosthenes successfully defended. The island to the north is Prote, where the Athenian fleet spent the night before taking on the Spartans in the Harbour.

helmsmen opportunities to dart through, then, picking a target, swing round sharply to ram it in the side or stern (the classic *diekplous*, 'sailing-through-and-out' manoeuvre). The Spartans' only option was to run for the shore, and, with this in mind, they probably had not pulled out very far into the bay to meet the Athenian attack. Thucydides undoubtedly talked to men who were there:

> The Athenians rammed many of them after they had got to the beach and some of them while the crews were still boarding and before they could put out to sea. They disabled others and began to tow them away after the crews had abandoned them. At the sight of all this the Spartans on the shore became frantic, realising that their comrades were about to be cut off on the Island, and they rushed to the ships' rescue. They dashed into the sea fully armed and tried to get hold of them and drag them back. Each one was so focused on this that he behaved as if he was engaged in the action all on his own. It was absolute chaos. (IV.14)

Thucydides' account of this action highlights the skill with which the Athenian seamen handled their triremes, the *techne* which Pericles identifies as making 'our citizen helmsmen and deck crews … our most powerful asset (and we have more of them, and of better quality, than the whole of the rest of Greece)' (1.142–43). They rapidly and decisively outmanoeuvred the Spartans in the open water of the bay. Then individual helmsmen swung their ships in close to the shore and across the bows or sterns of the beached enemy (those that had not yet launched would have had their rams pointing out to sea; those that had been chased back to the beach probably ran up it bow first and would have not got so far out of the water). They came in close enough to attach tow ropes and then turned sharply to drag their target off. The scene is reminiscent of the final phase of the battle of Marathon, when the victorious Athenians pursuing the Persians 'came down to the shore … and grabbed hold of the ships… Cunegirus son of Euphorion fell there, his hand cut off by an axe blow as he grabbed hold of a ship's sternpost' (Herodotus VI.113–14). It took a few men on the shore to help a beached trireme launch and it probably did not take many men, hanging on to the ship or hauling on ropes and digging their heels in, to prevent it.

Somehow the Spartans had blundered terribly. They must have known that the Athenian fleet had only withdrawn as far as Prote. This island could be closely observed from the mainland directly opposite, and was clearly visible from the north end of Pylos and the higher ground behind the Spartan encampment in the bay. Simple visual signals (fire or smoke, flags or polished shields) or messages carried by runners or horsemen could have promptly informed them of any movement.

Yet the Spartans, whatever their plan, were not ready for the Athenians when they entered the bay two hours or so after they had left Prote. Meeting them outside the bay could be reasonably discounted as an option. But it would have been easy to block the narrow Sikia channel and the Athenians would have been vulnerable to well-timed flanking attacks at the point where the southern entrance to the bay widened out, whether they entered it in columns or line abreast. Whether this was the vision of the unnamed Spartan generals who were in overall command of the operation, or the plan was simply to defend the northern end of the bay where their fleet was beached next to their besieging land army's encampment, it may be that execution was delegated to non-Spartan commanders of the allied contingents that made up most of the naval force, and there may have been a failure of communication and coordination.

The allies must have been demoralized by the failure of the seaborne assault on Pylos and probably also by the demand laid on them to show gratitude to Sparta by sacrificing their ships on the rocky shore. In any case, a degree of defeatism was understandable in the face of the navy that had Salamis as its most glorious battle honour, that had been the cutting edge of Athenian imperial expansion for the subsequent half century, and that had mauled them so terribly in their previous encounters in 429 BC during the current war. Thucydides, having already mentioned the Spartans' shocked realization of what was at stake, goes on to describe 'the bewildered determination' with which they fought to hold on to their triremes. This does suggest that naval operations had been delegated to the allies, who provided most of the ships, and that the Spartans themselves had remained on shore. He continues:

Bronze tip of a battering ram from the mid-5th century BC and thought to be Sicilian. The 'teeth' would have been effective against woodwork or mortar but it does not appear heavy enough to make an impression on substantial masonry. Olympia Museum.

> Each side put up a hard fight and there were many casualties. The Spartans managed to win back their unmanned ships except for those that had been taken at the beginning of the battle and both sides eventually broke off the engagement. However, the Athenians set up a trophy, gave the Spartans their dead and took possession of all the disabled ships. Then immediately they began patrolling around the Island guarding the prisoners they had cut off there. The Spartan army on the mainland, with all the reinforcements that had arrived from every direction, stayed where it was, facing Pylos. (IV.14)

Athenian victory was confirmed in the traditional manner, as after a land battle, by setting up a trophy, allowing the enemy to recover their dead and by collecting up the spoils from the battlefield; a disabled trireme could often be easily repaired and put back into service on the other side. But 'the men on the Island', the Sphacteria garrison, were the

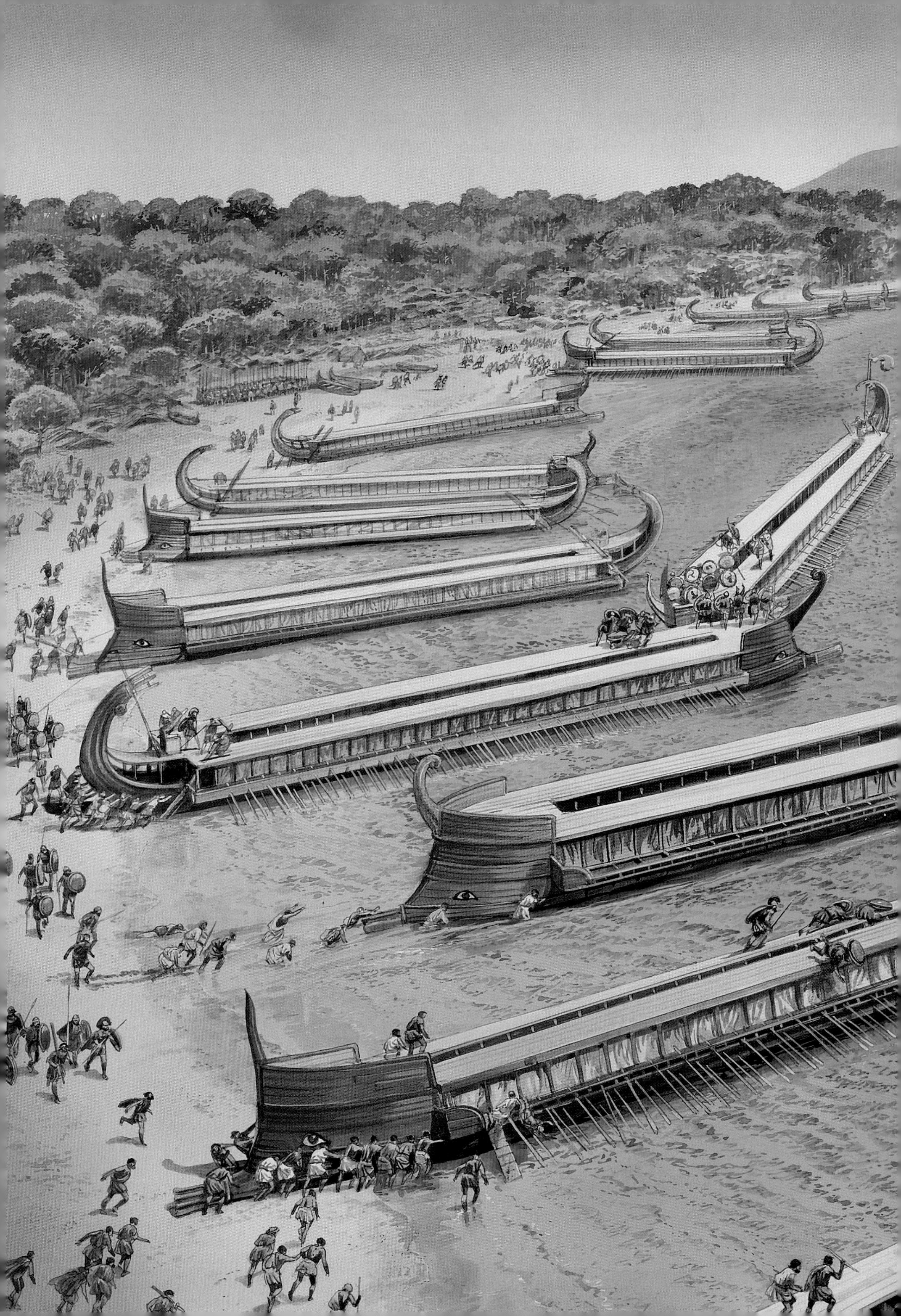

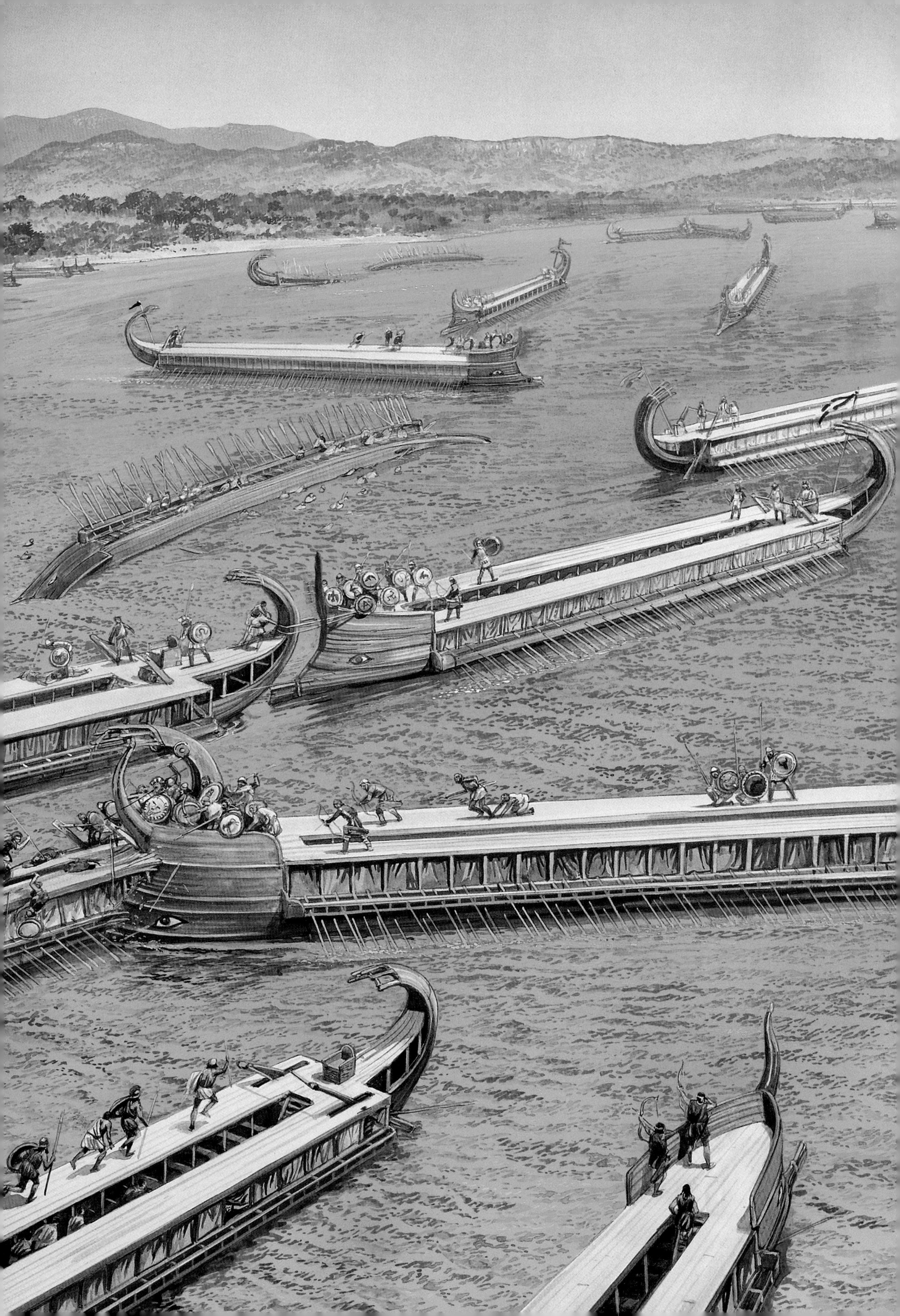

THE BATTLE IN THE HARBOUR (PP. 54–55)

The Spartans have been rapidly and decisively outmanoeuvred in the open water of the bay and run for the shore, having not had the confidence to pull out very far into the bay to meet the Athenian attack.

The Athenians rammed many of them after they had got to the beach and some of them while the crews were still boarding and before they could put out to sea. They disabled others and began to tow them away after the crews had abandoned them. At the sight of all this the Spartans on the shore became frantic, realising that their comrades were about to be cut off on the Island, and they rushed to the ships' rescue. They dashed into the sea fully armed and tried to get hold of them and drag them back. Each one was so focused on this that he behaved as if he was engaged in the action all on his own. It was absolute chaos (IV.14).

The ships that had not been launched would have had their rams pointing out to sea; those that had been chased back to the beach probably ran up it bows-first and would not have got so far out of the water. The Athenians picked their targets, rammed and boarded them, attached tow-ropes and dragged them off, rowing full astern (1). A rammed and holed trireme did not sink but was quickly immobilised as it settled in the water and might also capsize (2), particularly if the crew all made an undisciplined rush to one side. It was usual for the victors in a sea battle to tow these hulks away to repair them for their own use. The crews were generally not taken prisoner. Whilst the Athenians were displaying their superior naval skill and aggression the frantic Spartans' belated response probably reflected a desire to bring their hoplite strength to bear, arming and forming up on the beach (3) for a land battle that the Athenians had no intention of engaging in.

real prize. The most likely site for the trophy is the small island, now called Chelonisi (or Marathonisi), in the centre of the bay and provocatively close to the Spartan camp.

PEACE NEGOTIATIONS

The news of what had happened quickly reached Sparta. It was agreed that senior government officials, *ephors* or *gerontes* (life members of the *gerousia*, the 30-strong council of elders, which included the two kings), should go to the scene of the disaster with authority to decide on the spot on the best course of action. They immediately determined that it was not possible to rescue the men on the Island. But they were not prepared to let them be starved to death or massacred by the Athenians. So they decided to negotiate a local truce with the Athenian generals at Pylos and to send ambassadors to Athens to negotiate a wider understanding. They wanted to recover their men as soon as they possibly could. Thucydides does not use the precise terminology of a peace treaty at this point, but it becomes clear that the Spartans were indeed prepared to agree terms for ending the war in order to liberate the 420 hoplites. Elite Spartiates, the most precious of all their assets, made up about half this number; the rest were *perioikoi*.

The Athenian generals agreed with what the Spartans proposed on these terms: the Spartans were to hand over all the ships in which they had fought and any other warships in the general area and were not to attack the Athenian fort by land or sea; the Athenians would allow the Spartans to send daily supplies of food to the men on the Island under Athenian supervision, they would maintain their blockade of the Island as before but not actually land on it, and they were not to attack the Spartans on the mainland by land or sea. If any of these conditions were breached in any way by either party, the truce would be terminated. Otherwise it was to hold until the Spartan

A storming party attempts to scale a city's walls. The non-hoplite figures beneath the ladder are holding ropes to secure it against the parapet. Most sieges in the Peloponnesian War seem to have been more passive affairs with the objective of starving the defenders into submission. Bringing about betrayal from within was preferred to assault as an alternative. This is one of the many graphic images of late 5th–early 4th century warfare from the Lycian Nereid Monument. The Greek sculptors who worked on this had lived through the later years of the Peloponnesian War. British Museum.

Siege machinery and engineering on as large or elaborate a scale as seen on this 8th-century relief from the Assyrian palace at Nimrud was seldom, if ever, used by Greeks in the 5th century BC. British Museum.

embassy had returned from Athens, taken there and back in an Athenian trireme. Finally, it was agreed that the Athenians would return the Spartan ships in the same condition as they had received them when the truce came to an end. It would have taken a few days for the Spartan officials to get to Pylos and agree the truce, so the delegation sailed for Athens about a week after the battle.

The surrender, even temporarily, of 60 warships seems a massive concession. However, most of the triremes did not belong to Sparta but to her allies, and Sparta's current war strategy accepted the dominance of Athenian sea power, which had, in any case, once again been comprehensively demonstrated. Moreover, the Athenians could do nothing more than keep them at anchor in the sheltered northern area of the bay. They could not beach them on the Spartan-occupied shore (they could not beach most of their own ships on the very small piece of suitable shoreline that lay inside their perimeter); they did not have the manpower to put even skeleton crews on board; and they could not risk reducing their presence at Pylos by detaching men and triremes to tow them to Athens (if it was not a condition of the truce that the ships be kept at Pylos).

The allocation of rations was generous, even the half-quantities allowed for the Helots. The agreed individual portion of barley meal was about a kilogram, that of wine (which was normally drunk mixed with two or three parts of water) about 250cl. The barley meal was supplied as dough so that it could not be stockpiled but had to be baked into the Spartan barley cake staple for fairly immediate consumption; the small ration of meat included

The Sikia Channel looking across the Harbour from above the shore at Gialova. The Spartans should have been able to defend this narrow passage with little difficulty. The yachts at anchor, each a quarter to a third the length of a trireme, give an idea of how crowded this area would have been as the Athenians drove the Spartans back to the shore.

The small island, seen from Gialova and known as Chelonisi today, on which the Athenians probably set up their trophy after the sea-battle in the Harbour. This, and their surrendered fleet at anchor nearby, would have been in clear view of the Spartan encampment on the shore here.

would also have to be eaten quickly before it went off. There was a reasonable spring in the centre of the Island and the Spartans were actually more comfortably placed than the Athenians on Pylos; there was just a small spring up on the heights so most of their drinking water was obtained by scraping holes in the shingle along the shore and 'of the quality you'd expect', and their food supplies had to be brought in by sea.

Only a very few ships could be beached at a time so thousands of crewmen were spending uncomfortably long periods on board, day and night. Triremes were not built to provide accommodation. Thucydides makes no further mention of Prote, but the Athenians quite probably continued to make use of the large, sheltered bays to the south side of the island, where they could also obtain water.

The Spartan ambassadors arrived in Athens and addressed the Assembly. Thucydides has them giving a rather long-winded and patronising speech in which they acknowledge the Athenians' good luck but advise them not to push it too far on account of one acknowledged misjudgement on the Spartans' part:

> You are actually in a position to exploit this present good fortune and not only hold on to what you have won, but gain honour and glory as well. In this way you will escape the fate of those who receive some unexpected piece of luck and keep on overconfidently grasping for more simply because good fortune came to them so unexpectedly. Those who have often seen their fortunes sway either way are rightly suspicious of any success; this is surely something both your city and ours has learned from experience.

Here they generously bracket Athens with themselves, 'the city with the best reputation in all Greece'. Then there is a passage that reads like the pious musings of one of Sophocles' tragic choruses: 'Wise men invest their gains for the future and count them as provisional, and the same men also deal more intelligently with life's misfortunes. And, when it comes to war, they accept that their involvement will not be as limited as they might wish but will be determined by fortune. Such men are least likely to come to grief when carried away by success, but will have the wisdom to agree terms while their good fortune lasts.'

Chelonisi is also the site of the memorial to the British casualties at the 1827 battle of Navarino Bay, an even more one-sided affair.

Their offer was straightforward: 'The Spartans formally invite you to agree an armistice to end the war. They offer you peace and an alliance, and all other forms of friendship and neighbourliness that might exist between us. In return they ask for the men on the Island.' The speech concluded with a lofty vision of joint rule over the peoples of the rest of Greece 'who, in their inferiority, will respect us all the more'. (IV.17–20)

The Spartans thought that the Athenians would be willing to accept this offer of peace and to release their men in return for a declaration of mutual goodwill and a treaty that bound the two cities into an alliance. They expected the Athenians to vote in favour, just as they had voted to send an embassy to Sparta to sue for peace in 430 BC. But the Athenians responded in the same way as the Spartans had on that occasion, by demanding unacceptable terms of their own. As Thucydides put it, 'They reckoned that while they had the men on the Island they could have a truce with the Spartans any time they wanted, so they grasped for more'.

The Spartan delegation faced the people of Athens massed on the Pnyx, the small hill on which they had been gathering for their Assembly since the 6th century BC, against the backdrop of the Periclean and imperial Acropolis. The delegates' desire to pursue negotiations in more private surroundings was understandable.

The popular leader, Cleon, who was very influential at that time, drove the majority vote on this through the assembly. He persuaded his fellow

From the highest point at the north end of the Island and the position of the Spartans's northern outpost, looking towards Gialova. Simple signals using fire, smoke or polished shields would have been exchanged by the men on the Island and the main Spartan force on the mainland, and messages were also carried to and fro by boats and swimmers under cover of darkness. But the speed of events must have made meaningful communication impossible in the final 24 hours of the campaign.

citizens to demand, first, that the men on the Island must give themselves up, surrender their weapons and be taken to Athens; then, that Sparta must give back Nisaea, Pegae, Troezen and Achaea, places that had been ceded by Athens in 445 BC as part of the Thirty Years Peace. The Spartans could secure the return of their men and a treaty that would last as long as both parties thought fit when they had met these demands. Nisaea and Pegae, the two seaports of Megara, were of particular strategic importance. Troezen and Achaea would give Athens significant footholds on the Peloponnese; and the humiliation of surrender of their force on Sphacteria could not be countenanced. 'However, the Spartan envoys did not immediately respond to the Athenians but suggested that a committee be formed to discuss each point in detail in a calm manner, and to arrive at a mutually agreed set of decisions.' They thought the prospects of negotiating a more favourable outcome would be better away from the overheated Pnyx. They were also hoping that Nicias' faction with its more conciliatory attitude would have a strong voice in the committee. Finally, they were unwilling, for fear of damaging their reputation with their allies, to offer concessions publicly that might not be accepted (though they were quite willing to live with the consequences of selling out their allies if this proved a successful bargaining gambit).

Cleon spoke forcefully against this proposal, 'saying that he had always known that their intentions were devious, and this proved it. They were unwilling to speak out before all of the people but wanted to negotiate with just a small group. If they had proposals to make that were at all honourable, they should set them out before everyone.' The Spartans saw the bind they were in and accepted that they were not going to be able to persuade the Athenians to agree a treaty on terms that they thought were in any way reasonable, 'so they left Athens having achieved nothing'. (IV.22)

The truce at Pylos was immediately terminated and the Spartans asked for their ships to be returned. But the Athenians refused to give them back, alleging that the Spartans had breached the terms of the truce by carrying out a raid on their position and by other trivial infringements. The Spartans strongly objected and accused the Athenians of sharp practice, but they could do nothing about it and in any case would not have done any better if they had taken on the Athenian fleet a second time. The Athenian occupation of Pylos was now in its 12th week.

ATHENIAN BLOCKADE AND SPARTAN SIEGE

Hostilities around Pylos and Sphacteria were now resumed. An additional 20 triremes had been sent from Athens so the blockading fleet was now 70 strong. Thucydides tells us that the Athenians kept two ships continuously on patrol, circling the Island in opposite directions throughout the day; it is likely they also kept triremes positioned to cover the obvious escape routes to the north-east and south-east from the top and bottom of the Island. At night they anchored their ships in a cordon round the Island. However the gaps between the ships would have been quite wide and it was not possible to cover the western, seaward side when the wind got up.

On land, the Peloponnesians launched repeated attacks on the fort, but did not, it seems, bring much energy or ingenuity to bear, and the heavy timber for siege machinery called for weeks before never arrived, possibly because of the difficulty of transporting it by land. But they were prepared to wait.

For their part, the Athenians could not be any more proactive. Demosthenes now had over 1,000 hoplites at his disposal, but no Greek commander would have fancied his chances in a shield-to-shield confrontation with Spartan hoplites with odds not much better than two-to-one in his favour. And, though he knew from recent personal experience how effective *psiloi* could be against hoplites in the right tactical circumstances, he also knew that most of the large number he could put into the field lacked the required specialist skills or weaponry. Demosthenes would anyway have been worried by the largely overgrown, trackless state of the Island. He knew from recent experience, good and bad, that these conditions would favour the enemy. They would be able to ambush a landing army from hidden positions and do it great damage, and they would be able to keep the initiative, spotting weak points without being seen themselves and mounting surprise attacks at will.

The Athenians were now constantly short of food as well as water. All their supplies had to be brought in by sea. The single spring and improvised waterholes on the shore were far from adequate and would have deteriorated through heavy use. Living space was cramped enough for the garrison. Because it was possible only for a very few ships to beach at a time under the protection of the walls, the crews had to take it in turns to come ashore and eat while the majority had to stay at anchor offshore if they were not on patrol, though occasional 'shore leave' on Prote may have provided some relief. To make

Looking south from close to the north end of the Island. The cluster of larger trees in the middle distance marks the position of the spring, the only water source, and the stranded Spartans' main encampment. Their southern outpost was on the higher ground beyond. It was possible for a large number of triremes to disembark troops simultaneously along the western shore.

Athenian fortifications on Pylos

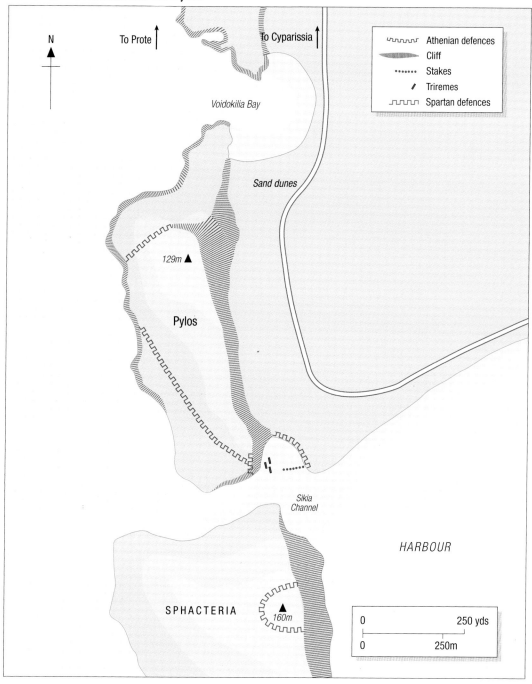

The island of Prote seen from the mainland north of Pylos. Thucydides only mentions it once, used by the Athenian fleet for one night as a base when preparing for the battle in the Harbour. But it is likely also to have been used as a solution to the problems caused by the very limited protected space for beaching ships at Pylos.

matters worse, the operation was taking an inexplicably long time. The men on the Island had been expected to surrender after just a few days, stranded as they were without food and with only brackish water to drink.

But the Athenians had perhaps made insufficient allowance for the Spartan warrior's powers of endurance, trained into him from childhood. Also, their Spartan commanders on the mainland had called for volunteers to take in supplies of barley meal, wine, cheese and other foodstuffs and offered generous rewards for anyone who succeeded in delivering them: money for citizens and freedom for Helots. There were plenty of volunteers, free men and especially Helots. They put to sea from various points along the coast and approached the western side of the Island from the open sea under cover of darkness. They met with most success when they had the wind behind them to carry them in, because the same wind made it difficult or impossible for the blockading triremes to hold their guard positions. The blockade-runners were also less motivated to take care of their boats because they were guaranteed compensation if they sustained damage when they beached on the rocky shore. The risk was greatest for those who attempted crossing in calm weather and some were caught, but the Athenians had a lot of sea to cover.

The Spartans also sent across swimmers with supplies. 'At first these were not spotted, but look-outs were then set to watch for them... Each side was very creative, the one in finding ways of getting food in, and the other in finding ways of stopping them... Divers swam out underwater, towing skins filled with poppy-seed mixed with honey and ground linseed on a cord behind them.' This concoction appears to have been for medicinal use, combining painkilling and emetic properties, and possibly easing the effects of dehydration!

There was growing concern in Athens about the situation. It was now August and late summer storms could add to the difficulty of keeping the occupying force supplied, which would become an impossibility with the approach of winter. They would have to give up the blockade and abandon Pylos. Their prisoners would go free and their extraordinary prize would be lost. It had become clear to them that this was what the Spartans were counting on, and they now understood why the Spartans had made no further attempt to negotiate. The Athenians began to regret the hard line they had taken when the Spartan ambassadors had addressed the Assembly and started to blame Cleon for advocating it.

Cleon's initial reaction was to try to play down the bad news by saying that the reports from Pylos were untrue. The men who had brought them suggested he went there with other observers to see for himself and report back personally. Cleon was backed into a corner, because he already knew very well how things were from his own direct communication with Pylos. He also knew that Demosthenes and his men, increasingly frustrated, were now eager to attempt a landing on Sphacteria, and he sensed that the people were now more inclined to agree to sending the reinforcements that would make this possible.

Cleon therefore proposed that an additional force be sent immediately, arguing that there was not time for a team of observers to carry out their mission, because by then there might no longer be any chance of taking the Spartans off the Island. He pointed out Nicias, one of that year's generals, and also a bitter political opponent whose aristocratic and property-owning faction still wanted to find a way of agreeing terms and ending the war. Cleon taunted him, challenging him and the other generals present to

prove their courage by leading a properly equipped force to the Island and forcing the Spartans on it to surrender: this is what he would do if put in command! Cleon was not a soldier and had never been elected general, yet the policies he favoured in pursuit of the war tended to be the most vicious and aggressive. Heckling broke out with people calling on Cleon to set sail and get on with it if he thought it was such an easy thing to do. Then Nicias weighed in and told him that he and the other generals were happy for him to take whatever troops he liked and have a try.

At first Cleon thought Nicias was bluffing, but when he realized that he was serious about handing over command to him, he became alarmed at the consequence of his rhetoric and conceded that it was Nicias who was the general and that he should lead. But Nicias repeated what he had said and offered his resignation as general, calling the Athenian people to be his witnesses. The harder Cleon tried to back down, the more the crowd, 'as is their way', roared Nicias on to hand over command and Cleon to lead the expedition. So Cleon finally had to agree to do it.

He came back before the assembly and, after declaring that he was not afraid of the Spartans, Cleon made the crowd-pleasing announcement that he would not be requiring a single Athenian to campaign with him. He would be taking only foreign troops who were in the city at the time from the Athenian colonies of Lemnos and Imbros, some peltasts from Aenis in Thrace and 400 archers, who might have been mercenaries from Crete or the Black Sea area. The make-up of this force would have been pleasing to Nicias and the other generals as well, because it did not reduce the hoplite strength available to them to respond to threats or aggression in other theatres.

The stranded Spartans could look down into the Athenian fort from their stronghold at the north end of the Island. The small bay and an area of ground behind it were protected by a strong stone wall that ran obliquely from the base of the cliff to the water's edge and the entrance to the small harbour this created was protected by stakes on its eastern side. (There was dry land between the north-west shore of the Harbour and Voidokilia Bay at the top of the Pylos ridge.)

One of the very few points on the eastern side of the Island at which the quick disembarkation and deployment of large numbers of troops would have been possible. This is the nearest to the likely position of the Spartan outpost at the southern end.

Cleon went on to promise that inside 20 days he would combine this force with the troops already at Pylos, make a landing on the Island and either bring back the Spartans alive or kill them there. This audacious undertaking caused a certain amount of laughter, and there were those in the crowd ('the more level-headed' as Thucydides describes them approvingly) who reckoned that there could only be two outcomes, both good: either they would soon be rid of Cleon, or, less likely, they would finally have those Spartans as true prisoners-of-war. After all the formalities had been completed to confirm these arrangements and the Assembly had voted for his expedition to be launched, Cleon asked for Demosthenes, who had now taken office as general for the year 425–424 BC, to share command with him and prepared to sail for Pylos as soon as possible. (IV.27–29)

Cleon had the good sense not to try to lead this mission without expert assistance, and Demosthenes was the ideal choice: he already had a plan of his own but needed extra resources to be confident of success. It seems Cleon knew about this plan and, whether or not he fully understood it, had faith in it. Also, he trusted Demosthenes, which was made easier by Demosthenes' apparent non-alignment in Athenian politics. Cleon was taking along exactly the kind of specialist troops that Demosthenes required. The 400 archers would double his strength in that arm. Peltasts were formidable javelin-fighters and Thucydides indicates there were over 400 of them, though his count could have included ordinary *psiloi* from Messenia, Lemnos and Imbros. He does not give a number for the latter two contingents, nor does he say what type of troops they were. However, Herodotus describes Samothracians, from a neighbouring island in the north-east Aegean, as 'javelin-fighters' (VIII.88).

These two contingents could have been a mix of conventional hoplites, javelin-fighters (either old-style hoplite or peltast) and archers. This force of approximately 1,200 men significantly increased Demosthenes' missile-fighting strength, and any extra hoplites amongst them would have been very welcome as he considered his options for mounting an attack on the Island whilst keeping enough men back to man his defences on the mainland.

Cleon would have needed at least 30 triremes to transport these troops if they did not double as rowers. However, this would have been such an exceptional measure for Athens at this time that Thucydides would surely have remarked on it. His later count of the Athenian fleet does not reflect the addition of any number as significant as this, nor does he make any comment about the greater overcrowding of the mooring area or about the thousands of extra mouths to be fed, which would have made the supply problem at Pylos even more acute. So it is likely that this substantial squadron sailed on to fend for itself by raiding the Peloponnesian coast after delivering Cleon and his troops.

It is intriguing that Thucydides says nothing about Cleon's apparent breach of his pledge to do the job without committing any more Athenian citizen manpower, passing up an opportunity to score a point against the one individual for whom he consistently shows dislike. However, whilst the officers and hoplites and the majority of the deck crew would have been Athenian citizens, the rowers would have include *thetes* (citizens from the lowest class), resident aliens (*metoikoi*) and public and private slaves. It could also have been argued that the crews would have no combat role in the mission.

In the meantime there had been developments at Pylos. Because of the cramped conditions on shore, Athenian ships had occasionally landed on the Island so that their crews could cook and eat their meals. They presumably chose spots as far away as possible from where they thought the main Spartan force was positioned, and relied on the protection of look-outs and the difficult terrain to give them time to board and row off if threatened. A trireme crew of 200 or so, including only a few hoplites and archers, would have been easy meat if less than half Epitadas' force had mounted an attack. However, it was probably Spartan strategy to avoid contact, which would have risked revealing their true strength or provoking a more proactive strategy on the Athenian side.

One of these crews started a brush fire. This was accidental, according to Thucydides, but Demosthenes, remembering his nightmarish defeat in Aetolia the year before, might easily have given the order for it to be done. A wind got up, the fire quickly spread, and large masses of the trees, bushes and undergrowth were burned away. With areas of shoreline cleared it was easier to pick out landing points that gave good access to the interior of the Island. Demosthenes could now also observe the Spartans' movements and positions and get a much better idea of their numbers. So when he received a message that Cleon was on the way, Demosthenes was already actively planning his own assault and beginning to make preparations, including calling in more support from the Messenians and other allies in the region.

The western side of the Island was much more accessible from the sea, but also more exposed to rough weather.

THE BATTLE ON THE ISLAND

It was now the second week of August and the Athenians had occupied Pylos in early May. As soon as Cleon and his men had arrived, the Athenians sent a herald to the Spartan camp on the mainland inviting them to instruct the men on the Island to surrender. Their personal safety would be guaranteed and they would be held in decent conditions whilst terms were negotiated along the same lines as offered previously at Athens. The Spartans swiftly rejected this.

Demosthenes and Cleon waited for a day, then embarked 800 hoplites on to a few ships under cover of darkness and put to sea. This was clearly not observed by Spartan watchers on the Island or the mainland and, if it was done from Demosthenes' small area of beach, it probably seemed no different from the launching of nightly blockade patrols, except that the ships may have been boarded later than usual to conceal the exceptional numbers on board. In order to transport hundreds of hoplites 'on a few ships' the Athenians would have embarked the maximum of 40–50 that could be safely accommodated on the deck of a troop-carrying trireme in calm weather. They may also have seated up to 62 hoplites on the top-tier rowing benches in place of the *thranites* oarsmen, reducing the need to as few as eight ships. This would have made it easier to disembark the entire force quickly, especially in the very limited space for landing on the Harbour side, and left more than enough ships to transport the much larger second wave. A little before dawn these ships put in to shore on the east and west sides of the Island and landed the men. It would have taken only a few minutes and could have been done quietly.

The Spartan force was now known to be divided into three. Epitadas, the commander, had most of his men concentrated in the centre of the Island around the spring. He had a small detachment positioned at the north end at the highest point, not named by Thucydides but known today as Mount Elias. This position was backed by high cliffs and reckoned to be impregnable on this, its eastern side. The remnants of the rough stone wall of an ancient fort and rocky outcrops reinforced the perimeter on the slopes of the other three sides. Thucydides mentions that Mount Elias had been identified by the Spartans as a good position to fall back on, if they were driven off the level ground on which they intended to fight. It also overlooked the Sikia channel

In the dawn light the Spartans on the mainland watched, powerless, as the Athenians made their landings on the Island, not knowing that they were coming ashore in much greater force on the seaward side. They were probably not yet aware of the night-time massacre of their outpost at the southern end.

and the Athenian camp, and needed to be permanently manned to cover what was otherwise a fairly straightforward line of attack from that direction. It was an excellent strongpoint, but with one significant drawback: there was no water apart from what could have been carried there for its modest garrison. The third detachment was stationed 500–1000m to the south of the main encampment to watch out for landings at that end and harass the enemy until the main force could join them and engage. This strategy had made sense whilst the Spartans had the advantage of the cover provided by the thick vegetation, but with that gone, they would have done better to adopt Demosthenes' strategy of meeting landings at the shoreline.

This southern outpost was manned by 30 hoplites and, presumably, an equal number of Helot *psiloi*. The detachment on Mount Elias was probably larger, perhaps 50, so Epitadas' central force would have totalled about 340 hoplites with their attendant Helots. Even if the Spartans' failure to observe that an assault force had been embarked the night before was reasonably understandable, it could only have been through incompetence or perhaps exhaustion that they were not in a higher state of alert on the Island. They are likely to have had word sent to them somehow of Cleon's arrival with reinforcements and of the latest offer of terms and its rejection. And intelligence of the debate in the Athenian Assembly, the decisions taken and Cleon's pledge would undoubtedly have reached the Spartans on the mainland before Cleon landed at Pylos. Any landing from now on was very likely to be concerned with more than finding space to prepare and eat a meal.

The Athenians now knew exactly where the southern Spartan outpost was, and movement was now much easier with trees and underbrush burned away. They advanced from their landing points at the double and overran the small detachment, only half-awake and groping for weapons. Then at sunrise Demosthenes put ashore his main assault force, consisting of 8,000–9,000 non-hoplite troops. As small a garrison of hoplites, archers and *psiloi* as could be risked had been left behind on Pylos. Thucydides explains the logistics. Everyone on each ship disembarked except for the *thalamioi* oarsmen on the lowest tier and the minimum number of crewmen needed to back off and hold the ship offshore until the time came to pick up the landing party. The balance of 130, consisting of 118 oarsmen, ten or so assorted seamen, the rowing master (*keleustes*) and the ship's commander (*trierarch*), went ashore to serve as *psiloi* along with the 40–50 archers, peltasts and extra *psiloi* that each ship could additionally take on board.

If Thucydides' statement that there were crewmen 'from 70 ships or more' is taken as meaning over 70 ships were actually involved in the landing, it would not have been necessary to load them so heavily if the additional troops were evenly distributed amongst them. However, the eastern shoreline could only accommodate a few ships coming ashore at one time and Demosthenes may have elected to use fewer ships on the western side as well so that he could disembark the men in larger concentrations and form them up and position them more quickly. He could have managed the landing with fewer than 50 ships.

The short, sharp opening action bore no relation to the nobler tradition of hoplite combat, and the Athenians were learning how to fight a different kind of war more quickly than the Spartans. Bronze cheek-piece from a late 5th–early 4th-century Phrygian-style helmet. National Archaeological Museum, Athens.

'The Athenians ran up to the outpost and slaughtered the men in their beds before they could reach for their weapons.' (IV.32) Relief from the Nereid tomb, British Museum.

The best of the few reasonable landing points on the eastern side of the Island. This is the Panagia landing, the site of the Russian memorial to their men who died in 1827.

To maintain surprise this substantial fleet must have been assembled outside the Harbour and Prote could have been the starting point. If the Spartans on the mainland had become aware of its approach, there was nothing they could do to prevent it and they clearly did not manage to get any warning across to the Island. Thucydides' narrative of what followed is vivid and exceptionally informative for an account of an ancient battle, and unquestionably based on conversations with combatants from both sides

Demosthenes organised his force into groups of 200, some larger, some smaller, and had them take up positions on areas of high ground up and down the Island in order to create the maximum uncertainty in the minds of the Spartans. The Spartans could not decide which way to turn to face the enemy forces now surrounding them on every side. They were completely enveloped by overwhelming numbers. If they charged out to the front, they were showered with missiles from behind; if they charged out on one flank, they were attacked on the other. Whichever way they turned, the enemy *psiloi* were always at their backs and very difficult to engage with because of their capability of fighting from a distance with arrows, javelins, stones and slings. The Spartans were quite unable to get to close quarters with them. When the enemy fell back, they outran the Spartans and when the Spartans backed off, they turned on them again. This was what Demosthenes had in mind when he first started planning a landing and this was the way he now executed it.

When the main contingent under Epitadas' command on the Island had seen that their guard post had been wiped out and that the landing force was moving towards them, they formed up and advanced on the Athenian hoplites with the objective of engaging them in close combat. The hoplites were directly to their front while the *psiloi* were on their flanks and behind them. But they were unable to get to grips with the hoplites and bring their expertise to bear. The Athenian *psiloi* kept them in check by showering them with missiles from all sides whilst the hoplites stayed out of the fight, making no move to meet their advance.

Whenever the *psiloi* came in close the Spartans drove them off, but then they would wheel and renew their attack. They were equipped for mobility and the Spartans with their heavy shields could not get to grips with them on this difficult terrain, which had never been cultivated. So, for a while, the two sides skirmished in this way but the Spartans were becoming tired and less able to dart out in response to each thrust against them. The Athenian *psiloi* saw that the Spartans' counterattacks were becoming increasingly sluggish and so grew more confident. They could now see how greatly they outnumbered the Spartans and began to realize that they were rather less formidable an enemy than universally reckoned. They were also encouraged by the fact that they had not suffered the casualties they had expected on first landing, overawed as they had been by the thought that it was Spartans they were taking on. Now they had less respect for them. So they gave a great roar and charged them in a mass, pelting them with stones, arrows and javelins, whatever they had to hand. The loud shouting and all-out assault were very unsettling for men who were not used to this kind of fighting. Also, clouds of ash from the brushfire were being kicked up. They could not even see what was right in front of their faces whilst the hands of many showered arrows and stones down on them through the dust storm. The engagement now became really difficult for the Spartans. Their *pilos* helmets could not protect them from the arrows and the heads of the javelins snapped off when they struck. The Spartans were helpless. They could not see what was in front of them; they could not hear commands called out to them above the louder shouts of the enemy. With danger on every side, they were losing hope of defending themselves or reaching safety. (IV.32–34)

Demosthenes' strategy was to avoid direct contact between his hoplites the Spartans. His hoplites outnumbered theirs by a factor of two, but whatever file-depth Demosthenes chose, Epitadas could match the length of his line by reducing his own in proportion and Spartan resolution, drill and supreme skill with spear and shield would more than counterbalance numerical advantage. In any case, the terrain 'which had never been cultivated', even if it had been cleared by fire, was unsuitable for phalanx combat, which had evolved through generations of fighting over level farmland. However, if they had engaged, the rough ground would have favoured the better organized and individually more highly drilled, trained and skilled Spartans. Demosthenes was clearly not assuming they had been significantly weakened by lack of food.

The units into which Demosthenes divided his very large light-armed force, if less than 200 strong, were probably formed as they were for embarkation on the triremes that carried them to their landing points on either side of the Island and north and south of the main Spartan position. The larger formations mentioned probably indicate that some of the specialist light-armed men were consolidated after landing from separate ships, though this would only have been practicable if the ships had landed at the

A *psilos*, typically armed with a rock and with a hide over his left arm as a basic shield. His *pilos* hat is very likely of the felt variety. The sword and leggings are not so typical. Most of his comrades would have been no more than stone-throwers, though some would also have carried edged weapons, spears or javelins. Kunsthistorisches Museum, Vienna. (Kunsthistorisches Museum)

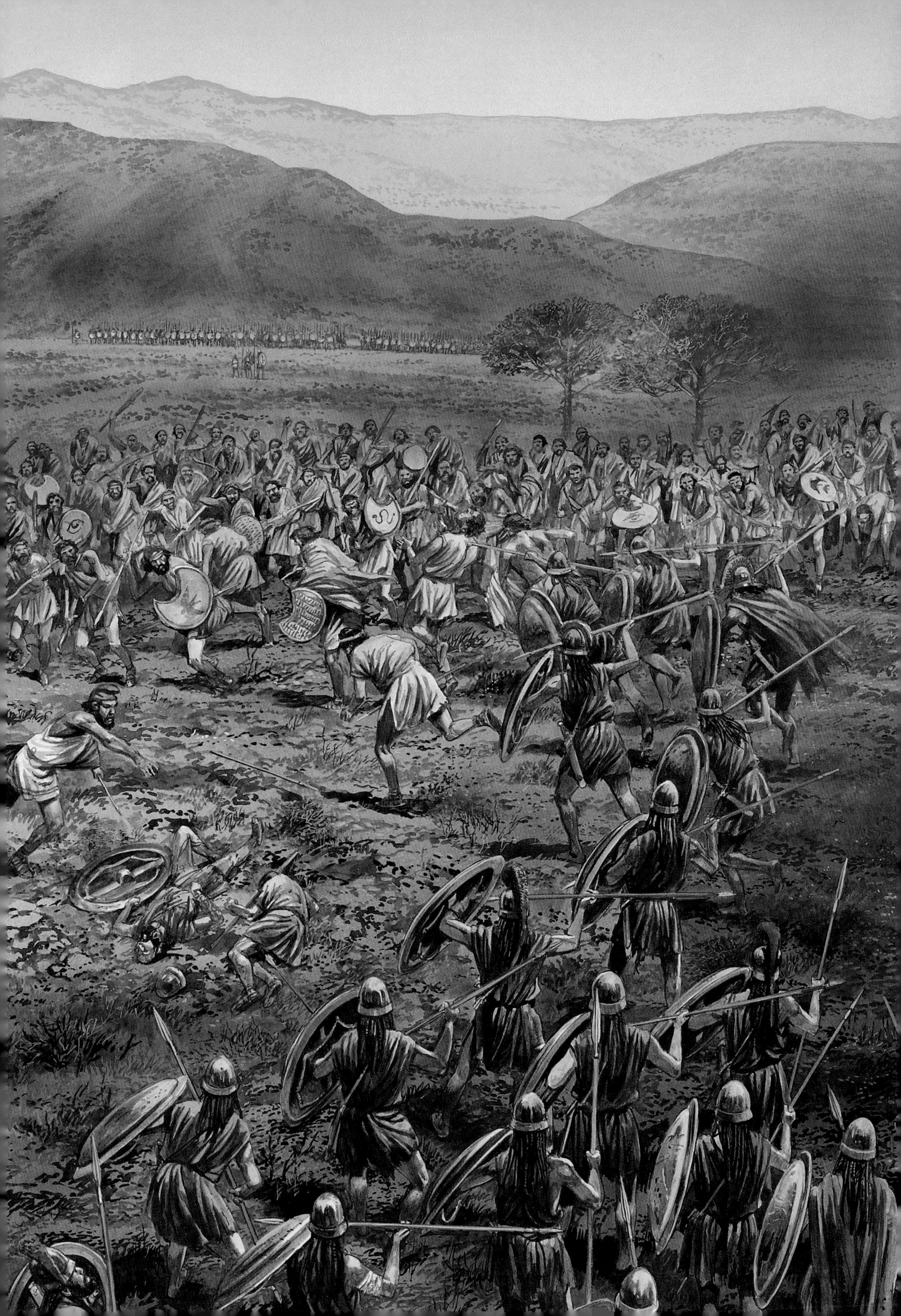

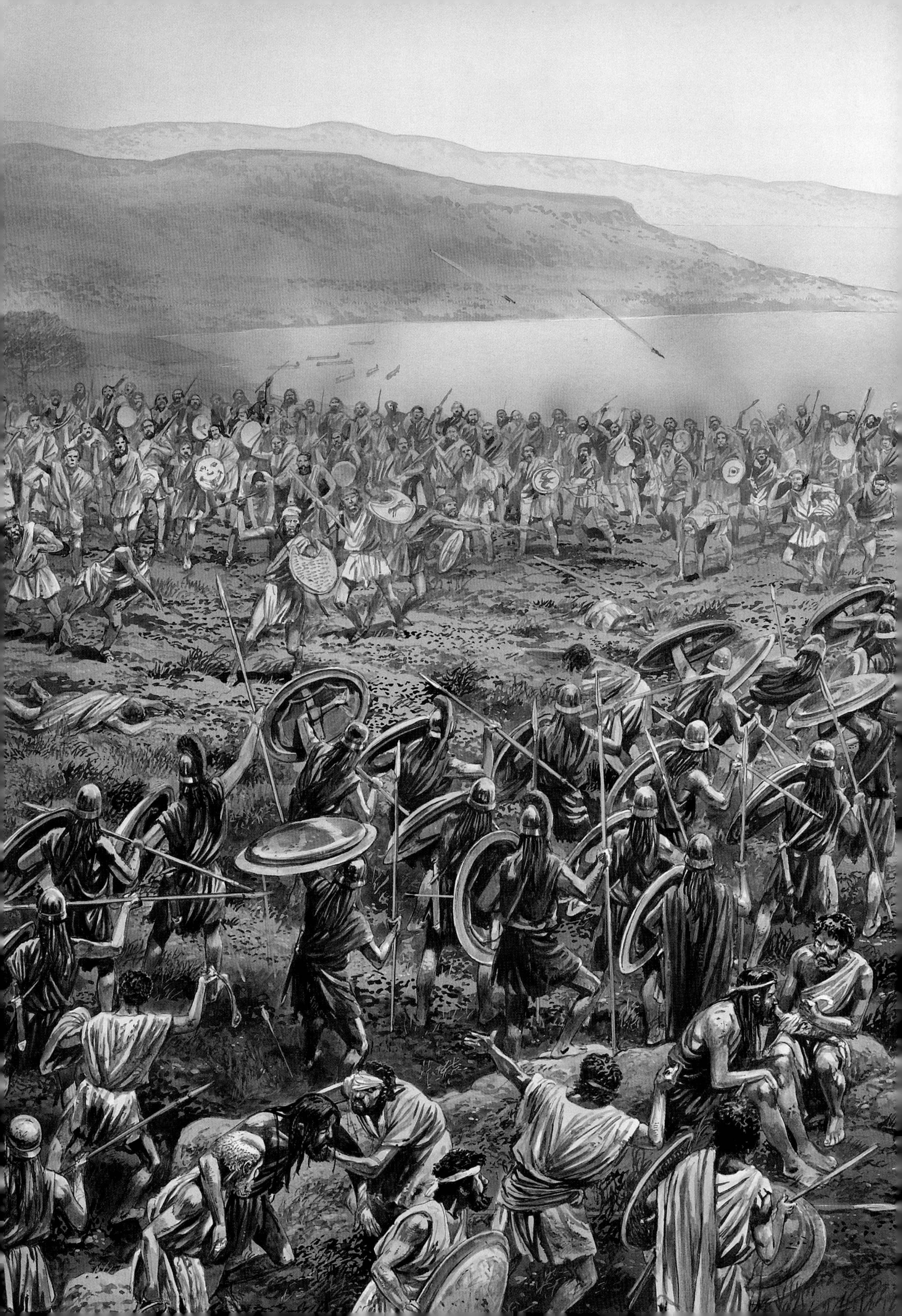

THE BATTLE ON THE ISLAND: *PSILOI* AGAINST HOPLITES (PP. 72–73)

'When the main contingent **(1)** under Epitadas' command on the Island had seen that their guard post had been wiped out and that the landing force was moving towards them, they formed up and advanced towards the Athenian hoplites **(2)** with the objective of engaging them in close combat. The hoplites were directly to their front while the *psiloi* were on their flanks and behind them. But they were unable to get to grips with the hoplites and bring their expertise to bear. The *psiloi* **(3)** kept them in check by showering them with missiles from all sides and the Athenian hoplites stayed away from the fight, making no move to meet their advance. Whenever the *psiloi* came in close **(4)** the Spartans drove them off, but then they would wheel and renew their attack. They were equipped for mobility and the Spartans with their heavy shields just could not catch up with them on this difficult terrain, which had never been cultivated. So, for a while, the two sides skirmished in this way but the Spartans were becoming tired and less able to dart out in response to each thrust against them.' (IV.33)

The Spartans, Spartiates in this section of the line, are in open order to offer a more difficult target for missile attack. Small groups **(5)**, generally of the youngest and fittest hoplites in the role of *ekdromoi* (runners-out), dash forward like snatch-squads in modern riot-policing. Helot attendants **(6)** provide support of various kinds, including fighting as *psiloi*. The Athenian peltasts **(7)**, here mingled with the mass of the *psiloi*, would have had a limited supply of javelins and would only contemplate hand-to-hand contact with Greece's finest hoplites if the prolonged skirmishing succeeded in breaking up their formation. The primary weapon for the *psiloi* was the rocks and stones at their feet. These had to be large enough and thrown at a range of no more than a few metres to be effective, giving the Spartan *ekdromoi* some opportunity to fight back.

Thucydides' remark about ground 'which had never been cultivated' is a reference to the ideal conditions for hoplite combat as satirised by Mardonius when making the case for the Persian invasion of Greece. Successive Spartan invasions of Attica had failed to provoke the Athenians into overriding one of the key principles of Pericles' war strategy and Demosthenes was not going to offer this kind of battle on Sphacteria. Some of the triremes that delivered the Athenian forces to the Island at daybreak are standing off the accessible western shoreline **(8)**.

same time or in quick succession on the same beach. The prolonged Spartan resistance and the final casualty rate could suggest that Demosthenes diluted his missile firepower by not concentrating his archers and peltasts sufficiently at the start of the battle.

Thucydides' description of a battle fought in 423 BC between a force under the command of Brasidas and a larger body of non-hoplite troops, in this case Illyrians, gives a little more detail on the tactics he describes Epitadas as using. 'Seeing that the Illyrians were about to attack, Brasidas formed his hoplites into a square and placed his contingent of *psiloi* inside it and prepared to retreat. He positioned the youngest soldiers where they could dash out to meet an attack from any direction and himself stood ready at the rear with 300 picked men to make a stand against the leading ranks of the enemy to screen the withdrawal.' (IV.125)

Epitadas used hoplite skirmishers (*ekdromoi*) in the same way, and his Helot *psiloi*, deployed within the main hoplite formation, gave him a little missile-firepower. However, it is unlikely he had a single archer in his ranks, and their response to the Athenian bombardment would have been mainly restricted to throwing the enemy's missiles back; nor did he have the men to form any kind of reserve (Brasidas' 300 picked men were key to his successful fighting retreat in Illyria). Clearly, it was not enough simply to deny Epitadas and his men a conventional hoplite engagement; the Spartans fought on, responding with these more fluid tactics. But, as Thucydides records, they were unsettled by the scale and din of the attack, fighting blind because so much dust and ash had been kicked up, and unable to co-ordinate their defence because they could not hear their officers' commands.

Thucydides' comment about the inadequacy of the Spartans' *pilos* helmets has been interpreted as evidence that they were made of felt or leather rather than bronze, allowing missiles to penetrate more easily. However, bronze was the material generally favoured by the Spartans, if not actually 'regulation issue', and the remark makes better sense if taken as contrasting the neck and face protection afforded by closed helmets such as the Corinthian type. Closed helmets had been generally superseded by the bronze open *pilos* except for ceremonial use, but may have been worn by some older soldiers on the Athenian side and perhaps by the generals.

The word translated as 'javelins' in the same sentence is *doratia* (literally 'little spears') and may imply a different kind of missile than the regular javelin (*akontion*), either light thrusting spears that could also be thrown or the smaller throwing spears, sometimes translated as 'darts'. Vase paintings show that the former were carried in pairs in Archaic times by hoplites and cavalry, and peltasts might go into battle with more than two of the latter. The point Thucydides may be making is that these weapons, some of which may have been

The piece of dry-stone walling here is unlikely to date back to the 5th century BC but it gives an idea of the way in which the Spartans could have reinforced the natural defences of their position.

Approaching the peak at the north end of the Island, today known as Mount Elias, from the south. The outcrops around the peak's base could have formed part of the southern section of the Spartan perimeter.

improvised, broke wherever they landed and could not be reused against the enemy, a design feature of the Roman legionary *pilum*.

> Eventually, after taking many casualties as they were pushed to and fro over the same patch of ground, the Spartans closed ranks and started to fall back towards their strongpoint, not far away at the top of the Island, to join up with the men guarding it. As soon as they began to retreat, the Athenian *psiloi* pressed forward with even greater confidence and louder shouts. Any Spartans they caught were killed, though most of them managed to withdraw to the fort and took up positions alongside the troops guarding it to defend it at every point that could be attacked. The Athenians were right behind them, but the strength of the position prevented them getting round it to encircle the Spartans, so they kept trying to dislodge them with frontal attacks. For a long time, indeed for most of the day, both sides held their ground, enduring the fighting and thirst and the heat of the sun, one side determined to drive the enemy from the high ground, the other determined not to give way. But it was now easier for the Spartans to put up a defence than before because their flanks were no longer unprotected. (IV.35)

Until the decision was taken to fall back, the Spartans fought in open order to give the enemy archers and javelin-throwers a less compact target and for greater ease of movement. Thucydides says their fort was 'not far away at the top of the Island'. In fact, their fighting retreat was carried out over more than half its length (a couple of hours' walk in normal circumstances) and with only minor losses. This was a very considerable achievement against such odds for men who were exhausted. The walls and natural defences around the peak of Mount Elias and the small number of fresh troops Epitadas' force joined there temporarily changed the situation. The Athenians' missile tactics could no longer be effective and the word translated as 'dislodge' (*osasthai*) shares its roots with *othismos*, the term for the phase of a phalanx battle when the opposing sides had come together and 'shoved' against each other, shield to shield and spear to spear. The Athenians were fighting uphill and the Spartans were holding them off with little difficulty. In any case, arrows and javelins must have been in short supply by now (resupply from offshore would have been quite a slow process), which may also explain the level of Spartan casualties sustained during the withdrawal.

When it seemed there could be no end to this, the commander of the Messenians [Pausanias gives his name, Comon] went up to Cleon and Demosthenes and told them they were wasting their time. But if they would give him a detachment of archers and *psiloi*, he thought he could find a way to get round to the rear of the Spartan position and mount an attack from behind. He got the men he asked for and set off over ground that was out of sight of the enemy so that they could not observe the movement. He worked his way around the steepest cliffs of the Island at points where the Spartans, relying on the natural strength of their position, had placed no look-outs. It was difficult going but (Comon) just managed to get round undetected. His force suddenly appeared on the peak to the rear of the Spartans. They were thrown into a panic by this shocking turn of events, but it was an excellent development for the Athenians, whose spirits were raised by the sight they had been waiting for. The Spartans were now under attack from front and rear and were in the same dire situation, to compare small things with great, as the men at Thermopylae. Just as those men were annihilated when the Persians outflanked them by taking that path, so these Spartans could not hold out any longer, caught as they were between two fires. They were few fighting many and weakened by lack of food, and they began to give way with the Athenians controlling every approach to their position.

Cleon and Demosthenes realized that if the Spartans collapsed any further they would be wiped out by their troops and so they put a stop to the fighting and held their men back. They wanted to deliver the Spartans to the Athenian people alive. They hoped that if the Spartans heard a herald's voice offering terms it would break their will and persuade them lay down their weapons and accept their terrible predicament. So a herald proclaimed that they could, if they chose to, lay down their arms and surrender to the Athenians, who would then decide what to do next. When they heard this, most of the Spartans put down their shields and raised their hands to signal that they accepted the terms that had been offered. A truce was agreed and Cleon and Demosthenes entered into discussion with Styphon son of Pharax representing the other side. Of the commanders appointed earlier the first in command, Epitadas, was dead, while his chosen successor, Hippagretus, had been laid among the corpses, taken for dead but actually still just alive. Styphon had been selected as third in succession, to take command, according to Spartan law, should anything happen to the others. Styphon and those with him said that they wanted to send a herald across to the Spartans on the mainland to ask for instructions. But the Athenians would not allow any of them to leave the Island and called for heralds to be sent over from the mainland. After two or three exchanges, the last herald to make the crossing from the mainland brought this message: 'The Spartans instruct you to decide for yourselves what to do, as long as this is nothing dishonourable.' After some discussion amongst themselves they surrendered and gave up their arms. (IV.36–38)

SPHACTERIA 425 BC

The Athenians launch a massive assault and, after a day's fighting over most of the length of the Island, finally force the surrender of the surviving 292 hoplites, including 120 elite Spartiates, who have been stranded there for 72 days since the sea-battle in the Harbour.

DEMOSTHENES

SPARTAN CAMP

SPARTAN OUTPOST

THE ISLAND

ATHENIAN FORCES
A 800 hoplites (probably without attendants)
B 8,000–10,000 rowers and sailors as *psiloi*
   700–800 archers
   800 peltasts
   400 others (mixed force of Messenians and
   other allies)
C Skeleton garrison

Note: Gridlines are shown at intervals of 500 meters (546.8 yards)

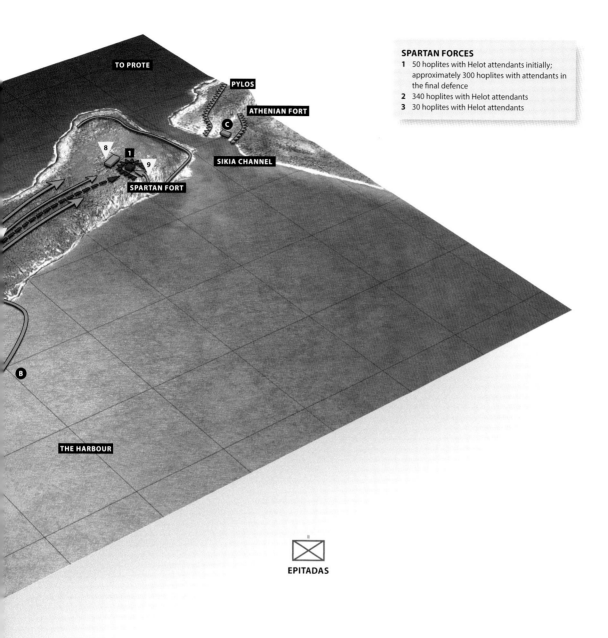

TO PROTE

PYLOS

ATHENIAN FORT

C

8 **1**

9

SIKIA CHANNEL

SPARTAN FORT

B

THE HARBOUR

EPITADAS

SPARTAN FORCES
1   50 hoplites with Helot attendants initially;
    approximately 300 hoplites with attendants in
    the final defence
2   340 hoplites with Helot attendants
3   30 hoplites with Helot attendants

▼ EVENTS

1   Before dawn: the Athenian hoplites land and
overrun the southern Spartan position.

2   They form up facing the main Spartan position.

3   The Spartans form up and advance towards them.

4   Dawn: the second wave of Athenian light-armed
troops comes ashore, in greater force on the much
more accessible western shoreline.

5   They rapidly surround the Spartans, attacking
them with missiles from all sides and preventing them
engaging with the Athenian hoplites.

6   Mid-morning: The Spartans abandon their attempt
to break through the skirmishing mass of *psiloi* to take

on the Athenian hoplites and begin a fighting retreat to
their stronghold at the north of the Island.

7   The Athenian *psiloi* harass them all the way whilst
the hoplites follow at a distance.

8   Afternoon: now reinforced by the fort's small
garrison, the main Spartan force holds out against the
Athenians' frontal attacks, which are carried out mainly
by their hoplites.

9   Evening: Comon the Messenian leads a small force
of archers and *psiloi* round behind the Spartans at sea
level to scale the cliff and attack them from the highest
point on the Island.

This view explains why the Spartans were not guarding their rear.

It had seemed as if the Spartans on Mount Elias were going to hold out until dehydration finished them off. Demosthenes would then have had problems of his own, keeping his much larger force fed and watered and with a concerted land-attack on his lightly guarded fort always a possibility. Comon's welcome initiative was probably inspired by some local knowledge, though Thucydides makes it clear that he could not say exactly where he would climb the cliffs in the Spartans' rear. Erosion, plant growth and the geological activity of two and a half millennia have brought about changes in the eastern cliff face that are more than superficial. But it is likely that there was a narrow path round its base similar to the goat track identified by Pritchett (1965) in the 20th century. Then as now, there were one or two places where it was relatively easy to scramble up from the water's edge to the ridge directly behind the peak of Mount Elias inside the Spartan perimeter, and not be seen by the defenders until it was too late.

Thucydides does not tell us whether Comon approached the start of this climb by working his way along the eastern side of the Island or by coming round from the west. There is plenty of dead ground to the west and north of the Spartan position and this would mostly have been easier going for a group of 30–40 men than the other route. Once Comon's men had worked their way round, made the climb undiscovered, and taken up position on the peak in the centre of their stronghold, the Spartans were finished. They could not protect themselves from the arrows, javelins and sling-stones coming in from above and behind at a range of 20–30m without turning away from the attackers in front of them and giving them the openings they needed to break through their perimeter.

When the truce was called, the Athenians found themselves dealing with the third in the Spartan chain of command, a glimpse of a level of military organization unmatched in any other Greek army of the time. Faced with two choices, surrender, which could be reasonably described as honourable in these particular circumstances, or a death at the hands of fellow-Greeks using barbarian tactics, which could not, they settled for the former with little hesitation.

That day and the following night the Athenians kept the Spartans under guard. Next day, after setting up a trophy on the Island, they made their preparations for sailing and distributed the prisoners amongst the trierarchs for them to guard. The Spartans sent a herald and took off their dead. The numbers killed and taken alive on the Island were as follows: 420 hoplites in all crossed over; of these 292 were taken alive, and the rest were killed; the number of Spartiates among the survivors was about 120. Not many Athenians were killed because the battle was not fought at close quarters. The men were blockaded on the Island for a total of 72 days from when they were stranded after the sea-battle to the land-battle on the Island. For about 20 of these days, while the ambassadors were in Athens negotiating, they had received regular supplies. For the rest of the time they had depended on what the blockade-runners could bring in and the Athenians collected up some grain and other food on the Island. Epitadas had issued rations to his men more sparingly than the level of supply actually permitted. (IV.38–39)

Mount Elias and the north-east corner of the Island from the Athenian position on the north side of the Sikia Channel. The Spartan perimeter encircled the peak but did not cover its rear along the top of the cliff. Comon and his men worked their way round to the base of the cliff, either from the south or perhaps more likely from the west (the right of the picture) where the approach could have been made over dead ground along the south side of the Sikia Channel. They climbed the cliff, which is, today, not as difficult as it appears from the top or from a distance at sea level, and emerged on to the saddle directly behind the peak and inside the Spartan perimeter. They were then able to take up a position on the peak, unopposed and not even observed till they started shooting arrows and throwing javelins.

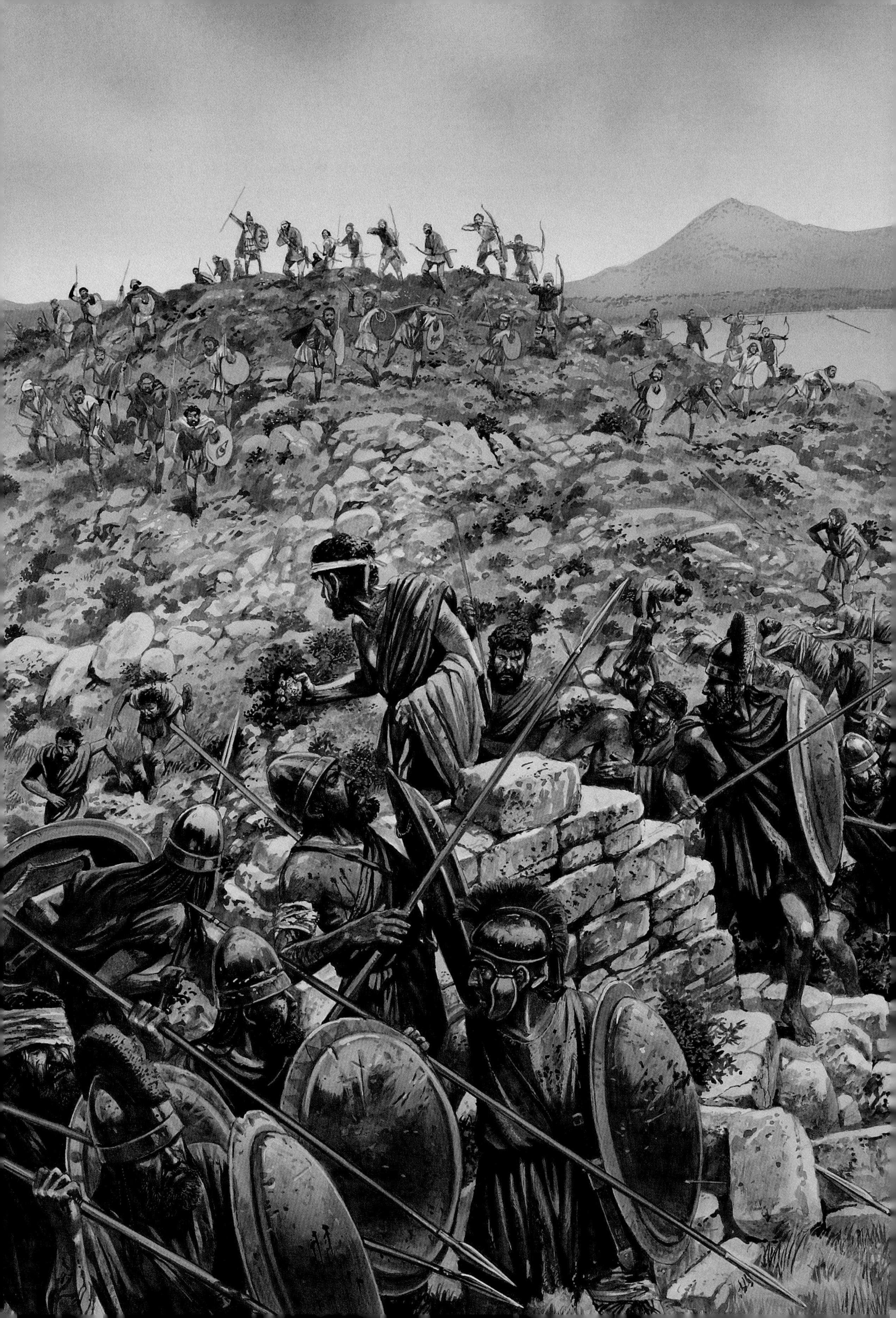

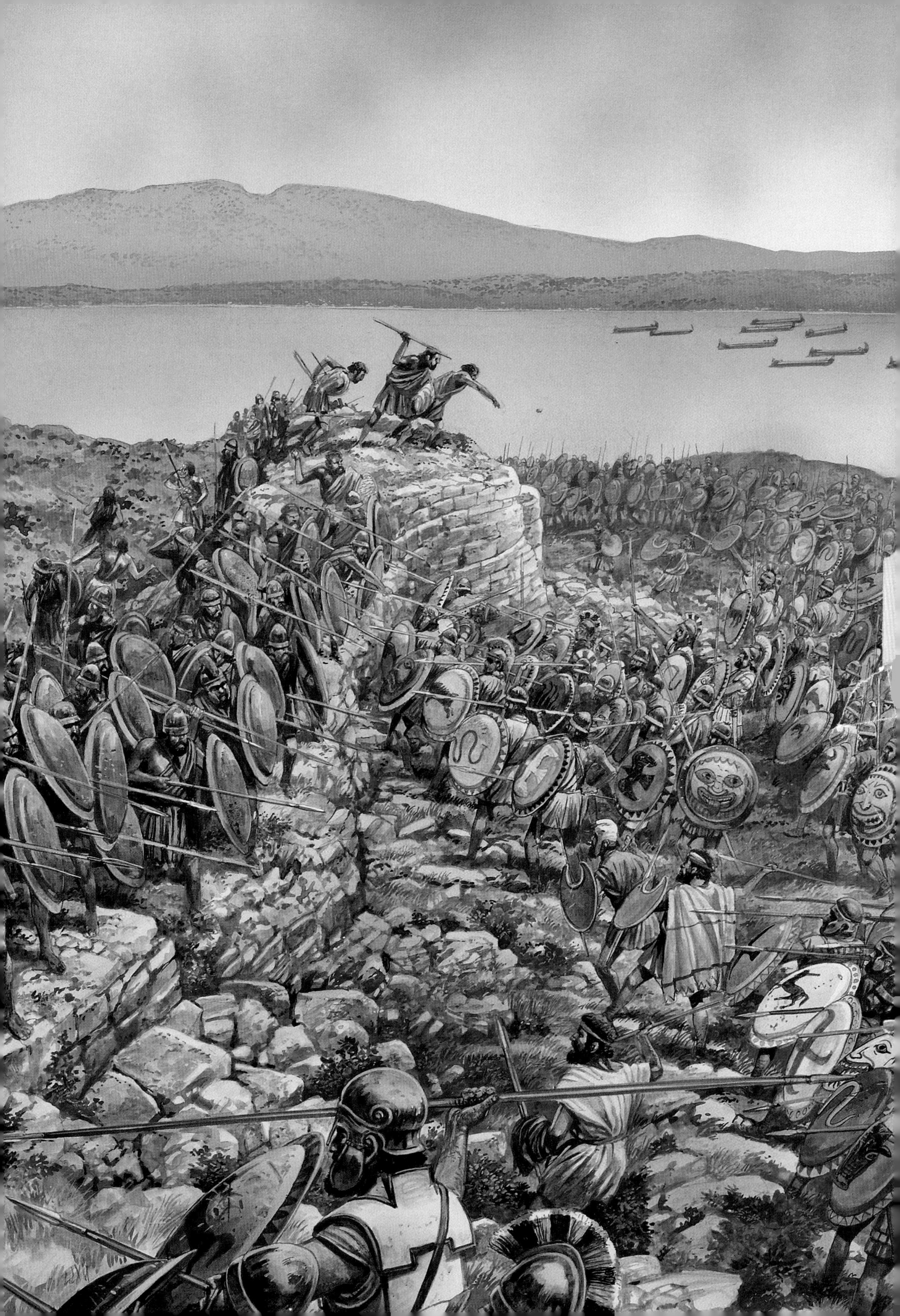

THE BATTLE ON THE ISLAND: THE SPARTAN LAST STAND (PP. 82–83)

After a fighting retreat over more than half the length of the Island the main Spartan force, depleted by casualties, joined the small garrison in their naturally defended and partly walled stronghold on the highest point at the north end, overlooking the Athenian position across the narrow channel separating Pylos from the Island. For most of the rest of the day they defeated all Athenian attempts to dislodge them. They were much less vulnerable to missile attack and were at last able to do what they did best to beat off efforts to force the position with spear and shield, but they now had little or no water. However, the Athenians could not afford to wait for them to collapse from dehydration because they too had supply problems with their much larger force. Then Comon the Messenian and his mixed, non-hoplite force, managed to work their way round to the rear and scale the cliffs without being seen. They crossed the dead ground in the saddle behind the peak in the centre of the Spartan position and occupied it **(1)**.

This is the moment when the small force of about 40 archers, slingers and javelin men attack the defenders from above and behind at a range of 20–30m. 'The Spartans were now under attack from front and rear and were in the same dire situation, to compare small things with great, as the men at Thermopylae. Just as those men were annihilated when the Persians outflanked them by taking that path, so these Spartans could not hold out any longer now, caught as they were between two fires. They were few fighting many and weakened by lack of food, and they began to fall back with the Athenians controlling every approach to their position' (IV.37). The Spartans' weakness would actually have been due to lack of water and probably sheer exhaustion. They may well have had nothing to eat all day but they were not actually starving; Thucydides later mentions that the Athenians discovered a stockpile of food on the Island. In the southern sector the thin Spartan line combining Spartiates **(2)**, *perioikoi* **(3)** and Helot attendants **(4)** is holding firm on the natural and man-made defensive perimeter while the more numerous Athenians hang back as the first missiles find their target. The Harbour with the captured Spartan ships at anchor **(5)** and the Messenian mainland **(6)** are in the background to the east.

It is only at this point that Thucydides gives the number of Spartan hoplites on Sphacteria but he does not mention their Helot attendants. One per hoplite, and a higher casualty rate, is a reasonable assumption, but this obviously was not a matter of much concern, though they probably fought and died loyally alongside their feudal masters. Of the 128 hoplite dead, 30 were killed in the first-wave attack on the Spartans' southern outpost. Probably most of the remainder died in the main battle before the fighting retreat; a number would, of course, have died from wounds later.

Leaving aside the death rate of 100 per cent on the final day at Thermopylae, where hoplite losses were not exceptional over the full three days, the 30 per cent death rate on Sphacteria had been exceeded previously in only one other reasonably well-documented battle. This was the defeat suffered by the Athenians only the year before under Demosthenes' command at Aegitium at the hands of overwhelming numbers of Aetolian javelin fighters. Here maybe 40 per cent of a 1,600-strong hoplite force had been lost. Demosthenes showed how well he had learned that hard lesson in his redeeming victory at Olpae later in the same year and on Sphacteria. If about half Epitadas' force were Spartiates, their death rate was around 40 per cent.

It is not surprising that Athenian casualties were light, not only because winning sides generally suffered significantly fewer, but also because of the

The area of dead ground that was left unprotected in the Spartan rear.

nature of the battle. The literal meaning of the Greek word *stadaia*, translated above as 'at close quarters', is 'standing up'. Thucydides uses it to contrast the conventional hoplite engagement that Demosthenes avoided with the running battle that he engineered. Hoplite casualties must only have been taken by the Athenians in the attack on the Spartan defences on Mount Elias. If *psiloi* were counted amongst the 'not many', most would have been caught in the early counterattacks of the Spartan *ekdromoi* before they tired. Thucydides' aside that the Spartans had managed to build up reserves of food is evidence of their strategy to sit out the blockade until autumn weather drove the Athenians home.

'And so Cleon's pledge, crazy as it had been, was fulfilled. He had brought the men on the Island back with him inside 20 days, just as he had promised.' (IV.39) The hawkish demagogue had disappointed his upper-class critics and rivals, strengthened his own political powerbase and made a name for himself as a general, even if victory truly belonged to Demosthenes. Thucydides' account of 'the Pylos affair' closes with this reflection on the Spartans' surrender.

> For the rest of the Greeks, this was the most unexpected event in the whole war. They had never thought Spartans would lay down their arms as a result of starvation or under any other form of compulsion, but expected them to keep their weapons and fight on in any way that they could, and die. They could not believe that the men who surrendered were the same kind of men as those who had died. Later, one of the Athenian allies tauntingly asked one of the prisoners from the Island whether his comrades who died were the 'fair and brave' ones (*kaloi k'agathoi*). The prisoner's answer was that a 'spindle' (*atrakton*), by which he meant an arrow, would indeed be worth a lot if it could pick out only the brave. His point was that it was chance that determined who was killed by stones and arrows. (IV.40)

The Greeks were amazed that Spartans, the most formidable warriors of their race, the heroes of Thermopylae and Plataea and victors in so many former Greek wars, could bring themselves to surrender in any circumstances. Surely the survivors had forfeited any claim to the manly virtue of *kalo k'agathia* that distinguished the elite they represented? The prisoner's answer is in the spirit of another Spartan saying, collected by Plutarch, 'It doesn't matter to me that I am dying, but it does that I have been killed by an effeminate arrow' (*Moralia* 234 E). This was the wrong kind of warfare and the old rules did not apply.

AFTER SPHACTERIA

When the men had been brought back the Athenians resolved to keep them in chains in prison until some deal could be done, but to take them out and execute them if the Peloponnesians invaded their land before this. They established a garrison at Pylos and the Messenians from Naupactus, who regarded Pylos as homeland (for it was once Messenian territory), sent out some of their most effective troops from there to plunder Laconia, and they were able to do a lot of damage as they spoke the local dialect. The Spartans had no previous experience of raiding and warfare of this kind. Helots were deserting and they were afraid that this might lead to more serious insurgency across the land. They were very worried and, although they did not want to reveal this to the Athenians, they kept sending embassies in an attempt to recover both Pylos and their men. But the Athenians, always grasping for more, sent the embassies back empty handed as often as they came. (IV.41)

Thucydides here tersely concludes his 10,000-word account of the campaign, 'This was what happened at Pylos'. The Athenians sailed back to Athens and the Spartans marched home. Thucydides does not say what the Athenians did with the captured ships that they had held at anchor in the bay for over two months. Triremes left afloat and neglected would deteriorate quite rapidly, especially any that were damaged or had already been at sea for a long period and some of them were probably not of very good quality in the first place. In any case, the Athenians would not have had the manpower to row them away, though they may have taken a few of the better hulls with them under tow. They probably left most of them behind to rot or perhaps burned them as a final gesture.

Nor does Thucydides tell us of any Spartan arrangements to contain or keep watch over the garrison and ships that remained. The fort was kept supplied by sea and probably served for the most part as a base for seaborne raids up and down the coast, because the closer hinterland was thinly populated and offered little in the way of assets to destroy or plunder.

Thucydides depicts the Spartans as reduced to near-paralysis at this time:

They were in a state of high alert, fearful of new threats to the established order of things. The disaster on the Island had been a huge shock; both Pylos and Cythera were in enemy hands, and they were hemmed in on all sides by a war that was fast-moving and unpredictable. Their attitude to military action had become even more cautious… The misfortunes that had come upon them, in such quick succession and against all reason, had filled them with

The bronze skin of a Spartan shield brought back to Athens as a trophy. It is tersely inscribed 'Athenians from Lacedaemonians at Pylos'. Agora Museum, Athens.

dismay, and they were fearful that another disaster might happen, just like the one on the Island. As a result, they had lost confidence in their fighting ability and they thought that any move they made would lead to catastrophe. Their morale was shattered because they had previously not known failure. (IV.55)

The continuing occupation of Pylos, that 'deserted spot' and the imprisonment of 120 Spartiates might seem less serious than the threat posed by the fort at Methana, near Epidaurus and occupied by the Athenians that same summer, to important allies in a more densely populated and prosperous area of the Peloponnese, or by the capture (in 424 BC) of the strategically and commercially important island of Cythera, or, indeed, by the loss of almost the entire allied fleet. However, Pylos was more dangerous as a rallying point and refuge for dissident Helots and other natives of Messenia than as a base for pirate raiders.

Even more potently, it was associated with defeat and humiliating surrender. The same applied to the 120 Spartiates. Disgraced as they may have been, the Spartans wanted these men released and home. Some of them were from the most prominent families, who applied influence, and they were all surviving members of a warrior caste that was dying out. There were about 8,000 Spartiates in 480 BC according to Herodotus, 2,500 in 418 BC according to Thucydides, and less than 1,000 in 371 BC according to Aristotle. Reasons for this decline included the deaths caused by the earthquake of 465 BC and the subsequent Messenian War, and the unintended effect of rigidly applied inheritance laws. The Spartans were strongly motivated to make peace and prepared to make significant concessions in order to include the release of the Spartiate prisoners as a condition, even before they were taken off the Island.

The Athenians were not interested in peace but wanted to carry on the war, improving their already strong negotiating position by building on their recent success. However, things began to go wrong for them in 424 BC. After capturing Cythera they made a surprise attack on Megara; Demosthenes was one of the generals leading the operation. Brasidas, who was raising an army in the area of Corinth and Sicyon, intervened and saved Megara for the Peloponnesians, though the Athenians managed to hold on to the port of Nisaea.

They developed a grander plan to detach Boeotia from the Peloponnesian alliance that winter by invading simultaneously from the west and directly from Attica. Demosthenes was to lead the thrust from the west but the Boeotians found out about the plan and blocked it. The army from Athens carried out their part of the plan but was bloodily defeated at Delium, losing 'their general, Hippocrates, just under 1,000 hoplites, and a great many *psiloi* and baggage carriers'. This was a large-scale hoplite confrontation with 7,000 on each side, but the Thebans on the Boeotian right did not follow the conventional pattern. They formed up 25-deep against the eight-deep Athenian left and 'got the better of them, shoving them back slowly at first then putting them to flight'. The Athenian right did better initially but was then broken by a well-timed cavalry attack. Ironically, the quality of the Boeotians' non-hoplite infantry, which included 500 peltasts alongside more than 10,000 *psiloi*, better organized and equipped than their Athenian counterparts, could have been a factor in their victory. (IV.93–96)

Meanwhile, Brasidas had made his way overland to Thrace, not setting foot in Attica and unable to go by sea. He had personally proposed this mission to undermine Athenian interests in the area and the government had given reluctant support in the shape of 700 Helot hoplites and funds to hire mercenaries elsewhere in the Peloponnese. He successfully forced or persuaded a number of cities, including the important colony of Amphipolis, to abandon their allegiance to Athens and, in early spring of 423 BC, Athens and Sparta agreed a one-year truce. The Athenians' purpose was to put a stop to Brasidas' campaign, which had been worryingly successful, and use the time to organize a response to it. The Spartans were well aware of this but had anyway anticipated that the Athenians would be more inclined to negotiate after Delium. For their part, they hoped that the truce would lead to negotiation of a longer-term peace and 'the recovery of the men was an even higher priority while Brasidas' run of success continued' (IV.117).

The peace did not hold in Thrace. Brasidas engineered the defection of another city, Scione, before he had been informed of the truce but then neighbouring Mende also defected to him. Then, while Brasidas was away campaigning in Macedonia and Illyria the Athenians took Mende back and afterwards blockaded Scione; Nicias was one of the generals in command of that expedition. In summer 422 BC Cleon persuaded the Athenians to send him to Thrace in command of a strong force. He retook Torone before Brasidas could come to the assistance of the small garrison and then established a base at Eion, close to Amphipolis, where Brasidas consolidated his forces.

Thucydides' brief account of Cleon's and Brasidas' final battle before Amphipolis probably takes a biased view of

The goddess *Nike* (Victory) by the sculptor Paeonius. This was commissioned around 420 BC by the Messenians of Naupactus to celebrate their successes in the Peloponnesian War, including their involvement at Pylos and Sphacteria. Olympia Museum.

the generalship on both sides, but it is clear that the latter's perfectly timed sally was decisive in his posthumous victory. Brasidas was one of the seven casualties recorded by Thucydides on his side whilst the Athenians lost about 600, including Cleon. The two leaders most opposed to peacemaking, as Thucydides observed, were now dead.

> Neither side pursued the war any further and both were now inclined towards peace. The Athenians had taken a beating at Delium and again, not long afterwards, at Amphipolis. They no longer had the faith in their powers that had given them the confidence to reject earlier peace overtures, when they believed their current success would take them on to victory. They were fearful that their setbacks would encourage allies to defect in greater numbers and were now regretting that they had not agreed terms after things had gone so well for them at Pylos. The Spartans felt much the same. The war had not turned out as intended. They had expected to overcome the power of Athens in a few years by laying waste their land. Instead, on the Island, they had met with disaster on a scale that Sparta had never experienced before; their own land was being raided out of Pylos and Cythera; the Helots were deserting, and there was always the threat that those who remained in the Peloponnese might be influenced by those outside to exploit the situation and rebel, as they had done before... Both sides carefully considered all of this and came to the conclusion that it was best to agree terms. The Spartans were particularly keen to do so in their desire to recover the men who had been captured on the Island. (V.15).

Under its terms the Athenians were required to give back Pylos, withdrawing its Messenian garrison, and to release all prisoners, including those taken on the Island. The returning Spartiates were initially stripped of some of their rights but were later reinstated, so they did not receive the very harsh treatment they would have suffered in earlier generations. Pylos was occupied again in winter 419 BC and held for Athens till winter 409 BC. At Mantinea in 418 BC, a massive hoplite confrontation, the Spartans emphatically restored their fighting reputation in a victory over Argos, her old enemy, and her allies, including Athens. (V.65–75) The Peace of Nicias was meant to last for 50 years. It did not bring peace to Hellas, and Athens and Sparta were formally at war again in 414 BC.

THE BATTLEFIELD TODAY

The 19th-century battle of Navarino Bay is commemorated by this obelisk in Three Admirals' Square in modern Pylos (established by the Venetians in the 16th century). It is guarded by captured Ottoman cannons and the portrait plaque of Admiral Codrington is flanked by portraits of his Russian and French co-admirals.

The village of Gialova is an excellent base from which to explore Pylos and Sphacteria and also the south-west and west of the Peloponnese. The area has a comprehensive history. 'Sandy Pylos' was Homer's description of Nestor's kingdom. There are remains of a fine Mycenaean tomb just to the north of 'Nestor's cave' in the northern cliffs of the Pylos ridge and the extensive excavations of the wise old king's palace are a few kilometres inland; he also has a nice Messenian chardonnay named after him. Gialova looks out across

Navarino Bay to Sphacteria and Pylos. There is a small river at the northern edge of the village and it is plausibly suggested that the besieging Spartan army camped here.

The Pylos ridge is topped by the walls of the Old Castle (*Paliokastro*), established in the 13th century by the Franks, later extended by the Venetians and then by the Ottoman Turks. The Turks abandoned it shortly after the battle of Lepanto in 1571. They replaced it with the New Castle (*Niokastro*) behind the 'new' town of Pylos, using European engineers to apply the latest principles of fortification and moving the axis of their defence of Navarino to the wide southern channel into the Bay. The Turks abandoned this castle in 1828 at the end of the Greek War of Independence. In the battle of Navarino the previous autumn, the last battle fought entirely between sailing ships but actually an almost static exchange of cannon-fire, a British–French–Russian fleet sank most of a considerably larger Ottoman–Egyptian fleet without losing a single ship. Timbers can still be seen on the seabed and there are a number of memorials.

Olympia, Sparta and Mystras are in easy reach for day-trips. The nearest airport is at Kalamata and Messenia is less than five hours drive from Athens.

Sphacteria is uninhabited, and a nature reserve. It is not difficult to cross the Sikia channel to the north end by wading some of the way and swimming the rest. However, as exploration calls for some hours of rough walking, boots and food and drink are a good idea and it is best to go by boat. Small motorboats can be hired from Pylos town harbour, but these are only suitable for the sheltered water of the bay. To go out into the open sea and make a complete circuit, it is necessary to hire something a bit faster and bigger.

The best starting place for a walk on the Island is the Panagia Landing, the site of the Russian Navarino memorial. It is on the east side, about a kilometre from the northern tip and is one of the very few points on the shoreline where a trireme could have disembarked and deployed troops with reasonable ease. A good track leads north, at first through mature woodland, up on to the ridge along the probable line of the Spartans' fighting retreat to their stronghold and last stand on the 152m peak now known as Mount Elias.

From here there are excellent views south along the length of the Island, east across the bay to Gialova and the mainland, and north across the narrow channel to Pylos and the site of Demosthenes' fortified section of beach. The peak is not quite as high as it was in the 5th century BC, having been flattened by Italian engineers in World War II to accommodate an artillery observation post, but the vegetation, sparser than on the deeper soil of the lower slopes, is probably much as it was then.

The site of the spring or well and the main Spartan position can still be identified a kilometre or so south of Panagia Landing, but this is apparently now very hard to find in the thick woodland.

Thucydides' description of the Island as 'densely wooded for the most part and without paths because it had never been inhabited' (IV.29) remains accurate. The interior is much more accessible from the shore for most of its western length but there are no obvious places where a trireme could have easily been drawn out of the water over the steeply shelved rock. The only stretch of suitable beach on the whole Island is at the base of its highest cliffs below Mount Elias.

Pylos can be approached on foot from Gialova along the curving beach, a walk of about 3km, or by road and then by a track that runs between the modern lagoon and the beach. From the southern end of the Pylos ridge it is possible to take a circular walk starting from Demosthenes' beach and going north between the base of the eastern cliffs and the western shore of the lagoon (strong mosquito repellent is recommended!). The beautiful Voidokilia beach lies beyond a cluster of sand dunes; these run up to the base of the cliffs, which are crowned by the northern ramparts of the Old Castle. A steep path leads up to the top and an easy walk down the ridge to 'Brasidas' Rocks' at the south-west end and then back to Demosthenes' beach.

Aside from the architecture and engineering of later wars and the comparatively recent flooding of the flat ground immediately to the east of the cliffs, the ancient battle landscape of Pylos and Sphacteria is exceptionally unaltered.

FURTHER READING

Thucydides, translations and editions

Gomme, A. W., *A Historical Commentary on Thucydides Volume III*, Oxford University Press, Oxford (1956)

Mynott, Jeremy, *The War of the Peloponnesians and the Athenians*, Cambridge University Press, Cambridge (2013)

Lattimore, Steven, *The Peloponnesian War*, Hackett Publishing, Indianapolis (1998)

Strassler, Robert B. (trans. Crawley), *The Landmark Thucydides: a Comprehensive Guide to the Peloponnesian War*, Free Press, New York (1996)

Wilson, J. B., *Thucydides Pylos 425 BC Book IV 2-41 with Translation and Historical Notes*, Aris & Philips, Warminster (1979)

Background

Best, J. G. P., *Thracian Peltasts and their Influence on Greek Warfare*, Wolters-Noordhoff, Groningen (1969)

Cartledge, Paul, *After Thermopylae; the Oath of Plataea and the End of the Graeco-Persian Wars*, Oxford University Press, New York (2013)

——, *Sparta and Lakonia: a Regional History 1300-362 BC*, Routledge, (second edition) London (2001)

Hanson, Victor David, *A war like no other: how the Athenians and Spartans fought the Peloponnesian War*, Random House, New York (2005)

Kagan, Donald, *The Peloponnesian War*, Penguin Books, London (2004)

Kagan, Donald and Viggiano, Gregory F., *Men of Bronze: Hoplite Warfare in Ancient Greece*, Princeton University Press, Princeton (2013)

Morrison, J. S., Coates J. F. and Rankov, N. B., *The Athenian Trireme: The History and Reconstruction of an Ancient Greek Warship*, Cambridge University Press, Cambridge (2000)

Lazenby, J. F., *The Spartan Army*: Aris & Philips, Warminster (1985)

Nicastro, Nicholas, *The Isle of Stone: a Novel of Ancient Sparta*, Signet Books, New York (2005)

Pritchett, W. K., *Studies in Ancient Greek Topography Part I*, University of California Press, Berkeley (1965)

——, *The Greek State at War Volumes I–V*, University of California Press, Berkeley (1971-1991)

Rankov, Boris, *Trireme Olympias: the Final Report*, Oxbow Books, Oxford (2012)

Rusch, Scott M, *Sparta at War: Strategy, Tactics and Campaigns*, Frontline Books, London (2011)

Sabin, Philip, van Wees, Hans and Whitby, Michael, *Cambridge History of Greek and Roman Warfare I: Greece, the Hellenistic world and the rise of Rome*, Cambridge University Press, Cambridge (2007)

Schwartz, Adam, *Reinstating the Hoplite: Arms, Armour and Phalanx Fighting in Archaic and Classical Greece*, Franz Steiner Verlag, Stuttgart (2010)

Shaw, Timothy, *The Trireme Project: Operational Experience 1987–90*, Oxbow Books, Oxford (1993)

Trundle, Matthew, 'Light troops in classical Athens' in Pritchard, David M., *War, Democracy and Culture in Classical Athens*. Cambridge University Press, Cambridge (2010)

van Wees, Hans, *Greek Warfare: Myths and Realities*, Duckworth, London (2004)

Westlake, H. D., *Individuals in Thucydides*, Cambridge University Press, Cambridge (1968)

INDEX

References to images are shown in **bold**.

CAMPAIGN • 224

MONS GRAUPIUS
AD 83

Rome's battle at the edge of the world

DUNCAN B CAMPBELL   ILLUSTRATED BY SEÁN Ó'BRÓGÁIN

Series editor Marcus Cowper

First published in Great Britain in 2010 by Osprey Publishing,
Midland House, West Way, Botley, Oxford OX2 0PH, UK
44-02 23rd St, Suite 219, Long Island City, NY 11101, USA
Email: info@ospreypublishing.com

Osprey Publishing is part of the Osprey Group.

A CIP catalogue record for this book is available from the British Library.

ISBN: 978 1 84603 926 3

PDF e-book ISBN: 978 1 84603 927 0

Editorial by Ilios Publishing Ltd, Oxford, UK (www.iliospublishing.com)
Page layout by: The Black Spot
Index by Mike Parkin
Typeset in Sabon and Myriad Pro
Maps by Bounford.com
3D bird's-eye views by The Black Spot
Battlescene illustrations by Seán Ó'Brógáin
Originated by PDQ Media
Printed in China through World Print Ltd.

11 12 13 14 15   11 10 9 8 7 6 5 4 3 2

The Woodland Trust
Osprey Publishing is supporting the Woodland Trust, the UK's leading
woodland conservation charity, by funding the dedication of trees.

www.ospreypublishing.com

DEDICATION

To Janet and Ruairi, who cheerfully agreed to spend a perfectly good
summer's day exploring the foothills of Bennachie with me, and kept
me supplied with wine during the writing of this book.

ACKNOWLEDGEMENTS

It is again a pleasure to acknowledge the kindness and generosity of friends
and colleagues who provided illustrations (or attempted to locate them)
for this little book: Tony Birley, for the Vindolanda tablets; Jim Bowers, for
his stirring photo montage; Julie Bronson, for never giving up the quest to
find the coin of 118 BC; Stephen Bull, for the Lancaster cavalry tombstone;
Ross Cowan, for finding some excellent coins; Donald Fraser, for the
reconstructed Roman field oven; Fraser Hunter, for items in the care of the
National Museums of Scotland; Lásló Kocsis, for the Carnuntum diploma;
Jona Lendering, for assorted photos (as always); Alan Leslie, for his photos
of Roman military ditches; Mike McCarthy, for the Carlisle photographs;
David Mason, for the Chester inscriptions; Joyce Reynolds, for valiantly
attempting to track down Julius Karus' lost tombstone; Alison Rutherford,
for trying so hard to locate the photo of the 'Agricola' writing tablet;
Manfred Schmidt, for CIL's drawing of the Tacitus inscription; Tony Spence,
for his excellent reconstructions of Iron Age chariots; Adrian Wink, for
supplying some splendid images of his fellow re-enactors; and David
Woolliscroft for some wonderful aerial photographs.

Stan Wolfson kindly permitted me to read his unpublished manuscript,
The Battle of Mons Graupius: Some problems of text, tactics and topography
(1999), from which I have benefited greatly. Of course, readers should not
assume that he agrees with everything that I have written, although I am
happy to acknowledge that I have usually accepted his emendations to
Tacitus' text (especially at 35.3, 36.3, 38.2 and 38.5).

A NOTE ON THE SOURCES

All ancient sources are referenced using the abbreviations listed on page
94. All translations are my own, although I have frequently benefited from
the suggestions in Ogilvie and Richmond's commentary, and readers may
notice that some passages from the *Agricola* bear a remarkable
resemblance to the excellent version of A. R. Birley, which I was often
unable to better.

ARTIST'S NOTE

Readers may care to note that the original paintings from which the
colour plates in this book were prepared are available for private sale.
The Publishers retain all reproduction copyright whatsoever. All enquiries
should be addressed to:

Seán Ó'Brógáin, Srath an Ghallaigh, An Clochan, Leifear, Tir Chonaill, Ireland

The Publishers regret that they can enter into no correspondence
upon this matter.

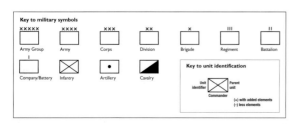

CONTENTS

The Roman Empire in the Flavian period, *c.* AD 80

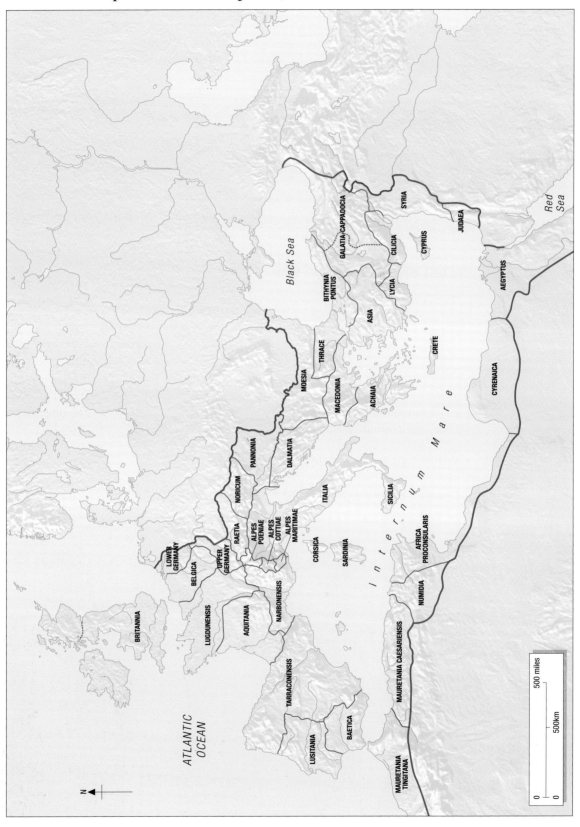

Red Sea

Black Sea

GALATIA-CAPPADOCIA

SYRIA

CILICIA

CYPRUS

JUDAEA

BITHYNIA PONTUS

LYCIA

AEGYPTUS

ASIA

THRACE

CRETE

MOESIA

MACEDONIA

ACHAIA

CYRENAICA

PANNONIA

DALMATIA

Internum Mare

NORICUM

ITALIA

SICILIA

RAETIA

ALPES POENIAE

ALPES COTTIAE

ALPES MARITIMAE

AFRICA PROCONSULARIS

LOWER GERMANY

UPPER GERMANY

CORSICA

SARDINIA

BELGICA

NUMIDIA

LUGDUNENSIS

AQUITANIA

NARBONENSIS

BRITANNIA

MAURETANIA CAESARIENSIS

TARRACONENSIS

ATLANTIC OCEAN

LUSITANIA

BAETICA

MAURETANIA TINGITANA

N

500 miles

500km

0

0

ORIGINS OF THE CAMPAIGN

By AD 83, Roman armies had been campaigning in Britain for 40 years. Throughout southern England, the process of romanization was gathering momentum, as the indigenous tribes welcomed the development of towns and took on some of the trappings of Roman civilization. But, although two generations of Roman soldiers had now fought and died in the province, whole tracts of Wales and northern England still required close military policing. At Rome, the reigning Flavian dynasty wished their legacy to include the final conquest of Britain and its absorption into the Roman Empire. The defeat of the Caledonian tribes at Mons Graupius in AD 83 brought that dream closer to fulfilment. But, in the words of the Roman historian Tacitus, 'Britain was completely conquered and immediately neglected' (Tac., *Hist.* 1.2: *perdomita Britannia et statim omissa*). The focus shifted to the great river frontiers of mainland Europe, where the threat to Rome seemed more pressing. Never again would a Roman army stand on the furthest edge of the world.

View of Bennachie from the north-east, across the site of the Roman marching camp at Durno. The suggestion of the late Professor Kenneth St Joseph, that this is the site of the battle of Mons Graupius, has become generally accepted. (Author's collection)

THE CLAUDIAN INVASION: PEOPLES SUBDUED AND KINGS CAPTURED

Coin of Claudius. Roman coins detail the official set of titles of the reigning emperor, in this case *Ti(berius) Claudius Caesar Aug(ustus) P(ontifex) M(aximus) Tr(ibunicia) P(otestate) Imp(erator) P(ater) P(atriae)*. (Author's collection)

The Romans invaded Britain in AD 43, on the orders of the emperor Claudius. The island was home to dozens of individual Celtic tribes, some of whom had long-established trading links with Continental Europe. The Greek geographer Strabo, writing around AD 20, recorded that British exporters were already paying large sums in customs dues: 'they submit to heavy duties on the exports to Gaul, and on the imports from there, which include ivory bracelets and necklaces, amber and glassware, and similar petty goods' (*Geog.* 4.5.3). It seems that the southern Britons, at any rate, operated an economy of some sophistication, and many British aristocrats were already profiting from their links with Europe.

One result of Julius Caesar's expeditions to Britain in 55 and 54 BC had been to bring these southern tribes into the orbit of Rome. Although Strabo claimed that little had been accomplished on the island, he admitted that Caesar had brought back hostages and slaves, which suggests that some form of client relationship had been established with some of the tribes at least. The *Achievements of the Divine Augustus* (*Res Gestae Divi Augusti, RGDA*), the lengthy catalogue of the first emperor's deeds, publicized on his death in AD 14, lists Britons amongst the kings who took refuge at Rome (*RGDA* 32), and Strabo claims to have seen British chieftains paying homage on the Capitol. It was not uncommon for the beleaguered princes of other nations to seek shelter at Rome; another Briton did so during the reign of Gaius Caligula (Suet., *Calig.* 44), and the historian Cassius Dio suggests that it was the presence of another at Claudius' court that presented the emperor with an excuse to invade the island (Dio 60.19).

So it is not at all surprising that, when Roman troops arrived on British soil in AD 43, several chieftains were willing to pledge their allegiance. According to the inscription on Claudius' triumphal arch, 'the Senate and people of Rome (set up this arch) because [the emperor Claudius] received the submission of 11 kings of the Britons, conquered without any loss, and because he first brought barbarian peoples beyond the ocean under the control of the Roman people' (*ILS* 216; cf. Suet., *Div. Claud.* 17, for his triumph).

One of these friendly kings must have been Cogidubnus (or Togidubnus), who seems to have ruled the area around Chichester; formally hailed as a friend of Rome, on one inscription he is even named 'great king of Britain' (*RIB* 91: *rex magnus Britanniae*). Other so-called client kingdoms were established to relieve the pressure of military garrisoning by devolving responsibility onto the local chieftains. For example, in East Anglia, King Prasutagus of the Iceni was happy to ally himself with the Romans; and in AD 51, Cartimandua, queen of the Brigantes in northern England, handed over the fugitive rebel Caratacus to cement her friendship with Rome. But these were temporary measures. The 1st century AD was a period of confident expansion for Rome. Developments documented elsewhere in the Roman Empire show that treaty arrangements were usually allowed to persist only during the lifetime of the friendly ruler. Thereafter, such kingdoms were usually brought under direct Roman control as imperial provinces.

Throughout the remainder of Claudius' reign, Roman rule was gradually imposed across southern England. 'Peoples were subdued and kings were captured', writes Tacitus (*Agr.* 13.3) in the biographical work entitled *De vita Iulii Agricolae* (*The Life of Julius Agricola*, usually called simply the *Agricola*, for convenience). This work, our main narrative for these events, was written around 50 years later, but Tacitus must have had impeccable sources; as a senator, indeed as one of the consuls for AD 97, he was well placed to consult original documents and to interview first-hand witnesses. Foremost among these was his father-in-law, Gnaeus Julius Agricola himself, who must have been extraordinarily knowledgeable about Britain, having served there at each stage of his military career.

Although geographically remote, the unfolding events in this far corner of the empire surely caught the imagination of ordinary Romans. On the death of Claudius in AD 54, Seneca listed amongst his greatest achievements (albeit satirically) his conquest, not only of the Britons who live beyond the shores of the known sea, but of the Ocean itself (Sen., *Apoc.* 12). Equally, in later years, it became well known that one of the participating legions, *II Augusta*, had been commanded by the emperor Vespasian, then known only as a middle-ranking senator of obscure ancestry. But in AD 69, when the Roman world was dividing along partisan lines, the army of Britannia was inclined to support Vespasian, 'because, having been given command of the Second Legion there by Claudius, he waged war with distinction' (Tac., *Hist.* 3.44).

Coin of Claudius. This reverse image celebrates the conquest of Britain by depicting the emperor on horseback, flanked by trophies of captured weapons, on top of a triumphal arch with the legend *De Britann(is)*, implying a victory 'over the Britons'. (Author's collection)

Because of this future emperor's involvement, historians of the day were moved to seek out and preserve details that might otherwise have been lost, such as the fact that Vespasian 'engaged the enemy 30 times. He reduced to submission two very powerful peoples and more than 20 towns, including the Isle of Wight near Britain' (Suet., *Div. Vesp.* 4). Although this summary makes the activities of *II Augusta* reasonably clear, unfortunately no record survives of the movements of the other legions, and of the dozens of auxiliary units that must have accompanied them. However, it is likely that, while Vespasian proceeded west from the Roman landfall in Kent or Sussex and the friendly kingdoms established there, his colleagues pushed north-west and north. 'Gradually', in the words of Tacitus, 'the nearest part of Britain was shaped into a province' (*Agr.* 14.1).

NERO'S GOVERNORS: CONQUERING NATIONS, STRENGTHENING GARRISONS

By the time Nero came to the throne in AD 54, the Roman province of Britannia extended up to the Severn estuary in the west and the Trent in the east (Tac., *Ann.* 12.31: *Trisantonam et Sabrinam fluvios*). Roman arms had overrun the territories of more than half a dozen tribes: the Cantiaci of Kent, the Atrebates of Sussex, the Durotriges and Dumnonii of the south-west, the Dobunni of Gloucestershire, the Catuvellauni, whose lands stretched from Oxford to Cambridge, the Trinovantes of Essex, the Corieltauvi (long thought to have been called the Coritani) of the East Midlands, and perhaps the Cornovii of the West Midlands, too. A succession of Roman governors came and went, commanding the large army of occupation for the standard three- or four-year period: 'nations were conquered', writes Tacitus, 'and garrisons were strengthened' (Tac., *Agr.* 14.3).

Engraving of an inscription from Chichester (*RIB* 91), mentioning a 'great king of Britain' (*rex magnus Britanniae*) on line 5. Unfortunately, his name has been damaged, so that he could either be [Co]gidubnus (as usually preferred) or [To]gidubnus (as seems more likely to scholars of Celtic languages). The inscription commemorates the raising of a temple to Neptune and Minerva (*templum Neptuno et Minervae*) by a guild of craftsmen (*[colle]gium fabror(um)*). (Author's collection)

However, in AD 60, when King Prasutagus of the Iceni died, the rebellion raised by his widow, Boudicca, set the process of romanization back. All this time, the tribes of modern-day Wales, the Silures in the south and the Ordovices in the north, remained defiant. But the Brigantes, who were 'said to be the most numerous people in the entire province' (Tac., *Agr.* 17.1), were quiescent, and no real contact had been made with the tribes further north, in their Caledonian fastnesses.

In AD 68, the reign of Nero ended in chaos, with rebellion in Gaul and civil war spreading across the empire. First, Galba, the aged governor of Tarraconensis in Spain, took the throne, but fell foul of his erstwhile associate, Otho. Then he, in turn, was challenged and defeated by Vitellius, one of the commanders on the Rhine. Finally, the veteran general Vespasian, then orchestrating Rome's Jewish War, was proclaimed emperor by the legions in the east. With his two sons, he established the Flavian dynasty and ushered in a generation of stability.

Meanwhile, the province of Britannia had been in the hands of ineffectual governors for some time. The elderly Marcus Trebellius Maximus, in charge from AD 63 until 69, had been consul in AD 56, but had served in no military capacity since holding a legionary command in AD 36. Yet here he was, commanding the four legions and mixed auxiliary garrison of a consular province. Tacitus condemned his term of office for its lethargy. In fact, it was on this account that the commander of *XX Valeria Victrix*, Marcus Roscius Coelius, stirred up trouble: 'there was a mutiny, for the soldiers were used to campaigning and became unruly from lack of activity' (Tac., *Agr.* 16.3). Some years later, writing his *Histories*, Tacitus claimed that 'Trebellius accused Coelius of sedition and upsetting military discipline, and Coelius blamed Trebellius for embezzling and weakening the legions' (*Hist.* 1.60). In any event, the governor was forced to flee for safety, leaving the province in the hands of Coelius and his two colleagues (there being only three legions in the province at this time).[1] He joined the pretender, Vitellius, in Gaul, early in AD 69 (Tac., *Hist.* 2.65).

1. See Fortress 43: *Roman Legionary Fortresses 27 BC–AD 378* (Osprey Publishing Ltd: Oxford, 2006) by the same author, p. 18

Tribes of Roman Britain

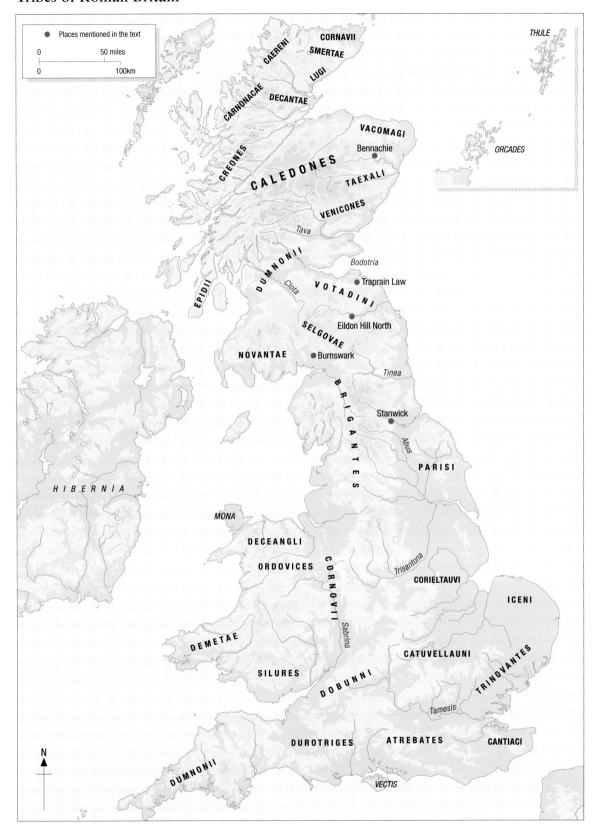

Places mentioned in the text

0   50 miles
0   100km

THULE

CORNAVII
SMERTAE
CAERENI
LUGI
CARNONACAE   DECANTAE

VACOMAGI
Bennachie

ORCADES

CREONES

CALEDONES

TAEXALI

VENICONES

Tava

DUMNONII

Bodotria

VOTADINI   Traprain Law

Clota

EPIDII

SELGOVAE   Eildon Hill North

NOVANTAE   Burnswark

Tinea

BRIGANTES   Stanwick

Abus

PARISI

HIBERNIA

MONA

DECEANGLI

ORDOVICES

CORNOVII   Trisantona

CORIELTAUVI

ICENI

DEMETAE   Sabrina

SILURES

CATUVELLAUNI

TRINOVANTES

DOBUNNI

Tamesis

DUROTRIGES   ATREBATES   CANTIACI

N

DUMNONII

VECTIS

9

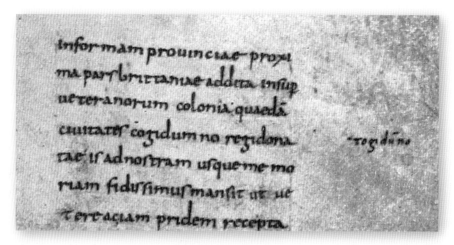

ROME AND THE BRIGANTES

Vitellius sent Marcus Vettius Bolanus to replace Trebellius as governor. If not exactly a military expert, at least Bolanus was no mediocrity; he had served with distinction as a legionary commander under the famous Corbulo during Nero's Parthian crisis, before proceeding to a consulship in AD 66. On his arrival in Britain, he preferred not to press his authority on the recalcitrant legions. Admittedly, the province must have been in some disarray. In around AD 65, Nero had already withdrawn an entire legion, *XIIII Gemina* (Tac., *Hist.* 2.11), which had subsequently wound up, with Otho, on the losing side at Bedriacum. And in the meantime, Vitellius had drawn off another 8,000 men, effectively halving the three remaining legions, in order to bolster his Continental army against the Flavian forces (Tac., *Hist.* 2.57).

Returning to Britain with Bolanus, *XIIII Gemina* was in a foul mood after its defeat by the Vitellian forces (Tac., *Hist.* 2.66); its support was soon canvassed by the Flavians (Tac., *Hist.* 2.86), so its sympathies most probably lay with Vespasian by now. As one of Vitellius' men, Bolanus will not have relished having the legion back in Britain. Nor can the other legionary commanders have been happy with their new governor. Probably appointed by Nero, they had perhaps developed Othonian tendencies; but they now found themselves reporting to a Vitellian governor and many of their men were off fighting for Vitellius in northern Italy (*Hist.* 2.100). Soon, however, Vespasian's old legion, *II Augusta*, embraced the Flavian cause (Tac., *Hist.* 3.44). And in case the subsequent death of Vitellius had not convinced the others to follow suit, in AD 70 the new emperor sent one of his supporters, the young Gnaeus Julius Agricola, to relieve the unruly Roscius Coelius as commander of *XX Valeria Victrix* (Tac., *Agr.* 7.3). Simultaneously, *XIIII Gemina* was again withdrawn for service on the Continent, never to return (Tac., *Hist.* 4.68).

Besides the shifting politics amongst the army commanders, there was an ongoing military crisis, for the client kingdom of the Brigantes was beset by its own civil war. It appears that Queen Cartimandua had divorced her consort, the warlord Venutius, and had taken up with his armour-bearer, Vellocatus. 'At first', writes Tacitus, 'the conflict was between themselves, and Cartimandua cunningly seized the brother and kinsmen of Venutius' (*Ann.* 12.40). She no doubt hoped that, by taking hostages, she could bring calm to the situation. But, as AD 69 wore on, and mutiny caused chaos amongst the queen's Roman protectors, Venutius declared open war on his estranged wife. In the pithy words of Tacitus, 'the kingdom was left to Venutius, the war to us' (*Hist.* 3.45).

It seems that the new governor Vettius Bolanus could rely only on his auxiliary troops, but he managed to rescue the queen. No doubt there was hard fighting across the Brigantian lands of Yorkshire, Lancashire and the north. Many years later, when the poet Statius came to honour Bolanus' son Crispinus in verse, he recalled the exploits of the young man's father in Britain. 'Here was your father accustomed to dispense justice, from this turf mound he addressed the cavalry; he planted watchtowers and forts far and wide – do you see them? – and surrounded these ramparts with a ditch. To the warlike gods he dedicated these gifts and these weapons – can you make out the placards? At the call to arms, he himself strapped on this cuirass, and this one he tore from a British king' (Stat., *Silv.* 5.2.144–49).

Archaeology has yet to identify Statius' watchtowers and forts with any degree of certainty, but it is likely that Bolanus' troops were obliged to extract Cartimandua from trouble. Her seat of power most probably lay at Stanwick (near Scotch Corner in Yorkshire), a site larger than any other in Brigantian lands by several orders of magnitude; imported fine wares and Roman-style building materials point to an owner of some authority, and whom better than Cartimandua? According to Tacitus, 'a powerful and exceptionally well-armed body of young warriors snatched her kingdom' (*Ann.* 12.40). Undoubtedly the supporters of Venutius, but modern claims that they were based around Carlisle in an area later known as the 'community of the Carvetii' (*RIB* 933: *civitas Carvetiorum*; cf. *AE* 2005, 922, for 3rd-century date) are purely speculative. At any rate, once Bolanus had rescued the queen, he was wise to refrain from any major campaigning if he lacked confidence in his garrison commanders.

Original manuscript page from the *Codex Aesinas*, folio 52 recto, the opening page of Tacitus' *Agricola*. The heading reads 'the book of Cornelius Tacitus concerning the life of Julius Agricola begins (here)' (*Cornelii Taciti de vita Iulii Agricolae liber incipit*). The task of decipherment is not helped by the small handwriting (the so-called 'Carolingian minuscule' script), along with frequent word breaks and peculiar abbreviations. (Author's collection)

TOP

Gate timbers exposed during excavations at Carlisle from 1998 to 2001. By use of the sophisticated tree-ring dating technique of dendrochronology, the timbers were found to have been felled late in AD 72. (© Carlisle Archaeological Unit. Photo: M. McCarthy)

BOTTOM

Roman timber floorboards belonging to the earliest fort at Carlisle, founded during the governorship of Petillius Cerialis (AD 70–73). In the foreground, a well was subsequently cut through the earlier levels. (© Carlisle Archaeological Unit. Photo: M. McCarthy)

VESPASIAN'S NEW ORDER: GREAT GENERALS AND ILLUSTRIOUS ARMIES

In AD 71, Vespasian inaugurated a new expansionist policy in Britain, sanctioning campaigns in the territory of northern England and Wales. Now, in the words of Tacitus, came 'great generals, illustrious armies' (*Agr.* 17.1). The first appointee as governor was Vespasian's kinsman (quite likely his son-in-law) Quintus Petillius Cerialis, who travelled directly from the Rhineland, where he had been suppressing a revolt. Previously, he had commanded *VIIII Hispana* during the Boudiccan crisis of AD 60; Agricola had been a legionary tribune at the same time, so the two men were again united. Along with Cerialis came a new legion, *II Adiutrix*, to replace *XIIII Gemina* and thus bring the garrison back up to four legions. And if his brief was conquest, he probably brought auxiliary units as well; there are several that make their first appearance in Britain at around this time.

Tacitus says that 'Petillius Cerialis immediately brought terror by attacking the community of the Brigantes' (*Agr.* 17.1). We have no idea how the campaigning of these years was organized, but the Roman legions must have ranged widely across northern England, crushing Venutius' revolt. A trio of marching camps (Rey Cross, Crackenthorpe and Plumpton Head) are thought to mark the passage of his army across the Stainmore Pass, the route later followed by the A66 highway from York to Carlisle. At 8–9.5ha (20–23 acres), they could be taken to represent the temporary accommodation of a legionary battle group supported by cavalry, perhaps totalling some 7,500 men. Although the camps cannot be closely dated, their morphology suggests that they belong to the earliest Roman activities in the area. Their squarish shape has been taken to indicate an early date, for later camps appear to be rather more elongated in their quest to attain a 'tertiate' layout, with sides following 3:2 proportions. More tellingly, they were planted on virgin soil; one of the camps, Rey Cross, is demonstrably earlier than the Roman road, which diverges from a straight line almost imperceptibly in order to enter one gateway and leave by another.

The legionary fortress at York, known to the Romans as Eburacum, is also usually attributed to Cerialis and his old legion, *VIIII Hispana*. Certainly, they left some epigraphic evidence of their presence there. The fortress they vacated at Lincoln (Roman Lindum) is thought to have been occupied by the newly arrived *II Adiutrix*. Meanwhile, the other two legions, *II Augusta* and *XX Valeria Victrix*, maintained watch over the west and south-west of the province. Tacitus says that, 'at first, Cerialis shared only hard work and danger, but soon glory as well' (*Agr.* 8.2), by which he implies Agricola's close involvement, so *XX Valeria Victrix* must have contributed an element at least to the campaigning army.

If the Stainmore camps can be assigned to Cerialis only on the basis of probability, the founding of a permanent fort at Carlisle can be attributed to him with absolute certainty. The dendrochronological dating of the gate timbers confirmed that Cerialis' army had felled the trees late in AD 72, finally vindicating the views of those whose suspicions had been raised by early pottery from the site. Another fairly large fort, extending over 3ha (7 acres) like Carlisle, was discovered at Blennerhasset, 30km (19 miles) to the south-west; subsequent fieldwalking recovered early Flavian material, quite in keeping with a Cerialian foundation.

Writing about Britain in around AD 77, the great encyclopaedist Pliny the Elder had mentioned 'the Roman forces, in almost 30 years, having extended our knowledge no farther than the neighbourhood of the Caledonian forest' (*Nat. Hist.* 4.102). This was certainly true in AD 77; but, strictly speaking, his words should relate to AD 72, almost 30 years after Claudius' invasion, when Cerialis' army stood at the point that later marked the Scottish border, and looked north into *terra incognita*.

By late AD 73 (or early 74), Cerialis had served out the standard governor's *triennium*. His departure drew a line under Brigantian affairs, and allowed the new governor, Sextus Julius Frontinus, to devote his attention to Wales. Garrisons were planted to hold down the volatile Silures in the south and Ordovices in the north, and *II Augusta* moved up from Exeter to a new fortress at Caerleon (transferring the name Isca from one to the other). At around the same time, it seems that either *XX Valeria Victrix* from Wroxeter, or *II Adiutrix* from Lincoln, began construction of a new fortress at Chester (Roman Deva), from where it could command both northern Wales and north-west England. By the time Frontinus left the province early in AD 77, the Roman legions were redistributed to dominate the north, and the new governor could plan for the conquest of present-day Scotland. His name was Agricola.

CHRONOLOGY

(All dates are AD)

40	Birth of Cn. Julius Agricola (13 June)
41–54	Reign of Emperor Claudius
43	Roman invasion of Britain
43–47	A. Plautius governor of Britannia
47–52	P. Ostorius Scapula governor of Britannia
52–57	A. Didius Gallus governor of Britannia
54–68	Reign of Emperor Nero
57–58	Q. Veranius governor of Britannia
58–61	C. Suetonius Paullinus governor of Britannia
60	Boudiccan revolt
61–63	P. Petronius Turpilianus governor of Britannia
63–69	M. Trebellius Maximus governor of Britannia
69	Civil war: 'Year of the Four Emperors'
69–71	M. Vettius Bolanus governor of Britannia
70–79	Reign of Emperor Vespasian
71–73	Q. Petillius Cerialis governor of Britannia
	Roman Army campaigns against the Brigantes in northern England
74–77	Sex. Julius Frontinus governor of Britannia

	Roman army campaigns against the Silures in south Wales and Ordovices in north Wales
77–84	Cn. Julius Agricola governor of Britannia
	Roman Army campaigns against the Caledonian tribes of Scotland
79–81	Reign of Emperor Titus
81–96	Reign of Emperor Domitian
83	Domitian campaigns against the Chatti; hailed as Germanicus ('Conqueror of Germany')
83	Battle of Mons Graupius (September)
84–87?	Unknown governor of Britannia
	Construction of legionary fortress at Inchtuthil begun; subsequently dismantled and abandoned
85	Hard fighting on Danube front
	Roman Army defeated in Moesia; governor (Oppius Sabinus) killed
86	Roman Army defeated in Dacia; Praetorian Prefect (Cornelius Fuscus) killed
87	*II Adiutrix* withdrawn from Britannia for service on Danube
93	Death of Agricola (23 August)
97–98	Reign of Emperor Nerva
98–117	Reign of Emperor Trajan
98	Tacitus completes Agricola's biography (*De vita Iulii Agricolae*)

OPPOSING FORCES

THE ROMAN ARMY: PILLAGERS OF THE WORLD

Since the days of Augustus, the Roman Army had been based around a core of 28 legions, distributed around the empire in readiness for further conquest. Each legion comprised 5,000 or so Roman citizens, equipped for battle as heavy infantry. The primary division of the legion was the *cohors* ('cohort'), which was further subdivided into six *centuriae* ('centuries'), each commanded by a centurion. But combat was not the legion's only role. Each unit was an army in miniature, with its own specialist technicians, craftsmen, medics and administrators; individual soldiers could be detailed to perform all manner of administrative or constructional tasks on behalf of the imperial government. During Agricola's governorship, there were still four legions in Britain: *II Augusta*, *II Adiutrix*, *VIIII Hispana* and *XX Valeria Victrix*.

In addition to these, and in order to achieve a balanced military establishment, the emperors continued to recruit smaller bodies of troops from the more warlike of Rome's allied and tributary nations. These men, largely Gauls, Germans and Spaniards, did not fulfil the citizenship requirement for service in the legions, so they were drafted into their own units, the so-called *auxilia* (which literally means 'assistance'). Veterans received citizenship, usually on completion of 25 years' service, and many were willing to pay for a bronze document (the so-called diploma, so named because it consisted of two bronze sheets, bound together and sealed) that legally proved the fact. Although they could be criticized as 'pillagers of the world' (Tac., *Agr.* 30.4), to outsiders they presented the unfamiliar and alarming image of a drilled and disciplined standing army.

Some of these auxiliary units were purely infantry, divided into centuries, like the legions, but organized as individual autonomous cohorts. Their status

Writing tablet from Carlisle. As at Vindolanda, the waterlogged conditions at Carlisle were found to have preserved organic remains amongst the rubbish dumped at the end of each occupation phase, including some ink tablets. It is a specialized task to decipher the Roman handwriting, often visible only under infrared light. This tablet, found amongst 1st-century material, is the start of a letter addressed to an unknown trooper 'of the *ala Sebosiana, singularis* of Agricola' (*[al]ae sebosianae sing(ularis) | Agricolae*). (Author's collection)

is generally considered to have been inferior to that of the legionaries. For example, it is thought that an auxiliary infantryman drew only ⅚th of the legionary's pay, and it is often stated that his equipment was not of the same high standard. Also, the *auxilia* often bore the brunt of garrisoning duties in order to release the legionaries for construction work, but each played a distinctive part in battle.

As the legions were predominantly infantry, specialized auxiliary units provided the cavalry component of any Roman army. Many of these were squadrons entirely of cavalry; known as *alae* (literally 'wings'), they were divided into 16 troops (*turmae*), each with its own decurion. More numerous than the *alae* were the *cohortes equitatae* ('equitate cohorts'), which were made up of both infantry and cavalry, roughly in the proportion of four to one. This mixture gave the equitate cohort more operational flexibility than a purely infantry unit. The cavalryman, whether he served in an *ala* or a *cohors equitata*, was generally more privileged than his infantry counterpart. A writing tablet from Vindonissa (Switzerland) seems to suggest that, on the eve of the Claudian invasion, a cohortal trooper (*eques cohortis*) received a salary of 900 sesterces (225 *denarii*) in three instalments (*AE* 2003, 1238). This was the pay of a legionary; the auxiliary cavalryman (*eques alaris*), by contrast, got ⅞th (1,050 sesterces, or 262½ *denarii*), while the auxiliary infantryman got much less.

It is likely that Agricola's cavalry forces included *ala I Hispanorum Asturum*, *ala I Thracum*, *ala I Tungrorum*, *ala Classiana*, *ala Petriana*, *ala Tampiana*, *ala Vettonum* and *ala Sebosiana*. Of these eight, only the last is directly attested at this time, through the find of a writing tablet at Carlisle (*AE* 1998, 852). But the tombstone of Flavinus (*RIB* 1172), *signifer* ('standard-bearer') of *ala Petriana*, should probably be dated to this time. And the other regiments appear on diplomas issued by the emperor Trajan to British veterans in AD 98 (*CIL* 16, 43), AD 103 (*CIL* 16, 48), and AD 105 (*CIL* 16, 51). The trend during the AD 80s and 90s was for troop withdrawals rather than new arrivals, so there is a good chance that the units discharging men around AD 100 had been in Britain under Agricola. However, the three diplomas do not give complete coverage of the provincial army. For example, a certain *ala Augusta* buried two of its troopers at Lancaster (*RIB* 606, now lost; and *Britannia* 37, 2006, 468ff.), probably during the Flavian period; if men were discharged from its ranks under Trajan, they must have appeared on a different diploma, hitherto undiscovered. Equally, *ala II Asturum*, which disappears from view between its early deployment in Pannonia and its appearance in Britain under Hadrian, may well have arrived with Cerialis in AD 71.

Some of these cavalry units had been rewarded for meritorious conduct. The men of *ala Vettonum*, which was originally recruited amongst the Vettones of central Spain, had received a block grant of Roman citizenship, most likely for bravery during the early years of the invasion. (The trooper commemorated at Bath, Lucius Vitellius Tancinus, seems to have taken his new Roman name from L. Vitellius, the Emperor Claudius' colleague in the censorship of AD 48; *RIB* 159.) The men of *ala Petriana* had received a similar award, but prior to their arrival in Britain. They are likely to have been one of the regiments that accompanied Petillius Cerialis in AD 71; *ala Sebosiana* was another.

Tombstone of Pintaius, standard-bearer (*signifer*) of *cohors V Asturum* (*CIL* 13, 8090). (Copy of an original in Bonn, Germany, on display in the Museo de la Real Colegiata de San Isidoro, León.) Pintaius' heir, who set up the tombstone, proudly states that his friend was an Asturian from Transmontanus (Trás-os-Montes in north-east Portugal), thus he was probably an original member of the cohort. (Author's collection)

Ala Classiana also received citizenship; probably raised in Gaul, it later calls itself *ala Gallorum et Thracum Classiana*, no doubt emphasizing its Gallic origins after an influx of Thracian recruits. These three units were entitled to add the letters *c.R.* after their name, indicating that each was an *ala civium Romanorum* ('squadron of Roman citizens'). At some stage, *ala Classiana* also acquired the honorific titles *invicta bis torquata* ('invincible, twice decorated'; *CIL* 11, 6033), but the occasions for these two grants of military decorations are unknown.

Infantry was always more numerous than cavalry. The three early Trajanic diplomas should again give a reasonable idea of Agricola's army, provided some care is exercised. For, although most of the named units could well have been long established in the province, one of the cohorts mentioned on the so-called Malpas diploma of AD 103 (*cohors I Alpinorum*) is known to have transferred *into* the province a few years earlier. The same may be true of a second unit (*cohors II Thracum equitata*), if its name has been correctly restored on the German diploma of AD 98. (There is a very slim chance of duplicate unit names, for those regiments raised in quantity from fertile recruiting grounds like Thrace and the Iberian peninsula; it is quite likely, for example, that a second *cohors II Asturum equitata* existed simultaneously in Lower Germany, but this is not the case with *cohors II Thracum*.)

An additional problem is posed, for those who would try to calculate the size of Agricola's army, by the possibility that some cohorts were at double strength, an innovation that was gathering momentum during the Flavian period. And finally, as with the *alae*, several units have probably evaded notice. In particular, although *cohors IIII Delmatarum* appears on one of our diplomas, we know nothing about the early history of *cohortes I* and *II Delmatarum*, which subsequently appear in Britain and may have been based here all along. (By contrast, *cohors III Delmatarum* is known to have been based in Germany.)

We can make an educated guess that Agricola's army included the following 20 cohorts: *cohors II Asturum (equitata)*, *cohors I Baetasiorum*, *cohors III Bracaraugustanorum*, *cohors I Celtiberorum*, *cohors I Cugernorum*, *cohors IIII Delmatarum*, *cohors I Frisiavonum*, *cohors I Hispanorum (equitata)*, *cohors I Lingonum (equitata)*, *cohors II Lingonum (equitata)*, *cohors III Lingonum*, *cohors I Morinorum*, *cohors I Nerviorum*, *cohors II Nerviorum*, *cohors II Pannoniorum*, *cohors I Tungrorum*, *cohors II Tungrorum (equitata)*, *cohors I Vangionum (equitata)*, *cohors I fida Vardullorum (equitata)* and *cohors II Vasconum*.

Again, as with the *alae*, we usually lack firm evidence for the presence of these units in Britain at this time. However, it seems certain that *cohors I Hispanorum* buried one of their number, a man named Ammonius, at the fort of Ardoch (*RIB* 2213) at around this time. And there is a circumstantial case (albeit a very good one) for the involvement of *cohors II Asturum* in the battle at Mons Graupius (as we shall see below). Furthermore, Tacitus specifically notes the presence of two Tungrian cohorts in Agricola's army, which are surely the two *cohortes Tungrorum* from the Trajanic diplomas; indeed, one of these has left evidence of its later occupancy at Vindolanda. Tacitus also mentions four Batavian cohorts (Tac., *Agr.* 36), so we may add *cohortes I* and *II Batavorum*, which are first attested in Pannonia in AD 98, but which must have been in Britain over a decade earlier, alongside *cohortes III* and *VIIII Batavorum*, which both left written records at Vindolanda.

Inner face of a diploma (*CIL* 16, 48 = *ILS* 2001) discovered near Malpas (Cheshire, England). Issued in AD 103 by Trajan (whose nomenclature has been lost in the damaged portion), it lists four of the *alae* and 11 of the *cohortes* that released veterans in that year from the army of Britain. The province is named towards the bottom of the sheet, where the regiments are said to be serving 'in Britain under Lucius Neratius Marcellus' (*in Britannia sub L(ucio) Neratio Marcello*). The text continues on the neighbouring leaf, which would have been securely bound to this one, and officially sealed. (© Jona Lendering)

(Oddly, there is no trace of Batavian cohorts bearing the intervening numbers.) One other cohort is mentioned by Tacitus, the *cohors Usiporum* which mutinied during its period of initial training (see below, p. 50); but, as the late Professor Sir Ian Richmond long ago wisely observed, this cohort can hardly be counted in the strength of Agricola's army.

As with the *alae*, some of these cohorts will have arrived with Cerialis in AD 71. In particular, the epithet *fida* ('loyal') uniquely applied to *cohors I Vardullorum* could have been earned on the Rhine during the events of AD 69. Other units may even have been newly raised in the aftermath of these troubles. Some likely contenders are *cohors I Baetasiorum*, *cohors I Cugernorum*, *cohors I Frisiavonum* and *cohors I Vangionum*, all raised amongst peoples who hailed from the Rhineland; perhaps also the *cohors I Morinorum* and the series of *cohortes Lingonum*, too. Wherever there had been trouble, it was only sensible to remove the men of fighting age from their homes, and channel any tribal aggression into the service of Rome.

The late Professor Richmond, in his posthumously published commentary to the *Agricola*, jointly authored with the late Professor Robert Ogilvie, was perhaps responsible for drawing attention to the British auxiliaries whom Tacitus mentions in the preamble to the battle of Mons Graupius (*Agr.* 29.2; 32.1, 3). In particular, Tacitus' claim that they had been 'tried and tested in a long period of peace' (*Agr.* 29.2: *longa pace exploratos*) showed that these were men from the south of England, which had long since been settled. Richmond thought it quite likely that these were entire units, newly recruited to bolster Agricola's army, and he duly compiled a list of likely regiments. Of course, Tacitus simply means that Britons were being recruited into the regiments already stationed in Britain, but Richmond's list is not without interest.

Amongst the regiments of Britons that he suggested were in existence during the reign of Domitian, *ala Brittonum* (*veterana*) seems out of place; it is not known before the 2nd century AD, when it was stationed in Lower Pannonia, so the balance of probability suggests that it was a Trajanic creation. Richmond's other cavalry unit, *ala I Flavia Augusta Britannica* is disallowed for a different reason: the title *Britannica*, unlike *Brittonum* ('of Britons'), indicates simply that the unit had previously served in Britain, perhaps during the initial invasion, before transferring to the Danube.

Of the several cohorts that Richmond listed, *cohors I Brittonum* is most promising, as it appears on a diploma of AD 85 (*CIL* 16, 31), so the time-served veterans of that year had been recruited in around AD 60. However, the diploma belongs to the army of Pannonia, and there is no sign that this cohort ever served in Britain. Similarly, the time-

Tombstone of Gaius Julius Karus (*AE* 1951, 88, now lost). The lettering is difficult to read, but would originally have been brightly picked out in paint. The inscription states 'For Gaius Julius Karus, son of Gaius, of the Voltinian voting tribe, from the province of Narbonensis, military tribune of the *III Cyrenaica* legion, prefect of the *Sixth Asturum equitata* cohort, decorated in the British war with a mural crown, a rampart crown, a gold crown, an honorific spear. The centurions and men of the *III Cyrenaica* legion and the *XXII* legion, sent into the province of Cyrene on account of the draft, (set this up)' (*C(aio) Iulio C(ai) f(ilio) Vo[l(tinia)]* | *Karo ex provincia Narbo* | *nensi trib(uno) mil(itum) leg(ionis) III Cy[r(enaicae)]* | *praef(ecto) coh(ortis) VI Astyrum eq[uit(atae)]* |₅ *donato bello Brittanico co[rona]* | *murali corona vallari co[rona]* | *aurea hasta pura* | *[c]enturiones et* | *milites leg(ionis) III Cyr(enaicae) et leg(ionis)* |₁₀ *[X]XII missi in provinciam* | *[C]yrenensem dilectus caussa*). (Author's collection, from *Quaderni di Archeologia della Libia* 4, 1961)

served veterans of *cohors II Brittonum*, who were released in Lower Moesia in AD 99 (*CIL* 16, 45), and of *cohors III Brittonum*, who were released in Upper Moesia in AD 100 (*CIL* 16, 46), must have been recruited in around AD 75; but again, there is no hint of service in Britain.

Scholars who have assumed that Agricola had 80 or 90 auxiliary regiments have surely overestimated the provincial army. During the reign of Hadrian, when Britain had one of the larger (if not, indeed, the largest) garrisons of the empire, there were still only a dozen *alae* and 30-odd cohorts, so it is unlikely that Agricola's army will have exceeded this. On the contrary, although we cannot be absolutely confident, it seems likely that, in the nine or ten *alae* and 24 cohorts listed above, we have identified the bulk of Agricola's army. Only further epigraphic discoveries will help to refine our list.

Roman officers and men

The long-service, battle-hardened legionary centurions were the real repository of experience in the Roman Army. Mostly promoted from the ranks after 15 or 20 years (although many were directly commissioned civilians of equestrian status), centurions could look forward to lifelong employment, culminating for a few in the coveted position of *praefectus castrorum* ('prefect of the camp'). After two or three years in this post, if the prefect was not tempted to retire from the emperor's service, he could hope for a highly paid procuratorial position.

Senior to the *praefectus castrorum*, but much younger and far less experienced, was the *tribunus laticlavius* ('broad-stripe tribune', drawing a distinction with the narrow stripe of the equestrian officer). Most aspiring senators spent one or two years in this post, having been directly appointed and assigned to a legion by the provincial governor. As in many areas of Roman life, patronage played an important role, and young men often secured a tribunate from a close relative, or were recommended by acquaintances.

In AD 58, at the age of 18, Agricola was granted a tribunate in Britain by the old warhorse Suetonius Paullinus. Tacitus tells us that Agricola refused to treat his military service as an excuse for larking about, as many young men seem to have done, and resisted using his rank to obtain leave of absence. On the contrary, 'he got to know the province, made himself known to the army, learned from those with experience, and followed the best examples' (Tac., *Agr.* 5.2). Ostensibly second in command of the legion, the tribune was more likely to be simply observing the practicalities of military life. Pliny the younger says that 'young men got their taste of service in camp in order to grow accustomed to command by obeying, and to lead by following' (Plin., *Epist.* 8.14.5). Unusually, in AD 82–83, we find the tribune of *VIIII Hispana*, Lucius Roscius Aelianus, conducting a detachment of his legion from Britain to the Rhine *in expeditione Germanica* ('on the German expedition': *ILS* 1025). As we shall see, this was the Emperor Domitian's campaign against the Chatti. We might have expected the more experienced *praefectus castrorum* to be entrusted with the responsibility of leading troops into a war zone (cf. Tac., *Ann.* 13.39).

Each legion was commanded by a *legatus legionis* ('legionary legate'), a senator usually aged in his 30s, whose previous military posting had been as a tribune, ten years before. In the meantime, he had been obliged to fill a variety of civil posts, underlining the fact that the senator was, first and foremost, a Roman magistrate, and only incidentally a military leader. As we have already seen, Agricola began his service as legate of *XX Valeria Victrix* in AD 70; he returned to Rome in AD 73, to continue his senatorial career.

The sons of equestrian families, by contrast, commanded the auxiliary units. These were wealthy municipal aristocrats who had elected to serve in the *tres militiae* ('three military grades'), either as young men at the start of their public career, or in middle age, having held a succession of magistracies in their local area. Traditionally, they began with the command of an infantry cohort, which carried the rank of *praefectus cohortis* ('cohort prefect'). The second stage of their military career was as a legionary tribune, with the rank of *tribunus angusticlavius* ('narrow-stripe tribune', drawing a contrast with the broad senatorial stripe). Besides the senatorial tribune, each legion also had five equestrian tribunes, whose duties largely revolved around representing the common men in judicial matters. Alternatively, the new 'double-strength' cohorts required a tribune as their commander, no doubt acknowledging the greater responsibility associated with their larger size. Many men elected to serve only as tribune before returning to civilian life, but for those who were determined to complete their military career the third

Tombstone of Insus, discovered in Lancaster in 2005. Almost 2m (7ft) in height, the sculpture depicts the cavalryman riding down a Briton, whom he has first decapitated. He describes himself as a 'Treveran citizen' (*cives Trever*) who served as the '*curator* of Victor's troop' (*[t(urmae)] Victoris curator*), the cavalry equivalent of a centurion's *optio*. (© Lancaster City Museum/Lancashire Museums)

stage was the command of a cavalry unit as *praefectus alaris* ('squadron prefect'). Promotion from one grade to the next depended as much on patronage as on the talents of the individual, for these posts were in the gift of the provincial governor.

Only two of Agricola's officers at Mons Graupius are known by name. The first is Aulus Julius Atticus, a young *praefectus cohortis* just beginning his career. (Tacitus simply calls him Aulus Atticus, but the family name Julius seems likely.) Like Agricola himself, he probably came from Narbonensis, where other Julii Attici are known.

The second is Gaius Julius Karus, who also came from Narbonensis. He was later buried in Cyrene, where as *tribunus angusticlavius* he was conducting a recruiting drive for the two legions of Egypt, *III Cyrenaica* and *XXII Deiotariana*. During his previous posting, as *praefectus* of *cohors II Asturum equitata*, he was decorated *bello Britannico* ('in the British war'; *AE* 1951, 88). His receipt of a *corona muralis* ('mural crown', usually given for storming an enemy town), a *corona vallaris* ('rampart crown', usually given for storming an enemy camp), a *corona aurea* ('gold crown', given for gallantry), and a *hasta pura* ('honorific spear', restricted to the officer class) seems lavish at a time when it was usual to reward deserving officers with one crown and one spear. To merit such rewards, he must surely have played a key part in Agricola's strategy.

THE CALEDONIAN FORCES: THE NOBLEST IN ALL BRITAIN

In contrast to the Roman Army, we know virtually nothing about their Caledonian adversaries. It is unfortunate, but inevitable, that much of our information about them derives from Roman sources, which are unlikely to be entirely impartial or even wholly accurate. To remedy this deficiency, scholars often extrapolate from later Pictish practices, or from the exploits of warbands in medieval Irish and Welsh literature, but the validity of this approach is questionable.

A generation ago, it was common to characterize the Iron Age peoples of Scotland as 'Celtic cowboys, footloose and unpredictable'. However, it has now been realized that, at the time of the Roman invasion, they had a long history of subsistence farming, harvesting barley and wheat, and herding cattle, goats, sheep and pigs. Extensive field systems, associated with roundhouse settlements, have come to light, dividing up great swathes of arable land in Angus, Fife and the Lothians. At the same time, pollen analysis suggests that this period saw widespread woodland clearance for cereal production. Linear alignments of pits perhaps represent the postholes of fence lines, segregating croplands from grazing pastures, while elsewhere, massive earthworks snaking across the countryside have been labelled as 'ranch boundaries'. And substantial stone-built underground cellars called souterrains (literally 'under the earth' chambers) provided the cool, dry conditions necessary for storing foodstuffs, certainly grain, perhaps even meat, milk and cheese.

In common with their Celtic cousins across western Europe, the north Britons were sophisticated craftsmen, builders and artisans, despite their lack of written records. Yet Mediterranean writers like Diodorus Siculus, a contemporary of Julius Caesar, were struck by 'their humble dwellings, being built for the most part out of reeds and logs' (Diod. Sic. 5.21.5). Certainly,

TOP

Aerial view of the souterrain at Shanzie, near Alyth (Perth). The curving stone-built structure, around 35m (115ft) in length, is typical of these underground storehouses. (© David Woolliscroft)

BOTTOM

Iron Age roundhouse, reconstructed at the Archaeolink Prehistory Park, near Aberdeen. Many of the Caledonian peoples who heeded Calgacus' call will have come from homesteads like this one. The mountain of Bennachie can be seen in the background. (Author's collection)

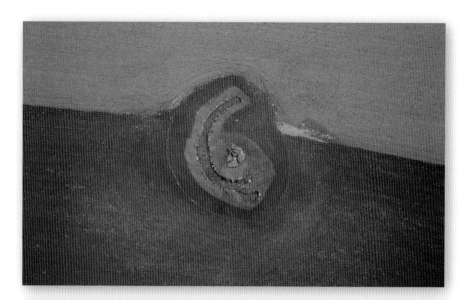

the peoples of lowland Scotland lived in settlements of roundhouses, sometimes fairly large with distinctive conical thatched roofs and earthen walls faced with wattle and daub. And in river- or loch-side locations, similar houses, called crannogs, were built in the water close to the shore, supported on timber platforms and connected to dry land by timber jetties. But their timber construction was in no way primitive, and in fact required advanced carpentry skills. Further north, the trend was towards building in stone.

Celtic society was tribal. Although Tacitus writes only of 'the peoples who inhabit Caledonia' (*Caledoniam incolentes populi*: *Agr.* 25.3), Ptolemy the geographer lists over a dozen tribes in Scotland: the Novantae of Galloway, the Selgovae of Dumfriesshire, the Dumnonii of Ayrshire and Stirlingshire, and the Votadini of the Lothians; then, beyond the Forth–Clyde isthmus, the Epidii of Kintyre, the Venicones of Tayside, the Taexali of Aberdeenshire and the Vacomagi of Strathmore; and finally, beyond the Great Glen, a welter of names (Creones, Carnonacae, Caereni, Decantae, Lugi, Smertae, Cornavii) centred on the Caledones (Ptol., *Geog.* 2.3.5–9). Incidentally, it is virtually certain that the tribe was known as the Caledones (not, as Ptolemy mistakenly records, the Kaledonioi), for the native Vepogenus, whose name occurs on an early 3rd-century inscription from Colchester (*RIB* 191), called himself a 'Caledo', not a Caledonius.

Ptolemy was writing around AD 150, but it seems that, for the geography of north Britain, he relied on information gathered by Agricola's army, decades earlier. For one thing, neither Hadrian's Wall nor the Antonine Wall appears in his listings, although both existed at the time of writing. But it is curious that, although Ptolemy had acquired the names of so many tribes, Tacitus avoids mentioning a single one. He repeatedly refers to the region called Caledonia, but only rather vaguely to 'the inhabitants of Caledonia' (*Caledoniam habitantes*: *Agr.* 11.2), whereas he happily names the individual tribes south of the Tyne–Solway line.

Archaeology has identified a cultural boundary in the vicinity of the Fife Peninsula, based on the distribution of various artefacts and settlement patterns. Such a boundary, perhaps marked by the Earn or the Tay, would separate the lowland grouping of the Novantae, Selgovae, Dumnonii and Votadini from the more northerly peoples, who inhabited Caledonia proper. It is interesting to note that, as we shall see, Agricola thought that he could have established a boundary in Central Scotland between the Clyde and Forth estuaries, effectively separating the lowlands from Caledonia.

The archaeology of the Southern Uplands shows a degree of centralization, with prominent hillforts at Burnswark (near Dumfries), Traprain Law (near Haddington, East Lothian) and Eildon Hill North (near Melrose in the Scottish Borders). Although small and seemingly insignificant by south British standards (Burnswark is only 7ha [17 acres] in area, Traprain Law is 13ha [32 acres] and Eildon Hill 16ha [40 acres]), each clearly represents the tribal focus for, respectively, the Novantae, the Votadini and the Selgovae. The Dumnonii of the Central Lowlands seem to have followed a different tradition, with an emphasis on the crannogs of the Clyde and the Tay.

Oakbank crannog, reconstructed on Loch Tay near Kenmore. The design of this Iron Age dwelling, situated in the water and entered by a narrow walkway, was naturally defensive, as well as being well placed for fishing. The inhabitants probably reared stock on the loch side, to judge from finds of animal bones and cattle teeth.
(Author's collection)

Denarius (silver coin) of D. Junius Brutus Albinus, one of Caesar's assassins, minted in 48 BC. The reverse image shows Celtic motifs of the crossed war-trumpets with an oval shield at the top and a chariot wheel at the bottom. (Author's collection)

By contrast, the many ring-shaped forts of the north, the so-called duns, indicate a greater degree of social fragmentation. Mostly enclosing less than 2ha (5 acres), these duns perhaps represent the defended homesteads of individual Caledonian family groups, although their formidable stone-built ramparts, often reaching 6m (20ft) in thickness and perhaps 2m (7ft) in height, represent a significant expenditure of time and effort. The precise dating of these can be problematic; in the absence of accurate archaeological dating techniques, it is usually only the presence of Roman items, whether looted or traded, that gives us some idea of chronology, and such finds are relatively sparse.

It is only natural, of course, that a landscape of mountains, bogs and woodland, sometimes cleared for agriculture, sometimes left as a wilderness, created pockets of habitation, with individual family units seeking the security of their own small fortified dwelling. Perhaps there was the danger of marauders from neighbouring communities, for the rearing of livestock probably encouraged rustling. Equally, a predominantly farming folk would have been conscious of the threat from wild bears and wolves.

Caledonian warriors

Greek and Roman writers characterized Celtic and Germanic peoples as being blue-eyed and blond- or red-haired with large physiques. For Tacitus, 'the red-golden hair of the inhabitants of Caledonia, and their massive frames, declare their Germanic origin' (*Agr.* 11.2). Tacitus, of course, went on to compose a discourse all about the tribes of Germany. 'Their physical appearance,' he wrote, 'is always the same: fierce blue eyes, red hair, and large bodies' (*Germ.* 4). It is interesting to compare the opinion of Strabo, who had painted a similar picture of the Germans as 'being little different from the Celtic race, with an excess of savagery, stature, and blondness, but otherwise similar' (*Geog.* 7.1.2). And in his description of Britain, he wrote that 'the men are taller than the Celts [i.e. the Gauls] and less golden-haired, but their bodies are rangier' (Strabo, *Geog.* 4.5.2). They were also thought to be rather boastful, as Tacitus implies when he has the Caledonian chieftain call his people 'the noblest in all of Britain' (*Agr.* 30.2).

Some scholars are inclined to reject these statements as 'topoi', the kind of stock descriptions that a writer could insert in his work to pad it out and add colour. But, of course, the mere fact that the blue-eyed, red-haired north Briton became a commonplace of ancient literature does not necessarily discount its accuracy. Equally, the ancient notion of environmental determinism, that a rugged country produced a rugged people, is not entirely fanciful.

Again, it is unfortunate that Tacitus is our only source for Caledonian warfare, but classical authors portrayed the Celts in general as formidable warriors. In battle, they made a terrifying noise, shouting 'in the barbarian fashion, with roaring, chanting and discordant cries' (Tac., *Agr.* 33.1), and blowing distinctive horns. The only ancient description of these horns comes from Diodorus Siculus, who wrote that 'they have peculiar and barbaric war-trumpets; for, when they are blown, they produce a harsh sound that suits the tumult of war' (Diod. Sic. 5.30.3). But archaeology can supply an actual example of such a trumpet, for an animal-headed horn known as a carnyx was discovered long ago at Deskford (near Elgin in Moray). It had been carefully dismantled and buried in a ritual act. Its multi-part sophisticated

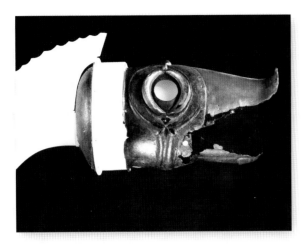

design, expertly crafted from copper alloy (perhaps ultimately of Roman origin), has been replicated in modern times to produce a functional musical instrument whose voice perfectly matches Diodorus' description.

If Tacitus is our only source for Caledonian warfare, other classical authors painted a more general picture of the Celts in battle.

> In their battles, the Celts use chariots drawn by two horses, which carry the charioteer and the warrior; when they encounter cavalry in the fighting they hurl their javelins at their opposite number and then climb down to join battle with their swords. Some of them despise death to such a degree that they step into danger unprotected and wearing only a loincloth. They bring with them free-born attendants chosen from the poor, using them in battle as charioteers and as shield-bearers. Those drawn up for battle are accustomed to step out from the line and challenge the most valiant of their opponents to single combat, brandishing their weapons and terrifying their adversaries. And when any man accepts the challenge to battle, they sing of the bravery of their forefathers and of their own excellence, and insult and disparage their opponent, by these words generally sapping their bold spirit. Having taken the heads of those who fall in battle, they fasten them to their horses' necks; they carry the arms stripped from the enemy to their attendants, covered with blood, chanting a paean and singing a victory hymn, and they nail these prizes onto their houses, just like those who catch a wild animal in the hunt.
> Diodorus Siculus, *Bibl. hist.* 5.29.1–4

The Celtic individualism described by Diodorus led to a very different type of fighting from the organized battle line of the Romans. In emphasizing fighting on foot, Diodorus has an ally in Tacitus, who held the opinion that the Germans and Caledonians were principally foot soldiers, and that 'their strength lies in their infantry' (Tac., *Agr.* 12.1; cf. *Germ.* 6.2). But one of the writing tablets recovered from the Roman fort of Vindolanda and dated broadly to the period around AD 100 sheds an interesting light on the matter. The tablet in question appears to be the final sheet of a memorandum, setting out information about the native Britons, perhaps on the occasion of a change of command at the fort. The first line is damaged, but the remainder states, in terse military style: 'there are very many cavalry; the cavalry do not use swords, nor do the wretched Britons (*Brittunculi*) mount in order to throw javelins' (*AE* 1987, 746 = *Tab. Vindol.* 164).

LEFT
Carnyx head from Deskford (near Elgin, Moray). Described as 'a pig's head with movable under-jaw' when it was discovered in the 1860s, it has been recognized as the distinctive boar's head bell of the Celtic war-trumpet known as a carnyx. Modern excavations at the find-spot concluded that the item had been carefully dismantled and buried as a votive deposit, perhaps around the time of Mons Graupius. (© National Museums of Scotland, by kind permission of Dr Fraser Hunter)

RIGHT
Silver cauldron from Gundestrup (Denmark), discovered in a peat bog where it had been carefully dismantled and buried as a votive deposit. Measuring 0.42m (17in.) in height and 0.69m (27in.) in diameter, the cauldron was perhaps used in ritual purification ceremonies. A warband accompanied by carnyx-players can be seen on the interior. (© National Museum of Denmark)

Broadly the same picture is painted by the geographer Pomponius Mela, writing during the reign of Claudius, who claimed that the Britons 'fight not only on horseback or on foot but also from two-horse chariots' (*Chor.* 3.6 = 52). As we shall see, the Caledonians certainly fielded horsemen at Mons Graupius in AD 83, but they were no match for the carefully drilled cavalry of the Romans, who quickly routed them.

Our Vindolanda tablet begins mid-sentence, but the damaged line appears to read *nudi sunt Brittones* ('the Britons are naked'). This should not be taken literally, because in a military context *nudus* simply meant 'lacking protection'. Caesar uses a similar description of Gauls whose shields had been rendered cumbersome and unusable because they were pierced by Roman javelins; they discarded the shields, preferring to fight 'with their bodies unprotected' (*BGall.* 1.25: *nudo corpore*). (The Greek version of the same word is used by Diodorus for the unprotected charioteers, quoted above, who wear only a *perizôsis*.)

It is quite likely that the majority of the Caledonian warriors had no armour. Tacitus speaks only of their 'massive swords and short shields' (*Agr.* 36.1). So it is interesting to note the custom, mentioned by several classical authors, whereby 'all the Britons actually stain themselves with woad, which effects a blue colour, and for this reason they appear more horrifying in battle' (Caes., *BGall.* 5.14). There may have been a ritualistic element to this tattooing. Indeed, we may even speculate that the tattoos were seen as magical protection, for woad, like urine, has anti-bacterial properties that must have been useful in dealing with wounds.

The Caledonian tribes also upheld the traditions of chariot warfare, 'just like the old Greek heroes in the Trojan War' (Diod. Sic. 5.21.5). Classical authors were astounded that the Britons still employed such an archaic style of fighting; so much so, that they made a point of mentioning it. 'As regards battles', writes Strabo, 'the Britons mostly make use of chariots, just like the Celts' (*Geog.* 4.5.2). Even Cicero warns one of his correspondents, Gaius Trebatius Testa, to be careful 'that you are not deceived by the charioteers in Britain' (Cic., *Epist. ad fam.* 7.6). And Caesar, too, was so fascinated by the British chariots, that he wrote a lengthy excursus:

TOP

Writing tablet no. 164 from Vindolanda (*AE* 1987, 746), thought to be a memorandum describing the nature of the native Britons. The famously patronizing reference to 'little Brits' (*Brittunculi*) occurs on the second bottom line. (© Vindolanda Trust, by kind permission of Prof. A. R. Birley)

BOTTOM

Bronze sword scabbard from Mortonhall (Edinburgh). Craftsmen used two different copper alloys to create the sophisticated decoration on this highly ornate piece, which is thought to date from around the time of the battle of Mons Graupius. Measuring 0.58m (2ft) in length, the matching weapon would perhaps not qualify as one of Tacitus' 'enormous swords'. (© National Museums of Scotland, by kind permission of Dr Fraser Hunter)

This is their method of fighting from chariots. First, they drive around in all directions and throw missiles and cause confusion in the ranks through fear of their horses and the din of their wheels; and when they have worked their way in between the cavalry squadrons, they jump down from the chariots and fight on foot. Meanwhile, the charioteers gradually withdraw from the fighting and position their chariots so that, if they are hard pressed by a host of enemies, they have an escape route to their own side. Thus they provide the mobility of cavalry and the stability of infantry in battle; and by daily practice and training they accomplish so much that, even on the steepest slopes, they can easily continue at full gallop, control and turn swiftly, and run along the beam, stand on the yoke, and from there quickly get back in the chariot.

Caesar, *BGall*. 4.33

Tacitus' brief note, that 'certain tribes also fight with chariots; the nobles are the charioteers, their clients the fighters' (*Agr.* 12.1), preserves an interesting detail that is at variance with the descriptions of Diodorus and Caesar (quoted above). It seems that the Caledonian nobility drove the chariots, while their social inferiors acted as warriors. Unfortunately, whether by accident or design, Tacitus (or, at any rate, the text of the *Agricola* that has come down to us) does not describe the precise activities of the chariots at Mons Graupius, besides the fact that they proved disappointing.

TOP
Denarius (silver coin) minted in 118 BC to celebrate the defeat of the Gallic tribes in 121 BC. The coin shows the Celtic motif of the two-horse chariot and, in the background, the carnyx or war-trumpet. (© McMaster University Collection, Hamilton, Ontario. Photo: Katrina Jennifer Bedford. Ref. 1946.001.0008C)

BOTTOM
Chariot burial at Newbridge (Edinburgh) during excavation in 2001. The grave preserves the shape of the vehicle, with the wheels nearest the camera and the yoke pole at the far end; iron terrets and two bridle bits were found. Unusually, the vehicle was not dismantled before burial. Although no body was found, comparable finds from Yorkshire were linked with high-status individuals. Radiocarbon dates obtained from the chariot wheels indicated that the chariot was around 2,400 years old. (© National Museums of Scotland, by kind permission of Dr Fraser Hunter)

TOP

TOP
Reconstruction of the Wetwang chariot, excavated in 2001 and found to date from around 300 BC. Unlike the Newbridge burial, the Wetwang chariot had been dismantled and the pieces arranged around the crouched body of its female owner. (© Tony Spence)

BOTTOM
Reconstructions of Iron Age chariots, based on the finds from Wetwang (Yorkshire) in 2001. Each one demonstrates a different method of suspending the floor from the double-arched sides, in order to absorb the shocks that are inevitably generated by driving on solid wheels. These models are of the *essedum* type, and lack the scythed axles of the *covinnus*. (© Tony Spence)

The status of the driver is not the only difference exhibited by the Caledonian chariot. For Caesar uses the word *essedum* to indicate the type of chariot that he encountered amongst the south Britons, and the same word is used by other classical authors, like Cicero, for example (in the letter mentioned above). But, in his report of the battle at Mons Graupius, Tacitus uses the word *covinnus*. This unfamiliar word is explained by Pomponius Mela, who notes that the Britons employed 'chariots armed in the Gallic fashion; they call them *covinni*, on which they use scythed axles' (*Chor.* 3.6 = 52). The singular design of the Caledonian chariots must have caused a sensation at Rome, for even the poet Silius Italicus, in his pro-Flavian epic, managed to include a reference to it, along with that other British peculiarity, woad tattooing: 'no differently does the blue-painted native of Thule, when he fights, drive around the dense battle lines in his scythed chariot (*covinnus*)' (Sil. Ital., *Pun.* 17.418–9). (By the time Silius was writing, his audience were familiar with Thule, the ancient name of the Shetland Islands.) Silius' contemporary, the poet Martial, even claimed (humorously, no doubt) to have received a *covinnus* as a gift from his friend Aelianus (Mart., *Epig.* 12.24).

Other classical authors periodically mention scythed chariots, dating back to Alexander the Great's encounters with the Achaemenid Persians. Frontinus, the one-time governor of Britain who wrote a book of military stratagems, believed that Caesar had encountered such vehicles in Gaul (Frontin., *Strat.* 2.3.18), a fact that receives an echo in the poet Lucan's reference to the *covinni* of the Belgae (Luc., *BCiv.* 1.426). Most interesting is the advice of the late Roman writer Vegetius on 'How scythed chariots and elephants may be opposed in battle' (*De re mil.* 3.24). Recalling how these vehicles had been used in the past by Antiochus III of Syria and Mithridates VI of Pontus, he writes that 'at first, they caused great terror, but after a while they attracted scorn; for it is difficult for a scythed chariot always to find level ground, and it is hindered by the slightest impediment, and is incapacitated if even a single horse is weakened or wounded'. Vegetius contrasts the initial psychological effect with the difficulties inherent in the design and the subsequent failure to perform. Almost the same sequence of events occurred at Mons Graupius, as we shall see.

OPPOSING COMMANDERS AND PLANS

Modern statue of Agricola, erected in his home town of Fréjus (ancient Forum Julii). He is depicted with one hand raised in salute, while the other holds his *mandata*, the instructions given to every provincial governor by the emperor. No ancient likeness of Agricola is known. (Author's collection)

AGRICOLA AND THE ROMANS

When Agricola arrived in Britain, accompanied by his family and probably (as was usual for a provincial governor) by an advisory staff of companions (*amici*), it was already midsummer AD 77. The Roman campaigning season ran from 22 March to 22 September, so the army had been sitting idly for some months. Agricola's predecessor in the governorship, Frontinus, had left the province earlier in the year, probably as soon as the sea lanes opened. Consequently, 'the soldiers turned to relaxation', writes Tacitus, 'as though campaigning had been cancelled' (*Agr.* 18.1).

Agricola will have made his way initially to the provincial capital at London, to meet his official staff (*officium*) and bodyguard (the *pedites* and *equites singulares*) and to liaise with the procurator, an equestrian officer in charge of finances. He surely carried orders (*mandata*) from the emperor Vespasian, whom we can imagine repeating Claudius' instruction to Aulus Plautius to 'conquer the rest' (Dio 60.21). He certainly remained in contact with Rome by sending at least two end-of-season reports and probably more.

Contact with Vespasian was critical. After all, the empire was a military dictatorship, in which the emperor relied on his governors to administer his various provinces for him. Minor areas with only auxiliary garrisons, or with none at all, could be entrusted to men of the equestrian aristocracy, who filled the posts as procurators or prefects, usually after completing the *tres militiae*. But provinces with important military forces were governed by senators. Many, like Britain, contained multiple legions, so they required a senator of some seniority to outrank the legionary legates under his command. Thus, only men who had held the consulship, the supreme magistracy at Rome, were eligible to govern these provinces, where they took the title of *legatus Augusti pro praetore* ('emperor's legate with the powers of a praetor', the usual formula to designate a provincial governor).

Agricola's consulship fell just before his appointment to govern Britain. The consular listings for the AD 70s and 80s, as we know them, have many gaps, and one of them relates to Agricola's term of office. Every year was divided, in theory, into six two-month periods, each to be occupied by two consuls; the year was officially named after the *consules ordinarii*, the 'ordinary' consular pair who held office in January–February. Consequently, and understandably, members of the ruling Flavian dynasty normally reserved the first few months in each year for themselves, sometimes up to April or

P·CORNELIO·P·F·   TACITO·CA   ·COS
XV·VIRO·SACRIS·FACIVNDIS·X·VIRO·STLITIBVS·IVDICANDIS·TRIB
MIL·LEG·   ·QVAESTORI·AVG·TRIBVNO·PLEBIS·PRAETORI

0   50   100 cm

even June. So-called 'suffect' consuls filled any subsequent slots, in a sequence that observed the unwritten rules of etiquette that were so important in Roman society. It seems quite likely that Agricola was one of these suffect consuls in AD 76, a year for which our consular listings exhibit several vacant slots.

'As consul', writes Tacitus, 'he betrothed his daughter, a girl of outstanding promise, to me in my youth, and after his consulship he gave her in marriage, and was immediately given command of Britain' (*Agr.* 9. 6). We know, from the poet Ovid, that it was unpropitious for marriages to take place before 13 June (Ovid, *Fast.* 6.223), and it was perhaps his daughter's wedding in the summer of AD 77 that delayed Agricola's journey to Britain. Of course, travel in the ancient world was slow: in 54 BC, a letter from Caesar in Britain took a month to reach Cicero in Rome (Cic., *Epist. ad Att.* 4.18.5). We may also speculate that the entourage of *amici* that accompanied Agricola on his journey north through Gaul included his new son-in-law, serving as military tribune with one of the British legions. Because tribunates were in the gift of the provincial governor, it was fairly common for young men to begin their military career serving with a close relative.

CALGACUS AND THE CALEDONIANS

By contrast with Agricola, we know virtually nothing about his Caledonian adversary. It seems that, to oppose the Roman advance, as it enveloped the lowland peoples, the Caledonian tribes had formed a confederacy, which enabled them to field a force of 30,000 individuals. Their leader was Calgacus, a man who was 'outstanding among the many leaders in courage and lineage' (Tac., *Agr.* 29.4). The name is thought to mean 'swordsman' (like the Irish *calgach*), and some have suggested that this was a title rather than a personal name. Indeed, some have even doubted that the man ever existed, claiming that he was a literary creation of Tacitus'; but of course, the Caledonians must have had a leader.

We have seen that, for Ptolemy, the Caledonians were only one of several peoples inhabiting the north of Scotland. So it is possible that the disparate tribes had been brought together under a single war leader, just as the Gallic tribes threatened by Caesar had rallied to the banner of Vercingetorix in 52 BC. Certainly, in later years, the peoples of the north would come together into the two great groupings of the Maeatae and the Caledones (Cassius Dio 76.12), repeating a phenomenon that can be observed on other Roman frontiers.

It suited Tacitus' oratorical style to portray Calgacus haranguing his assembled warriors before the battle, so he duly provided a stirring 70-line speech for the chieftain (Tac., *Agr.* 30–32). Other classical writers followed the same tradition of inventing speeches. Although, as Agricola's biographer,

Tacitus was obliged to deliver factual information about his subject, as a writer in the tradition of Cicero and Sallust, he was equally obliged to produce a work of literature. It is noteworthy that his friend, the younger Pliny, consciously emulated elements from the *Agricola* in his own *Panegyricus* to the Emperor Trajan. So we may well imagine generations of long-suffering Roman grammarians drilling their young charges with repeated recitations of Calgacus' speech.

The speech is clearly not a reliable statement of Caledonian strategy. However, it is interesting as a statement of what a contemporary Roman *thought* that an outsider's observations might be, even though they are wrapped up in the stereotype of the boasting barbarian. It may, indeed, have been Tacitus' own opinion of the Roman Army's behaviour, when he placed into Calgacus' mouth the following indictment: 'plundering, butchering, raping in the false name of empire (*imperium*), where they have created desolation they call it peace' (*Agr.* 30.4).

'Today', Tacitus imagines Calgacus saying, 'will mark the beginning of freedom for the whole of Britain' (*Agr.* 30.1). The preceding 40 years of Roman occupation had seen other battles fought, but now, at last, the Romans had reached the edge of the world. 'We are the last people on earth and the last to be free', as the historian A. R. Birley renders one of Tacitus' wonderfully concise epigrams (*Agr.* 30.3: *nos terrarum ac libertatis extremos*). He draws a distinction between peoples who, having been conquered, later rise in revolt once they have had time to regret their submission to Rome. 'We will be fighting, vigorous and untamed, for freedom not for regret' (*Agr.* 31.4). Whatever Calgacus actually said on the eve of battle, we can be sure that the Caledonian plan was to defend their homes in the face of Roman imperialism.

THE CAMPAIGN

Although Tacitus is our main source of information, he is not the only ancient author to mention Agricola's campaigns. They briefly feature in the *Roman History* of Cassius Dio, an enormous multi-volume work researched during the reign of Septimius Severus (AD 193–211) and written up during the following decade. Sadly, the section covering the history of the Flavian emperors has not survived, but a Byzantine summary, the *Epitome Dionis Nicaeensis* compiled by the 11th-century monk Johannes Xiphilinus, preserves the highlights.

Oddly, the section mentioning Agricola appears under the year AD 79, just before the description of the famous eruption of Vesuvius in August that year and the great fire of Rome in the following year. It was common during Dio's lifetime for governors to be sent to Britain in response to war and rebellion, so this perhaps coloured his account when he wrote that, 'as war had again broken out in Britain, Gnaeus Julius Agricola overran all the enemy's territory there' (Cass. Dio 66.20.1). In fact, it looks as though he has summarized the entire seven-year governorship in one sentence. And when he continues, 'he was in fact the first of the Romans, that we know of, to discover that Britain is surrounded with water' (ibid.), he refers to an event that seems only to have occurred in Agricola's final year, when his fleet circumnavigated Britain.

Members of the Roman Military Research Society, who re-enact as Batavian auxiliaries, photographed at The Lunt Roman fort, Coventry, in 2008. (© Adrian Wink)

Roman Britain, AD 77–78

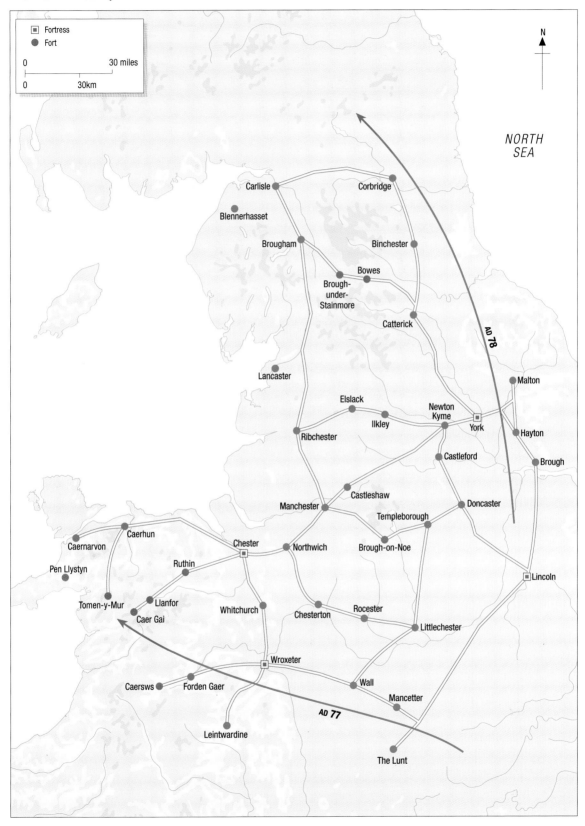

Fortress

Fort

0   30 miles

0   30km

N

NORTH
SEA

Carlisle

Corbridge

Blennerhasset

Brougham

Binchester

Bowes

Brough-
under-
Stainmore

Catterick

Lancaster

Malton

Elslack

Newton
Kyme

Ilkley

York

Hayton

Ribchester

Castleford

Brough

Castleshaw

Manchester

Doncaster

Templeborough

Brough-on-Noe

Lincoln

Caerhun

Chester

Northwich

Caernarvon

Ruthin

Pen Llystyn

Tomen-y-Mur

Llanfor

Whitchurch

Chesterton

Rocester

Littlechester

Caer Gai

Wroxeter

Caersws

Forden Gaer

Wall

Mancetter

AD 77

Leintwardine

The Lunt

AD 78

AGRICOLA'S FIRST SEASON (AD 77): SHARING THE DANGER

In the summer of AD 77, not everyone in the province was idly waiting for the new governor to arrive. The tribe of the Ordovices in north Wales had taken advantage of Roman lethargy to launch an attack on a cavalry regiment billeted nearby. The previous governor, Frontinus, had concentrated his efforts against the Welsh tribes, redeploying two legions in the process. But, when Tacitus specifically states that 'he subjugated the strong and warlike people of the Silures' (*Agr.* 17.2), his silence regarding their northern cousins is deafening.

Now, Agricola was faced with a serious problem. According to Tacitus, who (as we have seen) may well have been accompanying his father-in-law, 'not long before his arrival, the community of the Ordovices had almost completely destroyed an *ala* operating in their territory' (*Agr.* 18.1). Such impudence could not go unpunished. Nevertheless, there were those who pointed to the lateness of the season, for it was well into September by now, and they worried that conditions were no longer favourable for military action. Rather, they advocated keeping a watch on the suspects over the winter. But Agricola had other ideas.

Not only did he spring into action, despite the poor weather, but, when the Ordovices withdrew into the hills, he pursued them, 'himself at the head of the column' (*Agr.* 18.2) to share the danger. When Tacitus reports that 'almost the whole tribe was slaughtered' (*Agr.* 18.3), he perhaps saw it with his own eyes. But Agricola was not yet ready to return to winter quarters. He wished finally to stamp out any embers of rebellion that still smouldered on Anglesey, the holy island of the Druids. Tacitus elsewhere explains that it was 'a haven for refugees' (*Ann.* 14.29) and, although its heyday had been the Boudiccan revolt, Agricola had perhaps pursued the remnants of the Ordovices there.

This was not the first time that the Romans had approached Anglesey. Agricola himself may even have been there before, as a young tribune when Suetonius Paullinus attacked the island in AD 60. On that occasion, Paullinus 'built boats with flat bottoms to cope with the precarious shallows; thus the infantry crossed, while the cavalry followed by the shoals or, in deeper waters, by swimming between the horses' (Tac., *Ann.* 14.29). But this time, Agricola could not spare the time for boat-building, and threw his troops across, unencumbered by their packs and equipment.

The spearhead, comprising 'auxiliaries, specially selected from those who knew the shoals and were accustomed by tradition to swim with weapons while controlling their horses' (*Agr.* 18.4), were surely Batavians. Tacitus explains elsewhere that these particular troops hailed from an island in the Rhine delta, which explained their 'peculiar knack of swimming, even crossing the Rhine with weapons and horses, without breaking ranks' (*Hist.* 4.12). In fact, when he claims, earlier in the same passage, that they had 'increased their reputation in Britain', he may be thinking of the four *cohortes Batavorum* (above, p. 19) and their service under Agricola.

The surrender of Anglesey signalled the end of campaigning, and the troops were dispersed to their winter quarters. But, if this short and sudden episode shows us Agricola's vigorous temperament, the aftermath demonstrates another side of his character, for he 'did not exploit his success in vanity, but explained the campaign and the victory as keeping a conquered people down'. To underline the fact, 'he did not even report the affair in laurel-wreathed letters (*laureatae*)' (Tac., *Agr.* 18.6).

One of the lead pipes from the legionary fortress at Chester, stamped with Agricola's name. Three examples of the same inscription are known: *IMP VESP VIIII T IMP VII COS CN IVLIO AGRICOLA LEG AVG PR PR* (*RIB* 2434). (© David Mason)

For the significance of this particular detail, we must turn to the encyclopaedia of Pliny the Elder, where he explains that 'for the Romans especially, the laurel is a messenger of rejoicing and victory; it accompanies dispatches and decorates soldiers' spears and javelins and the *fasces* of generals' (*Nat. Hist.* 15.133). (The *fasces* were the symbolic bundle of rods signifying high office.) A pair of inscriptions from Ostia near Rome even record that, on 18 February AD 116, the emperor Trajan sent *laureatae* to the Senate 'on account of his having been hailed conqueror of Parthia (*Parthicus*)' (*AE* 1934, 97; 1939, 52). Clearly, Agricola was expected to report back to the emperor on the season's activities, but modesty prevented him from claiming too much credit.

AGRICOLA'S SECOND SEASON (AD 78): ESTUARIES AND FORESTS

The winter months were spent settling into the new posting. The first order of business for any new provincial governor was to organize his *officium*. A man of Agricola's seniority had a sizeable clerical staff to handle the day-to-day administration of the province. Something of the Roman Army's bureaucracy can be glimpsed in the mountain of writing tablets recovered from the Roman fort at Vindolanda. We can safely assume that the documentation generated by the governor's *officium* would have dwarfed the output from a single fort.

He also had his own domestic staff, as Tacitus reminds us: 'beginning with himself and his staff, he first checked his own household (*domus*), which for a good many people is hardly less difficult than governing a province' (*Agr.* 19.2). Tacitus was not exaggerating. The *domus* encompassed not only the immediate family, but also the slaves and freedmen, who could be numerous in a senatorial household; some of them were answerable to his wife, Domitia Decidiana, and will have organized her entertainment while her husband was on campaign.

When the campaigning season came around again, Agricola's first priority was to ensure that the Brigantes of northern England were suitably pacified, before any further advance could be contemplated. Tacitus writes:

> When summer came, having assembled the army, he was present everywhere on the march, praising discipline and preventing stragglers; choosing camp sites himself and personally reconnoitring estuaries and forests; and all the while giving the enemy no rest by launching sudden plundering sorties. And when he had sufficiently terrorized them, he showed them the attractions of peace, by using restraint instead. Consequently, many communities (*multae civitates*) that hitherto had conducted themselves as equals now renounced violence and handed over hostages.
>
> Tac., *Agr.* 20.2–3

Some have condemned this passage as a list of clichés, designed to disguise Agricola's lack of progress. Or more of the topoi that writers used to pad out their work, this time aimed at portraying the ideal general. But there is nothing inherently improbable in any of them. In fact, it is quite likely that, having traversed northern England in force, the Romans now made treaty arrangements with the peoples who inhabited the Southern Uplands of Scotland. The 'many communities' that Tacitus mentions, living in a landscape of estuaries and forests, surely lay amongst the Selgovae and Votadini, who probably entered into the same kind of client relationship that had earlier bonded Cartimandua and the Brigantes to Rome.

Tacitus also claims that these communities 'were surrounded by garrisons and forts with such care and attention that never before had a new part of Britain come over so quietly' (*Agr.* 20.3). We have seen that Petillius Cerialis

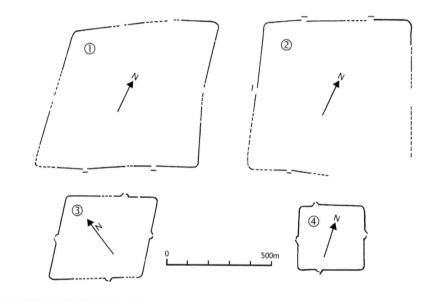

TOP
Comparative plans of some Roman marching camps.
1. Abernethy; 2. Dunning; 3. Stracathro; 4. Dalginross.
(© Author, after Maxwell)

BOTTOM
A length of rampart and ditch belonging to the north-west side of the Roman marching camp at Dunning, where they have been preserved in Kincladie Wood. (© Alan Leslie)

IMP CAES VESPASIANO AVG PM TR P P P COS VIIII ET TITO CAES
ARI IMP PONT TRP COS VII ET CAESARI AVGVSTI FILIO DOMITI
ANO BASILICAM ET BALNEVM THERMARVM LEG II ADIVTRIX PF
SVB GN IVLIO AGRICOLA LEG AVG PR PR PROV BRITANN FECIT

established a permanent fort at Carlisle. But archaeology seldom produces such an accurate foundation date, and other forts throughout the north of England can be assigned only very broadly to the Flavian period on the basis of their pottery and coins.

Nevertheless, it is unlikely that the Carlisle garrison lay unsupported so far north for very long, and Agricola's second season perhaps involved the organization of a logistically sustainable network of forts running back to the legionary fortresses at Chester and York. Certainly, both of the main routes north, on either side of the Cheviots, are dotted with half a dozen forts located at roughly 50km (30-mile) intervals to secure rearward communications, and it is likely that many of these were occupied at this time. Far from a season of relatively little progress, disguised by a list of topoi, it seems that Agricola was steadily laying the foundations for an invasion of Caledonia.

Imaginative reconstruction of an inscribed fragment found at Chester (*RIB* 463). Dedicatory inscriptions were very formulaic, and the list of titles of each emperor is well known from the general corpus of Roman inscriptions. Using clues from a similar dedication found at Verulamium, which actually names Agricola, this inscription has been restored to reflect the situation in AD 79, when Vespasian was consul for the ninth time and Titus for the seventh. (© David Mason)

AGRICOLA'S THIRD SEASON (AD 79): NEW PEOPLES AS FAR AS THE TAY

Modern writers often criticize Tacitus for his lack of geographical precision. But his readers in Rome were not interested in British geography, and the inclusion of strange place names would have made them none the wiser. Equally, Tacitus was not writing an itinerary. His readers expected not only to be informed, but also to be entertained, and if he occasionally dropped a few exotic names, that helped to sustain interest.

The account of Agricola's third season includes one of those exotic names, for he is depicted 'ravaging the peoples all the way to the *Taus* (the name of an estuary)' (Tac., *Agr*. 22.1). It is virtually certain that Tacitus here refers to the river Tay. Ptolemy, writing in Greek, records an estuary named Tava in the corresponding position (Ptol., *Geog*. 2.3.4: *Taoua eischysis*) and its similarity with the modern name is obvious (though ancient names often bear no relation to their modern counterparts). It would not be too far-fetched to speculate that Tacitus knew this particular place name because he had been there, standing at his father-in-law's side on the banks of the Tay. If he had accompanied Agricola to Britain, this could well have been his last season as legionary tribune before returning to a quaestorship in Rome, which was the next stage in the standard senatorial career.

The 'new peoples' (Tac., *Agr*. 22.1: *novae gentes*) encountered during this season were surely the Dumnonii, whose lands seem to have stretched across the Forth–Clyde isthmus into Stirlingshire and Perthshire. Campaigning in appalling weather, the Roman army sufficiently overawed them, and they perhaps handed over hostages, as their southern neighbours had done.

As we shall see (p. 51), campaigning armies based themselves, not in forts, but in marching camps, which were usually much larger and less formidably defended. Two camps in particular, recorded from the air in the 1970s, have been tentatively linked with Agricola's march to the Tay. The first, near the village of Abernethy (Perthshire) on the south bank of the River Earn, encloses 47ha (116 acres) within its squarish perimeter. Although nothing survives

Silver denarius of Titus, minted in AD 79. Previously, as Vespasian's colleague in power, he had shared each of his imperatorial acclamations (after his father's sixth). In AD 79, after Vespasian's death, he took his first acclamation independent of his father. This coin shows Titus as *IMP XV* along with his other titulature appropriate to that year. (Author's collection)

above ground, excavations across the south defences happened upon a sherd of Flavian pottery, which is suggestive of Agricolan occupation. Of the second camp, 15km (9 miles) west at Dunning (Perthshire), a 130m (425ft) length of rampart and ditch had long been known, running through the Kincladie Wood, where it had avoided destruction by the surrounding agriculture. It was found to belong to a similarly sized camp to the one at Abernethy, which was again broadly squarish in shape and probably exhibited the same doubled gateways on the north and south sides. (The find of a sherd of 2nd-century pottery from the west *titulus* ditch holds out the possibility of the camp's re-use during the Antonine occupation.) 'There was even time for the construction of forts. Experts commented that no other general selected suitable sites more wisely. No fort (*castellum*) established by Agricola was ever taken by enemy assault or abandoned either by capitulation or by flight. They could make constant sorties, for they were insured against long drawn-out sieges by supplies to last for a year. Thus winter was not feared there, for the garrisons (*praesidia*) were self-sufficient' (Tac., *Agr.* 22.2–3).

During this campaigning season, Agricola will have received word that his benefactor, the Emperor Vespasian, had died. The old man succumbed to illness on 23 June, in his 70th year, struggling to his feet and muttering that 'an emperor ought to die standing up' (Suet., *Div. Vesp.* 24.1). By midsummer, the news will have gone out to the provincial governors that Vespasian's elder son, the 39-year-old Titus, had succeeded to the throne. New *mandata* were perhaps issued. Certainly, we know enough about the new emperor to show that he did not simply slavishly follow Vespasian's policies. Equally, it is noticeable that the governors whom he found in place in key consular provinces, those like Britain, Pannonia and Syria, were retained there throughout his short reign. Nevertheless, it may be that he had other ideas for Britain, because Agricola's forward momentum certainly seems to have stalled.

At roughly the same time, Agricola received a legal assistant in the person of Gaius Salvius Liberalis, who held the new post of *legatus iuridicus* ('judicial legate'). Liberalis is known to have been an outstanding jurist who had been personally commended by the Emperor Vespasian (Suet., *Div. Vesp.* 13). Curiously, Tacitus does not mention him, and it is tempting to suggest that this was deliberate. At around the time when he was writing the *Agricola*, or just after, Tacitus and his friend Pliny successfully prosecuted a case in which Liberalis was the defence lawyer. So the two men perhaps did not see eye to eye.

Liberalis' career inscription (*ILS* 1011) reveals that, after serving as *legatus legionis* of *V Macedonica* in Moesia, he went on to hold the post of *legatus Augustorum iuridicus Britanniae*; the terminology implies service under successive emperors, so it seems that he was assigned by Vespasian and retained by Titus. He is known to have been absent from Rome from AD 78 until 81, so his legionary command can only have been for one year before he proceeded to Britain, on Vespasian's orders. If the old emperor had intended to free Agricola from the civic requirements of a developing province and allow him to concentrate on military tasks, the new emperor perhaps had different ideas.

Cassius Dio's brief account of Agricola's governorship, preserved by Xiphilinus, ends with the words, 'this took place in Britain, and as a result Titus was hailed as *imperator* for the fifteenth time' (Cass. Dio 66.20.3). As we noted above (p. 36), there is clearly some confusion in Xiphilinus' version (which may or may not reflect Dio's original). Nevertheless, Titus is known to have taken his 15th imperatorial acclamation late in AD 79. Did he perhaps assume that Britain was as good as conquered? Certainly, he and his father had not been averse to announcing *Iudaea capta* ('Judaea captured') in AD 71 with a great triumph (Cass. Dio 66.7.2), although the Jewish War was not over until the fall of Masada in AD 74.

AGRICOLA'S FOURTH SEASON (AD 80): SETTING A BOUNDARY

According to Tacitus, 'the fourth summer was spent securing what had been overrun' (*Agr.* 23.1). Whether or not Titus had actually called a halt, it was only sensible to ensure that lowland Scotland was firmly held. The lesson of the Boudiccan revolt was perhaps not lost on Agricola.

Equally, if Titus' plan was ultimately to complete the conquest, it would have been sensible to move the individual army units up within range of Caledonia. They were doing no good sitting in forts amongst the defeated Brigantes. Indeed, it seems that the task had already begun, with the previous season's fort building, and it surely continued into this new season, as Tacitus implies:

> If the courage (*virtus*) of the army and the glory (*gloria*) of the Roman name had permitted it, a boundary (*terminus*) could have been set within Britain itself. For the Clyde (*Clota*) and Forth (*Bodotria*), carried far inland by the tides of opposite seas, are separated by a narrow neck of land. This was, moreover, strengthened by garrisons (*praesidia*) and the whole sweep of country on the nearer side was secured, pushing the enemy back, as if into a different island.
> Tac., *Agr.* 23

Agricola's army had, by now, encompassed a huge area. Scholars have been quick to assume that the chieftain of the Votadini was treated as a friend of Rome, like the 11 kings who had earlier pledged allegiance to Claudius, or more recently Cartimandua of the Brigantes. But, unlike Claudius, the Flavians had shown themselves to be lukewarm about the concept of client kingship. In the east, Vespasian had incorporated the kingdom of Commagene into the province of Syria when he found that he distrusted the king (Jos., *Bell. Jud.* 7.219). And, although both the Votadini and the Selgovae appear to have handed over hostages in Agricola's second season, both must have had troops billeted upon them, whom they were obliged to feed.

Roman Scotland, AD 79–81

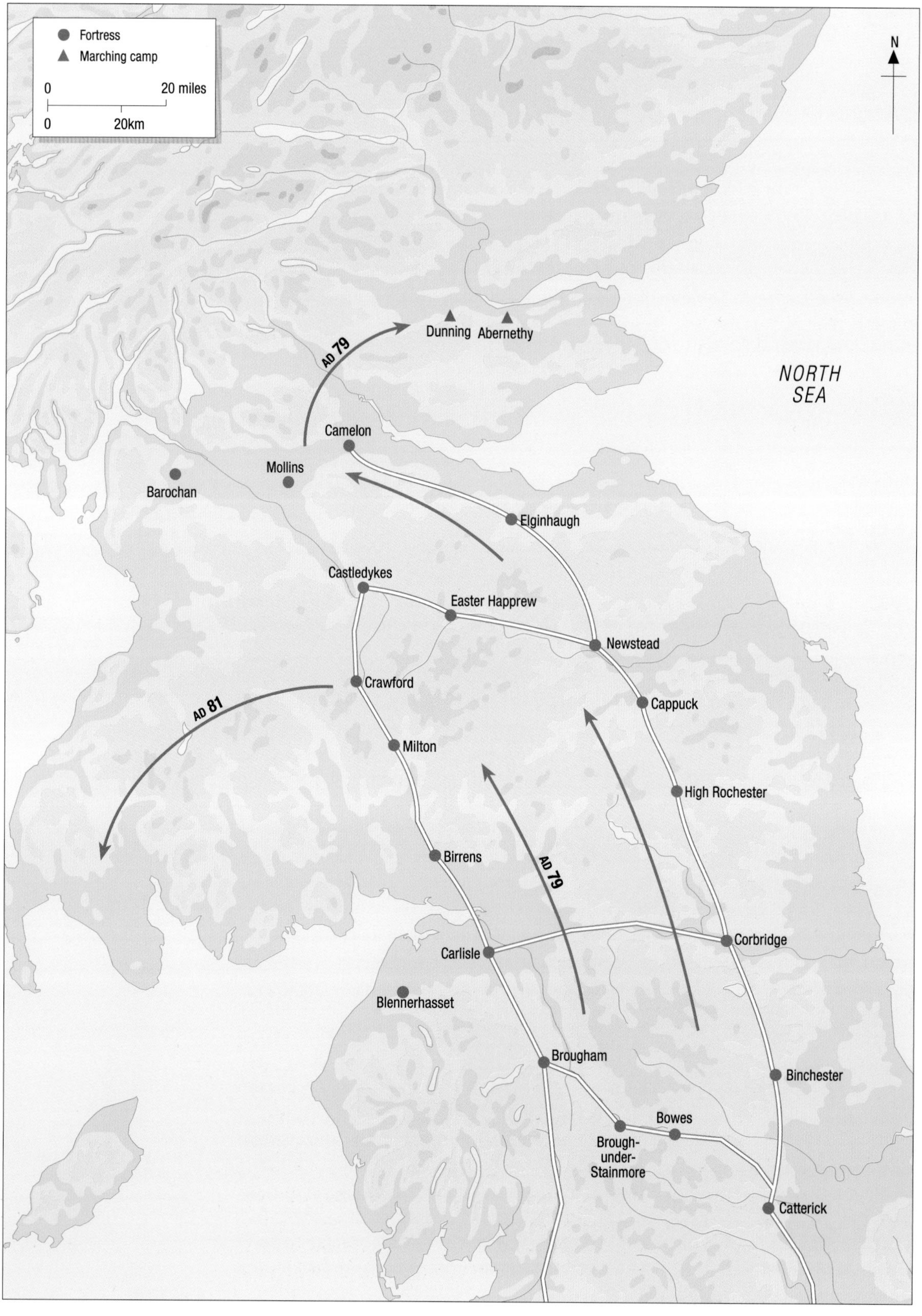
Fortress
Marching camp
0
20 miles
0
20km
N
NORTH SEA
Dunning
Abernethy
AD 79
Camelon
Mollins
Barochan
Elginhaugh
Castledykes
Easter Happrew
Newstead
Crawford
AD 81
Cappuck
Milton
High Rochester
Birrens
AD 79
Corbridge
Carlisle
Blennerhasset
Brougham
Binchester
Bowes
Brough-under-Stainmore
Catterick

Amongst the 'towns' assigned by Ptolemy to the Votadini is 'Kouria' (*Geog*. 2.3.7), by which he probably means Corbridge, known to the Romans as Coria. Here, a 10ha (25-acre) supply base was established at Beaufront Red House, some way to the west of the later fort and town. Likewise, one of the 'towns' amongst the Selgovae is 'Trimontion' (*Geog*. 2.3.6), corresponding to the 4ha (10-acre) fort at Newstead, which the Romans named Trimontium after the triple-peaked Eildon Hills; the fort lay at the centre of a sprawling marshalling ground for armies on the march. The main Roman road north, later known as Dere Street and nowadays followed by the A68, ran through both of these sites.

Other forts were well spaced along this route, and along the parallel route from Carlisle, now followed by the M74, in order to impose the minimum burden on the local economy, for Tacitus mentions that Agricola put an end to the abusive system whereby 'communities had to deliver supplies not to the nearest forts but to remote and inaccessible places' (*Agr*. 19.4). Along the western route, the sites of Birrens, Milton (Tassieholm), Crawford and Castledykes are normally linked with Agricola, while in the east, High Rochester, Cappuck and Easter Happrew completed the network. It was to these winter bases that the army retired after the summer's campaigning.

The 'garrisons' that strengthened Agricola's natural frontier between the Clyde and the Forth have always proved elusive, simply because nobody is very sure of the line that he envisaged for his *terminus*. It is probably too simplistic to suppose that the builders of the Antonine Wall, arriving at the same spot some 60 years later, planted their forts on top of Agricola's. For one thing, two of the likely candidates, Barochan (Renfrewshire) and Mollins (North Lanarkshire), forts of respectively 1.3ha (3 acres) and 0.4ha (1 acre), lie to the south of the line taken by the Antonine frontier, while a third, the so-called 'South Camp' at Camelon (near Falkirk), lies to the north. All three produced evidence of occupation within the Flavian period, and all three can justifiably be described as lying between the Clyde and the Forth. But it is not clear whether Agricola himself would have classified Elginhaugh (Midlothian), for example, as part of his *terminus*. The 1.3ha-fort there, lying to the south of the Forth estuary at the head of Dere Street, is thought to have been constructed in AD 79, which would place it in Agricola's third season. That season's fort-building activities may have accounted for other northern forts, as well.

AGRICOLA'S FIFTH SEASON (AD 81): CROSSING INTO TRACKLESS WASTES

Continuing the process of consolidation, Agricola must quickly have realized that, by advancing along Dere Street and distributing his army across the lands of the Votadini and Selgovae, he had entirely bypassed Galloway. This was the territory of the Novantae, amongst whom Ptolemy locates the place name 'Rerigonion' (*Geog*. 2.3.5), which is thought, on linguistic grounds, to be the present-day Loch Ryan, near Stranraer. If the Emperor Titus wanted all of lowland Scotland secured, then a foray into Galloway was required. 'In the fifth year of the campaigns, first crossing into trackless wastes, he subdued peoples up to that time unknown in several successful battles. He drew up his forces in that part of Britain that faces Ireland, more in hope than in fear' (Tac., *Agr*. 24.1).

Gold aureus of Domitian, minted in AD 88. (Author's collection)

This passage of Tacitus, more than any other, has caused great perplexity, and for a very simple reason. For, although Tacitus' style can often be intractable and his meaning obscure, there is an added complication caused by the physical state of the *Agricola*. In short, there are a few points in the text where the reading is uncertain. To explain this, a short digression on the manuscript tradition is required.

Most of the works that have come down to us from antiquity are preserved in handwritten manuscripts, which were jealously guarded in the monastic scriptoria of medieval Europe. In the case of the *Agricola*, we are reliant on the so-called *Codex Aesinas* (known to scholars as 'E'). This document was created in the 9th century AD by the monks of Hersfeld monastery in Germany, and was repaired in the 15th century by the creation of new pages to cover chapters 1–12 and 41–46, which must have been damaged in the meantime. Prior to the 20th century, scholars knew the *Agricola* only from two inferior 15th-century copies preserved in the Vatican, so the discovery of the original *Codex Aesinas* in 1902 was cause for celebration. But the handwriting is often difficult to decipher; so much so, that the 9th-century copyist even made some of his own suggestions in the margin.

The '*quinto expeditionum annonave prima transgressus*' of the *Codex Aesinas* (folio 59 recto) has often been suggested as a corrupt passage, where repeated miscopying has obscured the original meaning. At first sight, it means 'In the fifth year of the campaigns, crossing in the first ship...', but scholars baulked at the word order, pointing out that 'in the first ship' should be *prima nave*, not *nave prima*. And, in any case, where was Agricola going by ship? Down through the years, a variety of alternative readings has been proposed, none of which was entirely satisfactory. None, that is, until the recent suggestion of the archaeologist Gordon Maxwell, who suggested that Tacitus originally wrote *in avia primum transgressus*, 'first crossing into trackless wastes'. This would aptly describe an initial reconnaissance of the Galloway Peninsula.

The same passage is also well known for its mention of Ireland, and the fact that 'Agricola had received one of the minor kings (*reguli*) of this people who had been expelled in a family quarrel' (Tac., *Agr.* 24.3). We have seen that the emperors Augustus, Gaius and Claudius had received similar princes from Britain and elsewhere, and cultivated them in case their knowledge and contacts could be exploited. So it is entirely plausible that, on the Roman army's appearance in the lands of the Novantae, a disaffected Irish prince took the opportunity to present himself to the Roman governor.

Agricola's army must have returned to winter quarters by the time the news arrived of Titus' death on 13 September. Agricola himself was perhaps based at Carlisle. One of the writing tablets discovered there was addressed to an unnamed 'trooper of the *ala Sebosiana*, *singularis* of Agricola' (*AE* 1998, 852 = *Tab. Luguval.* 44). The members of the governor's horse guard (*equites singulares*) were drawn from the auxiliary *alae* under his command, so the rest of the *ala Sebosiana* may have been wintering elsewhere; though probably not at Corbridge, where an early tombstone (*RIB* 1172), now in Hexham Abbey, signals the presence of the *ala Petriana*.

Aerial view of the Roman fort at Ardoch, near Braco (Perth). This fine upstanding monument is one of the best-preserved forts in the Roman Empire. The visible remains date from the Antonine period, when the original Flavian fort was remodelled and extra ditches added. (© David Woolliscroft)

The new emperor's instructions were clearly to finish the job, for the one thing that Domitian lacked was military glory. Unlike his father and elder brother, he had never set foot in a military camp. His elevation to the throne, a month before his 30th birthday, allowed him to take his first imperatorial acclamation. He had a long way to go, before he would match the 17 taken by his brother, but subsequent events along the Rhine and Danube would give him ample scope. More immediately, his desire for glory was incompatible with the *terminus* imposed by Titus in Britain. It seems that it was not 'the glory of the Roman name' (Tac., *Agr*. 23) that baulked at an incomplete conquest, but Domitian (whose hated name Tacitus mostly avoids mentioning).

AGRICOLA'S SIXTH SEASON (AD 82): A WAR BY LAND AND SEA

'During the summer in which he began his sixth year of office', writes Tacitus, 'he enveloped the communities located beyond the Forth (*Bodotria*)'. Of course, in his third season (AD 79), Agricola had penetrated as far as the Tay (*Taus*), and had perhaps received hostages from the Dumnonii. So it was probably the Dumnonian communities of Stirlingshire and Perthshire that were now 'enveloped' or surrounded by forts in preparation for the final push into Caledonia. If this is the case, the series of forts along the road running north from Camelon, at Doune, Ardoch, Strageath and Bertha on the banks of the Tay, should date from this year. Situated at the limits of Dumnonian lands, these forts were well placed to draw supplies from the rich hinterland of Fife. 'Because an uprising was feared amongst all the peoples living beyond [the Dumnonii] and communications might be threatened by an enemy army, he reconnoitred the harbours with the fleet (*classis*), which had been deployed by Agricola for the first time as part of his forces, and was making a splendid impression in support, since the war was being pushed forwards simultaneously by land and by sea' (Tac., *Agr*. 25.1).

Tacitus goes on to describe how 'infantry, cavalry and seamen often mingled in the same camp, sharing supplies and banter' (*Agr.* 25.1). The early history of the *classis Britannica* ('British fleet') remains shadowy, but this was perhaps its first real taste of action. Agricola must have realized its value in maintaining contact with his northernmost garrison, at Bertha on the river Tay, even if the land route was impassable. Having sailed this far, it is unthinkable that the fleet would not have taken the opportunity to continue their exploration northwards, past Montrose, Stonehaven and Aberdeen.

Tacitus later imagines Calgacus lamenting that 'There is no land beyond us, and even the sea is no safe refuge when we are threatened by the Roman fleet' (*Agr.* 30.1). He was quite right, that the land of Caledonia stretched to the end of the island. 'There is no people beyond us, nothing but tides and rocks' (*Agr.* 33.1), as the Roman fleet was to discover so spectacularly in the following season.

It is quite understandable that 'the Britons, as was learned from prisoners, were dumbstruck by the sight of the fleet, for it was as if, now that the secret places beside their own sea had been opened up, the last refuge for the vanquished was closed' (*Agr.* 25.2). The small 3.2ha (8-acre) temporary camp at Dun, on the north coast of the Montrose basin, may have figured in these operations. The fragment of Flavian pottery found in the ditch would support the general dating, while the surrounding complex of circular houses, some 10–15m (33–50ft) in diameter, suggests contemporary Caledonian habitation. It seems that the Roman warships had struck a psychological blow here, by delivering troops to a hitherto inaccessible location, one of the 'secret places beside the sea'.

Finally, the peoples of Caledonia realized that there was no safe haven to rely upon, no secure refuge, so they finally went to war. 'The peoples who inhabit Caledonia', writes Tacitus, 'resorted to warbands and weapons, with great preparations, exaggerated by rumour, as is usual when the facts are unknown' (*Agr.* 25.3). Their opening gambit was to attack the northernmost forts, which prompted faint hearts on Agricola's staff to recommend an evacuation back to the Forth Estuary.

But, at this point, Agricola's scouts reported an imminent attack by several warbands. Tacitus explains that, 'so that he would not be outflanked by superior numbers who were familiar with the country, he himself divided his army into three groups and advanced' (*Agr.* 25.4). Such a tripartite division is a curious strategy, perhaps even risky in the face of uncertain enemy numbers; in the event, Agricola's forces almost came to grief.

> When the enemy found this out, in a sudden change of plan, they advanced together by night against the Ninth Legion, since it was especially weakened. Slaughtering the sentries, they burst in amongst the sleeping and the alarmed. There was already fighting inside the camp when Agricola, who had been informed of the enemy's movement by his scouts and was following in their tracks, ordered the swiftest of his cavalry and infantry to attack the rear of the combatants, and presently to raise the battle cry from the whole army.
>
> Tac., *Agr.* 26.1

Caught between two armies, the Caledonian warband fought their way back out of the camp, despite the crush in the gateway, and fled into the night. The Romans, for their part, were anxious to come to grips with their adversaries. 'They clamoured to drive on into Caledonia', writes Tacitus, 'and, in an incessant round of battles, finally to reach the furthest limit of Britain' (*Agr.* 27.1). They perhaps sensed the hand of history on their shoulders, with the fabled edge of the world almost within reach.

DOMITIAN'S CHATTAN WAR: A CONFLICT OF INTERESTS

While Agricola's army were keenly anticipating warfare in Caledonia, other events were afoot elsewhere in the empire. One of these in particular was destined to exert a critical influence on the conquest of Britain, although Tacitus only hints at the facts.

In composing the *Agricola*, Tacitus was not writing a straightforward history, but rather a celebration of his father-in-law's life. It is fortunate that he chose to illustrate that life with glimpses of current events, although his brevity of expression, often for rhetorical effect, can be frustrating. One example of this is the remark that the *VIIII Hispana* was 'especially weakened' (Tac., *Agr.* 26.1: *maxima invalida*), which has been taken to mean that, of all the legions, this one was particularly under-strength. But Tacitus gives no explanation.

The curious Debelec diploma (*ILS* 1995), issued to time-served auxiliary veterans of the Rhine army on 20 September AD 82, shows that the governor of Upper Germany, Quintus Corellius Rufus, was discharging men from three Moesian regiments alongside the regiments from his own province. The implication is surely that they were on temporary transfer at the time. The reason must have been Domitian's war against the Chatti, belittled by Cassius Dio (or his epitomator, Xiphilinus) as 'plundering some of the tribes across the Rhine' (Cass. Dio 67.3.5). At any rate, it seems that troops were being assembled during AD 82 for the following year's campaign in Germany, even from far-off provinces.

Britain was not exempt from this, despite Agricola's ongoing campaigns. For the tombstone of a certain Lucius Roscius Aelianus shows that he had been 'military tribune of the *VIIII Hispana* and of its detached troops in the German expedition' (*tribunus militum legionis IX Hispanae vexillariorum eiusdem in expeditione Germanica*: *ILS* 1025). It is tempting to suggest that this was the reason for *VIIII Hispana*'s numerical weakness during the Caledonians' night attack in AD 82.

Nor is it certain why Agricola divided his army into three groups. It would have been logical to place a legion at the core of each group, so it has been suggested that only three of the four British legions were on campaign. If this is the case, the fourth legion might have been dispersed to complete the task of fort building, for it is true that legionary craftsmen usually bore the brunt of any construction work. Unfortunately, Tacitus once again gives us a tantalizing glimpse, without providing the details that we would like.

THE MUTINY OF THE RECRUITS: A BOLD AND REMARKABLE CRIME

Tacitus relates another curious event during this season, which can have served only as an unwelcome distraction for Agricola. It seems that a regiment raised from the Usipi of Germany decided to mutiny, killing a centurion and the instructors who had been seconded for their basic training. 'They embarked on three small warships (*liburnicae*) dragging the helmsmen along by force', writes Tacitus (*Agr.* 28.1), and follows up with some lurid details of their clumsy voyage, before concluding with the remark that 'in this way, they sailed around Britain' (*Agr.* 28.3).

The tale of this 'bold and remarkable crime' (Tac., *Agr.* 28.1) became so famous that Cassius Dio incorporated it into his *Roman History*, from where it was excerpted by Xiphilinus, in the mistaken belief that it was only on account of their voyage that Britain was found to be an island. However, as we shall see, Agricola himself arranged for a seaborne reconnaissance to complete his governorship. Dio's version also illustrates how minor details can become corrupted by transmission, for he records that 'they killed their centurions and a tribune' (66.20.2). However, it was unnecessary for Dio to invent a tribune as their commanding officer, for it is quite likely that a unit in training could be entrusted to a legionary centurion. Such officers are frequently found in positions of authority, where they describe themselves as *curam agens* ('acting in charge'), or as the *praepositus* (literally 'one placed in command') of a unit, while retaining their rank as centurion.

BELOW LEFT

Aerial view of the Roman marching camp at Raedykes (near Stonehaven), looking south. The camp occupies the fields and moorland on the right of the photo. Its east rampart can be picked out where it runs along the west side of the wall extending from Broomhill Cottage. A large clump of trees marks the camp's north corner. (© David Woolliscroft)

BELOW RIGHT

Plan of Raedykes Roman camp (inverted to show south at the top) from General William Roy's *Military Antiquities of the Romans in North Britain*, completed in 1773 and posthumously published in 1793. The camp is not mentioned in the text, which prompted the eminent Scottish archaeologist Sir George MacDonald to suggest that Roy may have drawn the plan himself in the 1780s, as a late addition to the book. (Author's collection)

The tale also illustrates an interesting feature of conscription into the Roman Army. For, as well as drawing upon provinces with a large pool of available manpower, like Spain, Gaul and Thrace, auxiliary units were deliberately recruited from Rome's more warlike neighbours. The Usipi (also called the Usipetes elsewhere) should have been an ideal choice. Their lands lay in Germany along the river Lahn, which flows into the Rhine near Koblenz. During the events of AD 69, when German warbands crossed over to join the Batavian revolt and attacked the fortress at Mainz, the Usipi were drawn along by their larger, more unruly eastern neighbours, the Chatti (Tac., *Hist.* 4.37). Afterwards, the fighting men of other tribes in the general area, the Baetasii, Cugerni and Frisiavones, for example, were formed into individual cohorts and transferred far from their homelands. We would have expected the Usipi to be treated likewise. The only surprise is that their conscription was delayed so long – by almost a generation, in fact.

MARCHING CAMPS:
LIKE TOWNS PRODUCED IN A MOMENT

It is clear that, by March AD 82, as Agricola embarked on his sixth season, a few forts had been established as far north as the Tay estuary, to provide some of the troops with winter quarters. Agricola himself was perhaps based at Carlisle, if not further back in the fortress at York, but the bulk of his army occupied the forts of the Central Lowlands and Southern Uplands. These forts were intended to provide tolerable winter accommodation in timber buildings, and their turf and timber ramparts could be guaranteed to stand safe and sound all year round, maintained by only the smallest of caretaker garrisons, who were, themselves, secure behind sturdy timber gates. However, the onset of the campaigning season meant that troops were on the march for months on end; and as they moved around in search of their enemy, they required only makeshift accommodation.

Decades of aerial reconnaissance, photographing the unspoilt farmlands of Perthshire, Angus, Aberdeenshire and Moray, have revealed the telltale rectilinear traces of Roman marching camps by the dozen. Unlike the permanent forts, these were temporary enclosures, intended to marshal the troops under canvas or, strictly speaking, 'under leather' (*sub pellibus*: Caes., *BCiv.* 3.13), the true fabric of Roman tents. Even the officers lived in tents, but larger and more elaborate as befitted their elevated rank and status, with the commander occupying the largest, situated in the centre. The marching camp was no doubt primarily designed to preserve a degree of organization within a campaigning army, by providing familiar surroundings in an often-unfamiliar landscape, but it has been observed that its closely guarded boundaries also made clandestine desertion difficult.

Usually, the defences consisted only of a shallow perimeter ditch, from which the spoil was thrown up to form an earthen rampart; a palisade may have been planted on top. Gaps were left for the gateways, normally one in each side, although longer lengths of rampart might have two. These were covered, not by timber gates, but by an extra length of rampart and ditch, which either curved outwards in a semicircular extension of the camp rampart, or sat, detached, some way in front of the gap. The soldiers referred to the first of these as a *clavicula*, or 'little key', probably from its resemblance to the rather clumsy curved keys of the ancient world. In addition, the thought of securing a camp entrance with a 'little key' no doubt appealed to

The type of field oven discovered in Kintore marching camp, reconstructed at the Archaeolink Prehistory Park, near Inverurie. First, a pit is dug into the ground shaped as a figure-of-eight, of which one side is stone-lined for cooking; the soldier crouches in the other side, while tending the oven. This can be seen in the second view, showing a legionary re-enactor using the oven. (© Archaeolink Trust, by kind permission of Donald Fraser)

soldiers' humour. The second type of gate defence was known as a *titulus*, perhaps implying that it resembled a placard (the usual meaning of the word) lying on the ground; but, again, the name also satisfied soldiers' slang by naming the feature as a 'little Titus'.

An observer of the Roman army in action some years earlier, during Rome's Jewish War (AD 66–74), claimed that 'it is as if a town is produced in a moment' (Jos., *Bell. Jud.* 3.83). This observer, the historian Josephus, described how the ground was levelled, the perimeter marked out, the interior divided into tent lines, and the rampart thrown up, 'quicker than thought, thanks to the great number and skill of the workers' (Jos., *Bell. Jud.* 3.84). In the course of his brief description, he adds that 'they also create four gates, one facing each direction on the perimeter, convenient for draught animals to enter and wide enough for sorties in emergencies' (Jos., *Bell. Jud.* 3.81).

While broadly conforming to Josephus' description, no two marching camps in Scotland are exactly alike, and degrees of variation exist. For example, the 38ha (94-acre) camp at Raedykes in Aberdeenshire (which is clearly the Roman Army's handiwork despite the desire of 18th-century antiquarians to see it as Calgacus' stronghold) is broadly rectangular, but skewed in such a way that the north rampart has a pronounced re-entrant, centred on the north gate, and the west side gradually wanders eastwards, so that the south side is considerably shorter than the north. And, rather than the four gates of Josephus' account, Raedykes has six, with two on each of the long sides; but each one would be quite convenient for wagons, at around 15m (50ft) wide and protected by a *titulus* situated some 11m (36ft) outside. Indeed, a complete wheel was recovered from the camp during 19th-century investigations, but has since decayed from lack of conservation.

Roman Scotland, AD 82–83

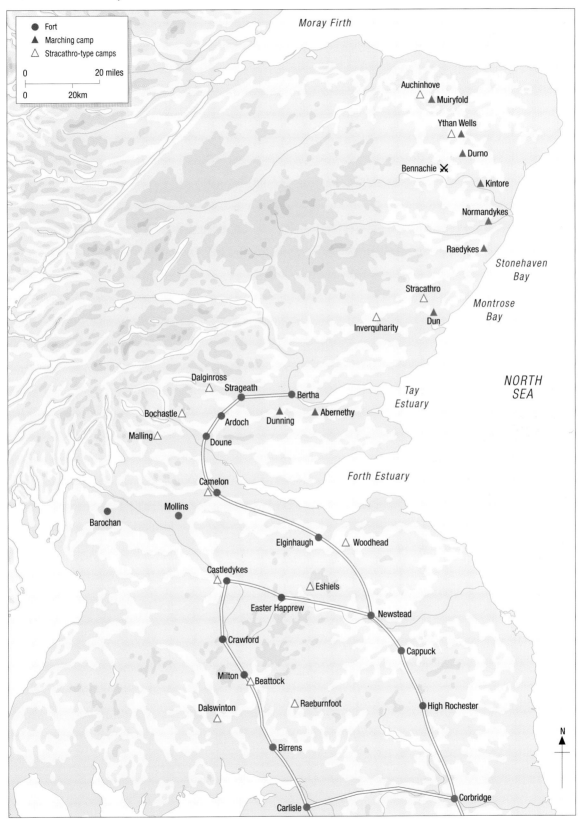

Fort
Marching camp
Stracathro-type camps

0   20 miles
0   20km

Moray Firth

Auchinhove
Muiryfold
Ythan Wells
Durno
Bennachie
Kintore
Normandykes
Raedykes

Stonehaven Bay

Stracathro
Inverquharity
Dun

Montrose Bay

NORTH SEA

Tay Estuary

Dalginross
Strageath
Bertha
Bochastle
Ardoch
Dunning
Abernethy
Malling
Doune

Forth Estuary

Camelon
Mollins
Barochan

Elginhaugh
Woodhead

Castledykes
Eshiels
Easter Happrew
Newstead

Crawford
Cappuck

Milton
Beattock
Raeburnfoot
High Rochester
Dalswinton

Birrens

N

Carlisle
Corbridge

The regular placement of the gateways, with each pair directly facing one another, served to define two main thoroughfares through the camp (or three, where there are six gates), so that each camp had a main longitudinal pathway (known to the Roman surveyors as the *via praetoria*) and one or two lateral pathways (the main one of which, running past the commander's tent, was known as the *via principalis*). These roadways formed the basis of a notional grid for the pitching of the soldiers' tent lines. 'Having entrenched themselves, they encamp in companies, in a quiet and orderly manner. They manage all their other affairs with discipline and security, obtaining wood and provisions, as needed, and water for each company. For nobody has supper or breakfast simply when they wish, but all together, and trumpets announce the times for sleeping, guard duty, and awakening, for nothing is done without such a signal' (Jos., *Bell. Jud.* 3.85–86).

Traditionally, archaeologists have concentrated their limited budgets on examining the defences and the gateways of marching camps, as the most obvious features visible on aerial photographs. The interior space was usually ignored, on the grounds that, most probably, it would be archaeologically sterile, since it had contained only tents. The occasional observation of lines of rubbish pits, notably inside the camps at Glenlochar, Dalginross and Stracathro, was dismissed as an aberration, without exploring the possibility that temporary accommodation could mean days or weeks, rather than the assumed overnight stop.

However, in 2000, when part of the camp at Kintore (near Inverurie, Aberdeenshire) was threatened with destruction by road building, much more solid evidence came to light. Besides general-purpose pits, thought to have been used as latrines, archaeologists unearthed over 120 stone-lined field ovens. It is not yet clear how the ovens were arranged in relation to the soldiers' tent lines, but their existence indicates that marching camps were rather more sophisticated than many have believed up until now.

AGRICOLA'S LINE OF MARCH: PASSING FORESTS, CROSSING ESTUARIES

Marching camps of various sizes have been identified as far north as Bellie (near Elgin, Moray) on the flood plain of the river Spey. Over the years, archaeologists have tried to make sense of them by assigning individual camps to different historical periods. This task has become synonymous with the name of the late Professor Kenneth St Joseph, one of the pioneers of aerial reconnaissance, who, between 1950 and his retirement in 1980, proposed various groupings of camps.

Although these were chiefly based on an analysis of surface area, with a nod to morphology, one of St Joseph's groupings is based on neither of these, but rather on the design of the gate defences. For the so-called 'Stracathro' gateway, combining both an internal and an external *clavicula* with an added oblique spur designed to further narrow the entrance on the outside, occurs in only around a dozen camps, all of them located in Scotland. Although examples at Beattock, Dalswinton and Castledykes are broadly similar in size, and their geographical distribution is contained within the south-west, yet the diversity of the rest of these Stracathro-type camps argues against a single coherent grouping. Nevertheless, its relationship to known Flavian forts at the type-site of Stracathro, and also at Dalginross, where it was actually observed as an upstanding monument by William Roy, demonstrate the likely dating of this type of camp to the period around Agricola's governorship.

Comparative plans of some Roman marching camps. 1. Raedykes; 2. Ythan Wells; 3. Durno. (© Author, after Maxwell)

Of the other groupings proposed by St Joseph, the most robust is the series of so-called '110-acre camps' at Raedykes, Normandykes, Kintore, Ythan Wells and Muiryfold. The line thus runs in a roughly north-westerly direction, from the Mounth, where the Grampian mountains come down almost to the sea, and skirts the Highland massif to arrive in the vicinity of the town of Keith. The five large camps, arranged at roughly 20km (12-mile) intervals, average 44.5ha (110 acres); although Raedykes is a poor fit at only 38ha (94 acres), the eccentricities of its layout perhaps account for its reduced size. No real dating evidence has yet come to light, but the big camp at Ythan Wells appears to overlie a 'Stracathro-type' camp there.

St Joseph noted that the extra long 25km (16-mile) interval between Kintore and Ythan Wells could be bisected, by taking a slight westward detour to Durno. Here, a 58ha (143-acre) camp, laid out as a slightly twisted rectangle, was first noticed in 1975. Like other camps in the '110-acre' series, and incidentally complying with standard Roman practice (e.g. Hyg., *De mun. castr.* 57), it lies near a watercourse, in this case the little river Urie, which flows past the long west rampart, about 200m (650ft) away. And like others in the series, it has six *titulus*-guarded gates. It was immediately noted that this largest camp north of the Forth–Clyde isthmus clearly ought to betoken special circumstances, further emphasized by its proximity to the distinctive mountain of Bennachie, and it has become almost universally accepted as the Roman mustering point for the battle of Mons Graupius.

THE BATTLE

Tacitus preserves no hint of the events in Britain through the winter of AD 82, but we can be sure that construction and maintenance continued apace. The garrisons strung out along the Strathmore road at Ardoch, Strageath and Bertha will have been especially keen to keep their defences in good condition. Work may even have been continuing on the legionary fortress at Deva. That water pipes were being laid in AD 79, 'during the ninth consulship of the Emperor Vespasian and the seventh of Titus, while Gnaeus Julius Agricola was the emperor's propraetorian legate', is demonstrated by the official stamp that appears on the lead pipes themselves (*AE* 1975, 554; *ILS* 8704a; *RIB* 2434). It is quite likely that work was continuing intermittently there, while the troops were not on campaign.

In the meantime, Agricola's wife, Domitia Decidiana, had given birth to another son earlier in the year. Their first son had died shortly after the birth of their daughter, Tacitus' wife, in AD 63–64, and the couple now lost this second son, early in the new year. Infant mortality in the ancient world was notoriously high. Perhaps for this reason, the Emperor Augustus had

View across the battlefield, looking south-west along the curving north face of Bennachie, like the tiers of an amphitheatre. The mountain's distinctive profile can be recognized from miles around. (Author's collection)

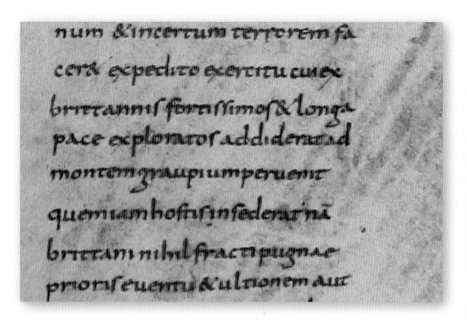

Extract from the *Codex Aesinas*, folio 60 recto (right hand column), where Tacitus first mentions Mons Graupius: 'he came to Mons Graupius, which the enemy already occupied' (*ad montem graupium pervenit quem iam hostis insederat*). (Author's collection)

legislated to grant certain privileges to those with children. His *ius liberorum* ('law concerning children') laid down, amongst other things, that the age limit for each stage of the senatorial career would be reduced by one year for each child. So Agricola had reached the praetorship in AD 68, two years earlier than the stipulated 30th birthday, because his wife had borne two children. Of course, it was important for a senator to have a son to carry on the family name, as well as a daughter to forge alliances with other families, so the premature death of another boy will have been particularly distressing.

Meanwhile, the Caledonians must finally have realized that battle was inevitable, for they began to assemble a host from their divided communities. 'They had at last learned', writes Tacitus, 'that a common danger must be repulsed by a common effort' (*Agr*. 29.3). So, sending out embassies far and wide, alliances were invoked or renewed, and the tribes of Caledonia gathered in strength. No doubt, warbands assembled from the various peoples listed by Ptolemy in his *Geography*. Some of these, the Venicones of Angus, the Taexali of Aberdeenshire, and even the Vacomagi of Moray, will have seen the Roman forces at first hand. Agricola may, in his sixth season, have marched as far north as Fochabers, where archaeology has revealed the likely site of a marching camp at Bellie. His fleet had almost certainly reconnoitred as far as the Moray Firth. But other peoples from more far-flung parts of Caledonia, the Cornavii of Caithness, for example, or the Creones of Lochaber, may have needed coaxing, cajoling even threatening, before they would mobilize for war.

In the end, Tacitus claims that more than 30,000 warriors, young and old, heeded the call, although the magnitude of the number has been doubted. The warriors were 'illustrious in battle and each wearing his decorations' (*Agr*. 29.4); if these are not the painted designs and tattoos favoured by the Celtic peoples, they may be the massive bronze armlets, collars and torcs which archaeologists periodically find on sites of the Scottish Iron Age. Writing over 200 years earlier, the Greek historian Polybius had been impressed by the Celtic warriors, 'richly adorned with golden torcs and armlets' (Plb. 2.29.8); on that occasion, it was the Gallic tribes at the battle of Telamon in 225 BC. The Caledonians at Mons Graupius must have presented a similar sight.

It is clear from Tacitus' account that the Caledonians selected the battlefield. Their choice of site was no doubt dictated by three considerations. First, in assembling a host from all over Caledonia, a reasonably central point was required, one which the more far-flung communities would still have a chance of reaching on time. Second, the hosting place had to be topographically distinctive, so that strangers could find it without difficulty. And third, as a proportion of the Caledonian fighting strength consisted of chariots, the battlefield required a reasonably flat plain. Mons Graupius must have satisfied all three of these factors, and, as we shall see, the site of Bennachie is an admirable fit.

THE LONG MARCH

On the morning of the battle, Tacitus represents his father-in-law sympathizing with the troops, saying 'Many a time on the march, when marshes or mountains and rivers were tiring you out, I have heard the bravest of you exclaim, "When will we get at the enemy? When shall we have a battle?"' (Tac., *Agr.* 33.4). Even if skirmishing might have occurred during this final season, the army will have been keen to exact revenge for the Caledonians' night attack on the *VIIII Hispana*. They wanted a full-scale battle to underline the conquest of Caledonia.

We have seen that the general line of Agricola's march was largely dictated by the topography, for the route north, from Camelon on the Forth–Clyde isthmus to the river Tay at Perth, is constrained by the presence of the Highland front, and is still followed to this day by the A9 highway. But, while the modern highway heads off through the Grampian Mountains towards Inverness, the evidence of Roman marching camps confirms what logic would suggest, that Agricola's army took the more coastal route, where they could maintain contact with the fleet. The camp at Raedykes is particularly relevant, lying only 5km (3 miles) inland from Stonehaven Bay. 'He sent the fleet ahead to spread great panic and uncertainty by plundering at various points; and with the army, marching without baggage and reinforced by the bravest of the Britons, picked out in a long period of peace, he came to Mons Graupius, which the enemy already occupied' (Tac., *Agr.* 29.2).

Arriving finally at the fateful battlefield, Agricola comments on the long months of campaigning. 'While we were advancing', Tacitus represents him saying, 'it is noble and splendid to have accomplished such a long march, bypassing forests and crossing estuaries' (*Agr.* 33.5). But if the battle should go badly, he warns his men, there would be a long and perilous trek back. Apart from the obvious danger of leaving an undefeated foe in the rear, the lateness of the season would complicate matters, because Tacitus tells us, in the aftermath of the battle, that 'the summer was already over' (*Agr.* 38.2).

Agricola's army was 'marching without a baggage train' (*expeditus*). If he wished to maintain maximum flexibility and speed, he had perhaps ordered the wagons to follow on, under separate guard. Usually, Roman armies on the march followed more or less the same form. A brief description was recorded by the Greek writer Onasander, in a work entitled *The General* (*Strategikos*), dedicated to Quintus Veranius, one-time legate of Britain, perhaps on the occasion of his taking up the governorship in AD 57. He recommended that an army should advance 'prepared at the same time for marching and for battle' (*Strat.* 6.1). This is perhaps his version of *expeditus*.

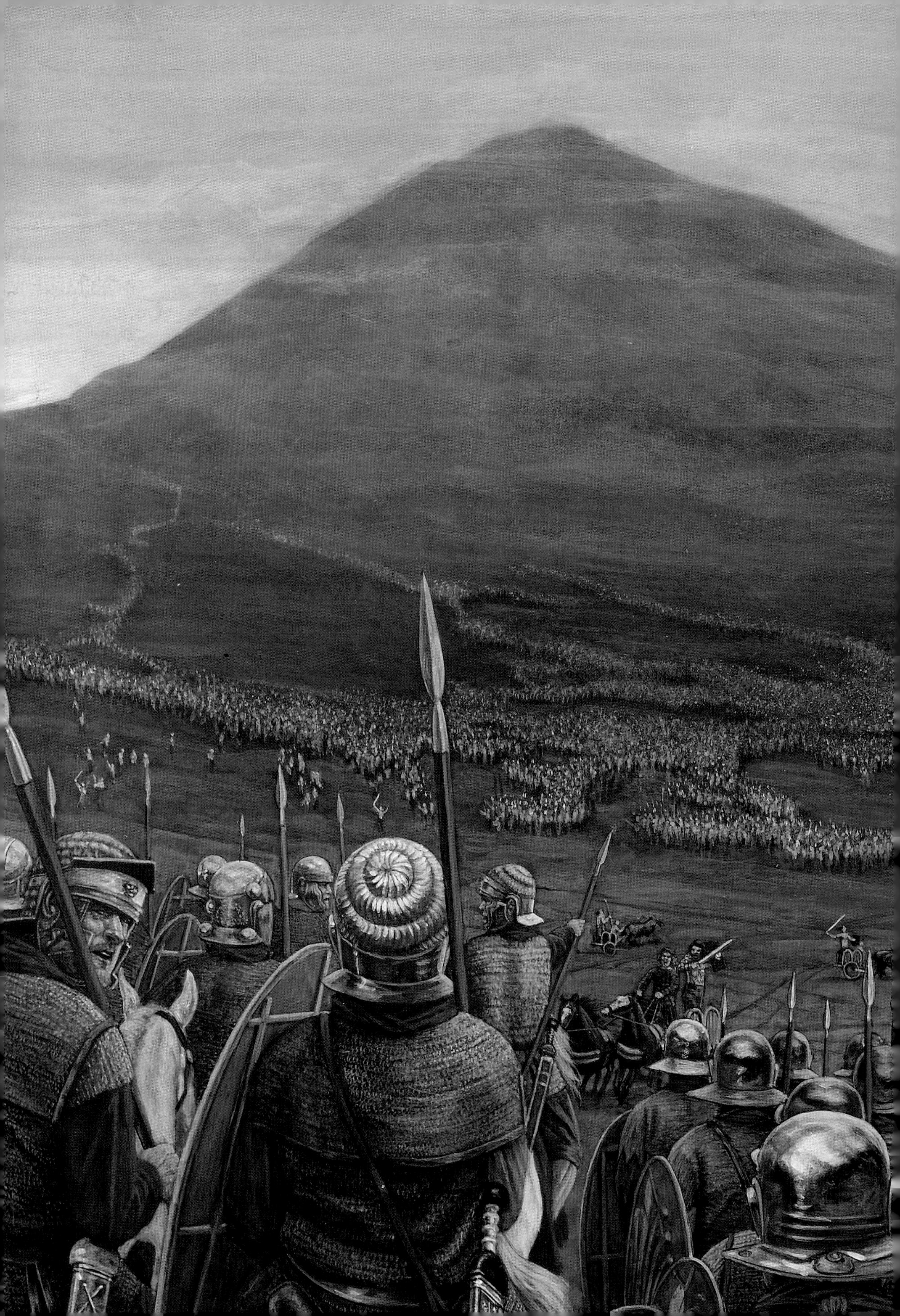

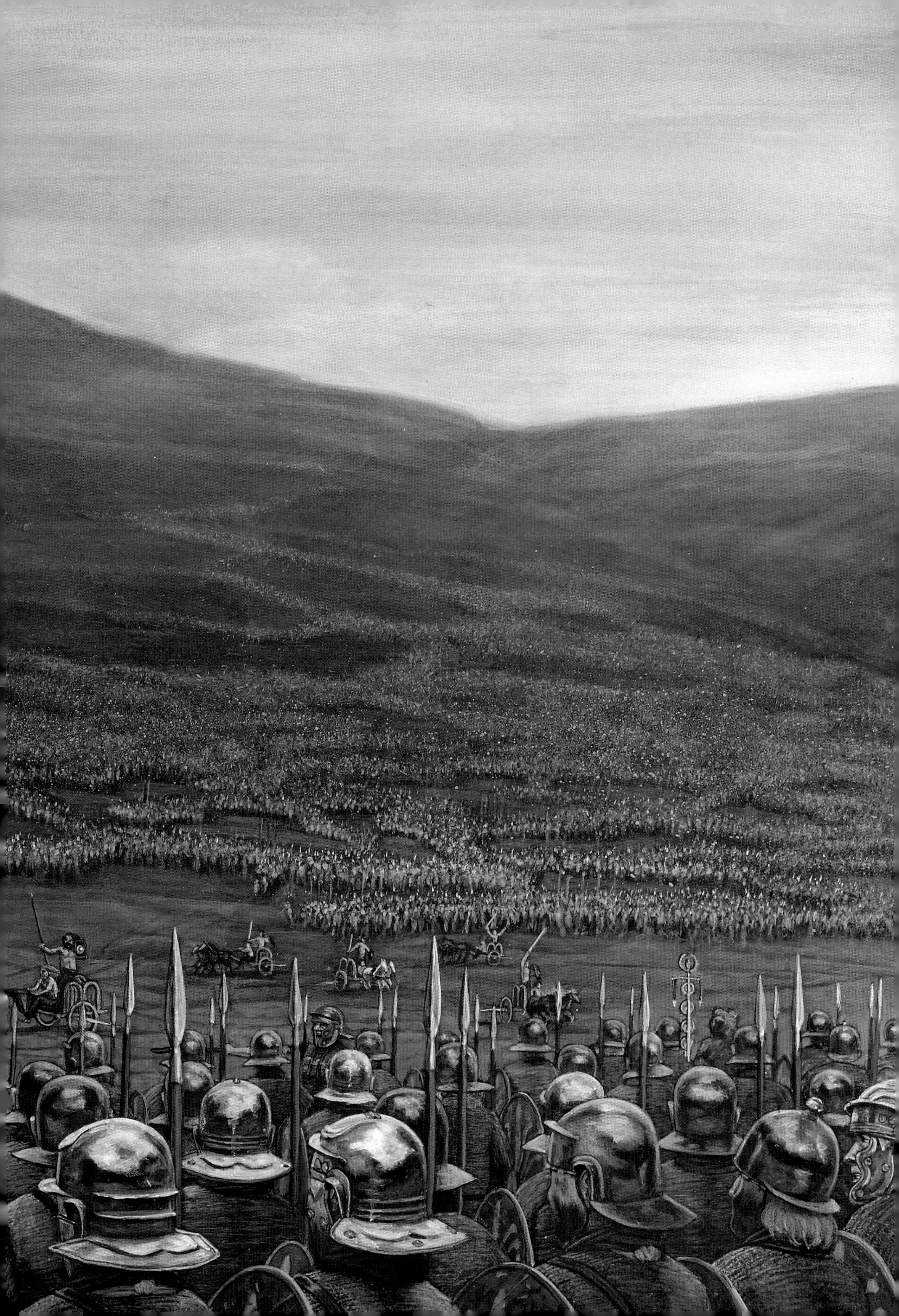

AGRICOLA'S ARMY IS DRAWN UP IN THE FACE OF THE CALEDONIAN HOST, WHICH HAS TAKEN UP POSITION ON MONS GRAUPIUS (pp. 60–61)

Late in the campaigning season of AD 83, Agricola's army finally confronted the massed Caledonian forces. The historian Tacitus claims that more than 30,000 warriors, young and old, gathered on the slopes of Mons Graupius for the climactic battle with the Roman invaders. Whereas the Caledonians probably assembled in their individual warbands, Roman discipline obliged Agricola's men to draw up in rank and file: 8,000 auxiliary infantry formed the core of his formation (1), supported by 3,000 cavalry, spread out on the flanks (2).

The Caledonian host, mostly infantry warriors, were drawn up on the lower slopes of the mountain (3) with small groups of horsemen, while their chariot-borne chieftains careered back and forth across the plain. Their purpose was evidently to intimidate the Romans and shake their resolve, while indulging in an ostentatious display of skill and force. Now, the front ranks of the Romans caught perhaps their first sight of the Caledonian chariots (covinni) with their scythed wheels, as they rattled and rumbled past (4).

The customary silence of the Roman ranks must have contrasted eerily with this din, amplified by the Caledonian horde, where individuals were shouting their war cries or blasting out tunes on the distinctive carnyx war-trumpets

At this stage, Agricola ordered his men to adopt a wider formation by opening out the ranks. Tacitus believed that the reason for this manoeuvre was the need to match the wide frontage of the Caledonians. However, the deployment of an open order formation may have been Agricola's intention from the start, along with his choice of auxiliaries in preference to the classic dense shield-wall of the legions. The flexibility of the auxiliaries as individual fighters must have seemed ideal in combating the threat posed by the Caledonian chariots, and Agricola may have envisaged a scenario not unlike Alexander the Great's battle of Gaugamela, where similar scythed chariots had been drawn into the front ranks, surrounded and overpowered there.

Onasander is quite clear that the good general should send cavalry scouts ahead of the main force to reconnoitre. But, beyond that, he simply notes that 'a marching formation that is compact and rectangular and not too long is easily manageable and safe' (*Strat.* 6.5). He further recommends placing the medical equipment and the baggage in the centre, but presumably Agricola's army lacked these. We know that, when he arrived at Mons Graupius, he deployed 8,000 auxiliary infantry and 5,000 cavalry; the size of his legionary force remains unknown, but we may legitimately infer that it broadly matched the auxiliary infantry.

Roman re-enactor equipped as an auxiliary infantryman, wearing a replica of the segmental arm guard (*manica*) discovered at Carlisle in 2001. He wields the short sword (*gladius*) usually (wrongly) associated only with legionaries, and wears a fur cap, which may have been a Batavian tradition. (© Adrian Wink)

ROMAN FORCES
1 Auxiliary cavalry (left flank)
2 Auxiliary cavalry (right flank)
3 Auxiliary infantry cohorts
4 Auxiliary cavalry reserve
5 Legionary vexillations

CALEDONIAN FORCES
A Chariots
B Infantry
C Cavalry

CALGACUS

BENNACHIE

ROMAN CAMP

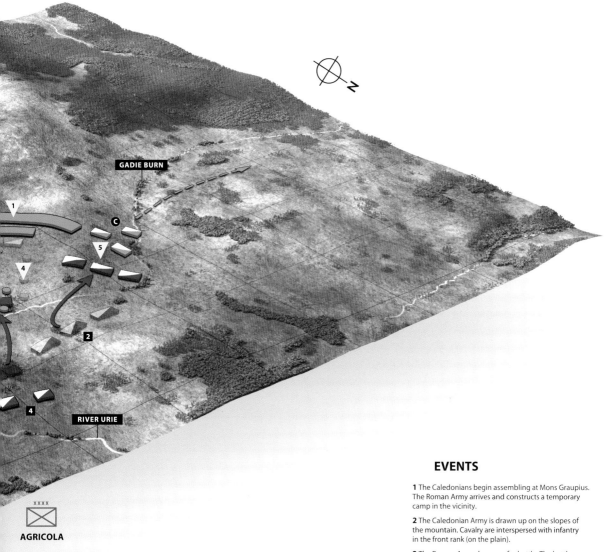

Note: Gridlines are shown at intervals of 1km/1093yds

GADIE BURN

RIVER URIE

AGRICOLA

EVENTS

1 The Caledonians begin assembling at Mons Graupius. The Roman Army arrives and constructs a temporary camp in the vicinity.

2 The Caledonian Army is drawn up on the slopes of the mountain. Cavalry are interspersed with infantry in the front rank (on the plain).

3 The Roman Army draws up for battle. The battle line is composed of auxiliary infantry and cavalry. The legionary vexillations form a reserve with four units of cavalry. Agricola takes up position with the reserve.

4 The Caledonian chariots drive back and forth across the plain to intimidate the Romans.

5 The Roman auxiliary infantry envelops the Caledonian chariots and advances to engage the Caledonian front ranks. Meanwhile, the Caledonian cavalry flees, pursued by Roman auxiliary cavalry.

6 Caledonian chariots are embroiled in the infantry battle; their wreckage obstructs the infantry.

7 The Caledonian rear ranks remain on the hillside.

MONS GRAUPIUS, SEPTEMBER AD 83: THE OPENING STAGES.

The forces are drawn up, the Caledonian cavalry is routed by the Roman cavalry, and the Roman infantry neutralises the Caledonian chariots while advancing to meet the Caledonian infantry.

An interesting parallel might be drawn with another army on the march, this time 50 years later in the eastern province of Cappadocia, where the governor, Arrian, was making plans to counter a threatened invasion of his province. His army, described in a text known as the *Expedition against the Alans* (*Ectaxis kat'Alanon*), involved cavalry scouts, in compliance with Onasander's recommendation. The column proper was spearheaded by a force of cavalry, comprising two regular squadrons (*alae*) and a composite force drawn from five equitate cohorts (*cohortes equitata*), probably totalling some 1,600 men. A body of around 2,000 auxiliary infantry followed them, made up from four cohorts, the last of which was a *cohors sagittariorum* ('cohort of archers'). Then, at this point on the march came the general himself, with his *equites singulares* ('mounted bodyguard') leading the cavalry component drawn from each legion under his command; in Arrian's case, this meant two legions, *XV Apollinaris* and vexillations of *XII Fulminata*, whom he specifies marching four abreast. After the legions came another grouping of auxiliary infantry, this time apparently mixed with the contributions of allied states and perhaps numbering another 2,000 men. Bringing up the rear of the column were two further cavalry squadrons, adding 1,000 to the cavalry total; one accompanied the baggage train, while the horsemen of the other rode in single file along the sides of the marching column.

Arrian's army was a smaller force than Agricola's, but it illustrates the kind of formation that the governor of Britain might have adopted in his march to Mons Graupius. Although smaller, it is still reckoned to have taken up almost 6km (4 miles). Agricola's army may have stretched for double that distance, so that his rearguard had barely left the gates of Kintore when his surveyors were already laying out the new camp at Durno, beneath the quadruple peaks of Bennachie.

THE GRAUPIAN MOUNTAIN

It was long ago conjectured that the name 'Graupius', which has no meaning in the Latin language used by Agricola and Tacitus, must have been a corruption of a Celtic word, 'Craupius'. This, it was argued, had the same derivation as the Welsh word *crwb*, meaning a hump, since Welsh also has roots in the ancient Celtic tongues. However, it now seems that the Welsh word is neither ancient nor Celtic, but probably derives from the Old French word *courbe*, meaning 'bent'. Consequently, any linguistic similarity with current place names (for example, Duncrub, a hill in Strathearn) seems purely coincidental.

The search for parallels with modern place names is, in any case, a fickle process. We have seen that the estuary named *Tava* by Tacitus has been identified with the river Tay, chiefly because the two words are similar. For the same reason, Tacitus' *Trisantona* is thought to be the river Trent, and his *Sabrina* the Severn. However, other ancient geographical names differ radically from their modern counterparts. Thus, although the river Clyde is recognizable in the name *Clota*, *Bodotria* is less obviously the river Forth. And, completing Tacitus' list of geographical features, *Thule* is almost certainly Mainland, the largest of the Shetland Islands, although the names are in no way similar.

More recently, it has been suggested that the name 'Craupius' might originally have been 'Cripius'. *Crip*, an ancient Welsh word for 'comb', is often applied to mountain ridges, such as the rock faces on Snowdon. It is quite possible that Agricola (or Tacitus himself) may have heard a Celtic place name meaning 'hill of the ridge'; and, if they Latinized it as *Mons Cripius*, it is easy to see how the name was later miscopied by the generations of medieval scribes who wrote the work out by hand. Worse corruptions have appeared in Latin manuscripts.

The name Mons Cripius, if it means 'hill of the ridge', is particularly well suited to Bennachie, with its 6.5km (4-mile) ridge running from east to west. Furthermore, the ridge is divided into the four summits of Hermit Seat, Watch Craig, Oxen Craig and Mither Tap, so that its profile is strikingly reminiscent of a cock's comb. If we can no longer explain Mons Graupius as a 'humped' hill, it seems very likely that it was a 'ridged' hill, which resembled the crest of a bird, just as does Bennachie. And it is noteworthy that its distinctive silhouette is visible for miles around. St Joseph noted it as far south as the Mounth, near the camp of Raedykes, and as far north as Keith, near the camp of Muiryfold. As a Caledonian mustering point, it seems ideal.

THE GENERAL'S SPEECH

The speech by a general to his troops was a feature of ancient warfare. Alexander the Great harangued his troops before Issus and Gaugamela (Curt., *Hist. Alex.* 3.10; 4.14); Hannibal and Scipio Africanus both addressed their troops before Zama (Plb. 15.10–11), and Caesar similarly before Pharsalus (Caes., *BCiv.* 3.90).

> The (enemy) battle line was already being drawn up when Agricola addressed his soldiers like this, thinking that, although they were cheerful and hardly able to be restrained within their defences, they needed to be encouraged still further. 'It is now the seventh year, fellow soldiers (*commilitones*), that, under the auspices of the Roman Empire, through bravery and loyal service, you have been conquering Britain.... We have surpassed the limits reached by earlier legates and previous armies, and the furthest point of Britain is no longer a matter of report or rumour, for we hold it with camps and with arms. Britain has been discovered and subjugated.
> Tac., *Agr.* 33.1–3

In his jointly authored commentary to the Agricola, which has become the standard text, Professor Ogilvie cautiously noted that 'Agricola may well have made a speech before the battle but we cannot tell whether Tacitus preserves anything of it'.

We can certainly be sure that Agricola made a speech, for it would have been remarkable if he had *not* addressed his troops at this most critical juncture of his entire governorship. The Greek writer Onasander advised that the general should be 'a competent speaker; for… if the general is drawing his men up for battle, the encouragement of his words makes them despise the danger, and long for the glory' (Onas., *Strat.* 1.13). The general's exhortation, he continues, is more encouraging than the very trumpet blast that signals the start of battle.

If we can be certain that Agricola addressed his troops, we are less sure of his precise words. Ogilvie points to the artificially rhetorical structure of the speech that Tacitus preserves. But, as an important public address, wouldn't Agricola have spent time planning it? Of course, in the end, Ogilvie is quite

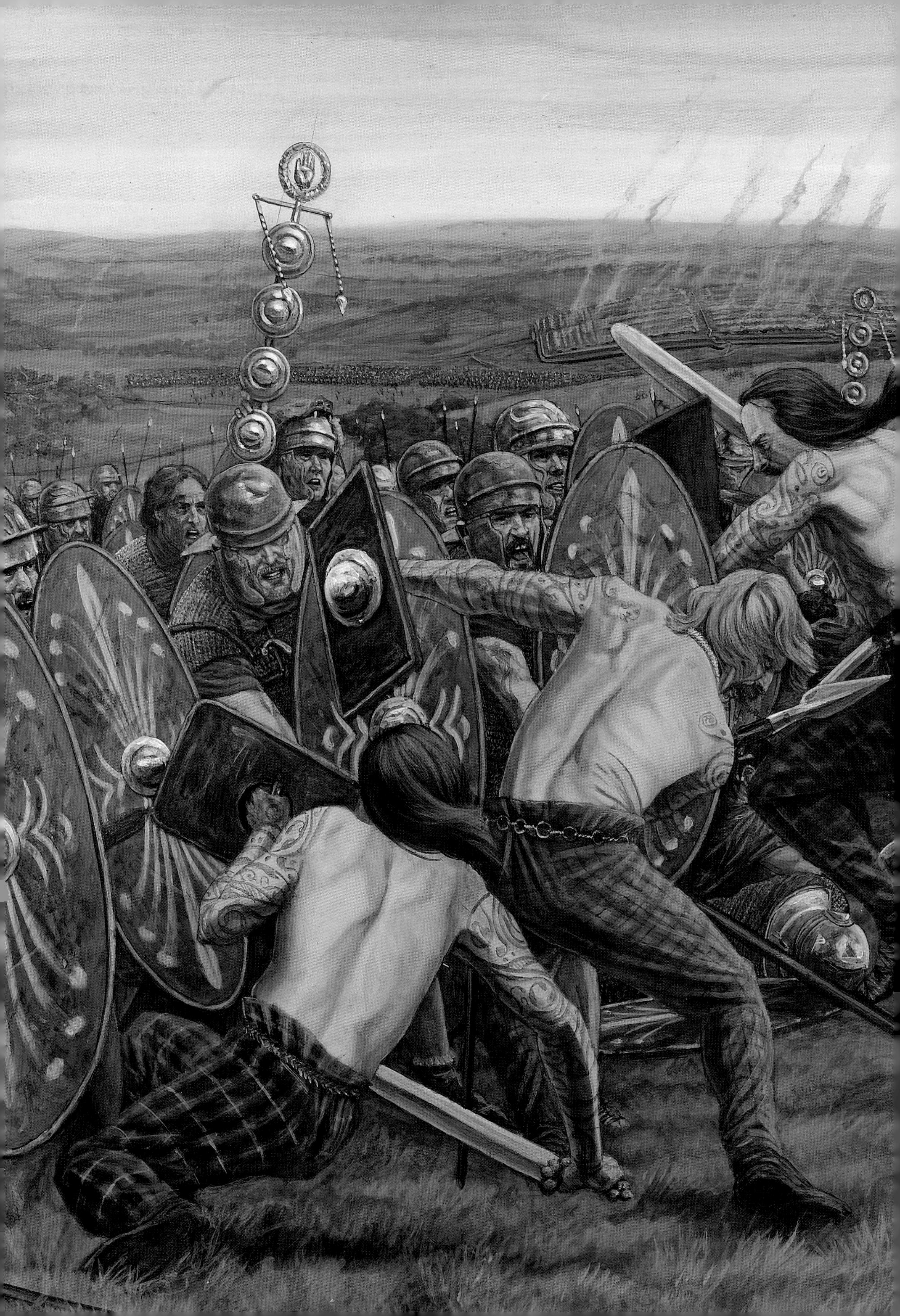

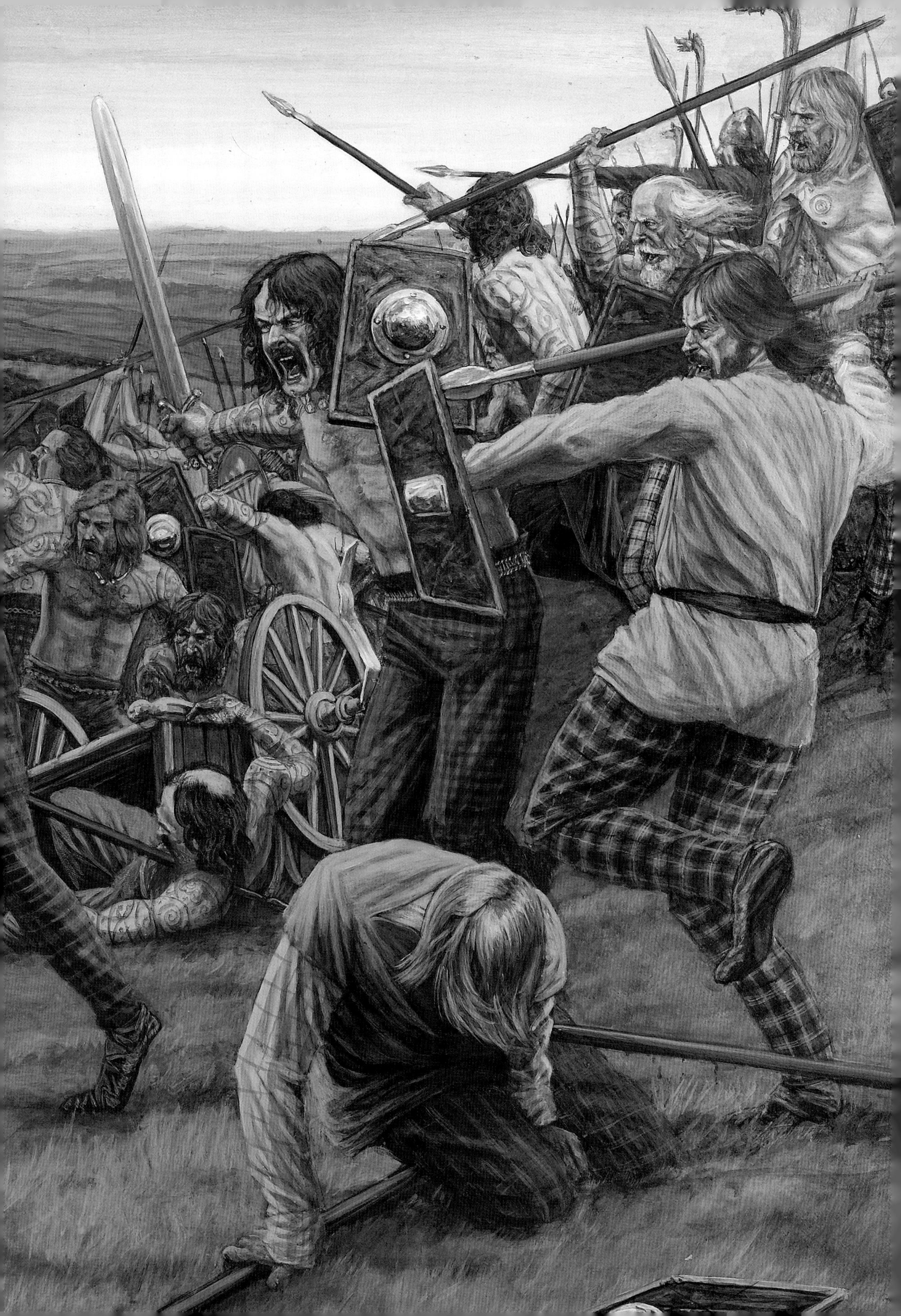

AGRICOLA'S BATAVIAN INFANTRY ADVANCES AGAINST THE CALEDONIANS (pp. 68–69)

The battle was joined with the traditional exchange of missile weapons. The flying spears of Agricola's auxiliaries would have thinned out the front ranks of the Caledonians, while many on the Roman side probably fell victim to the British spears. Tacitus makes it quite clear that the Caledonian horse had left the field, probably routed by the better-disciplined Roman cavalry, and the chariots, which had previously enjoyed the freedom of the plain, were now obstructed by the infantry advancing on both sides.

Once the auxiliaries had cast their spears, the real business of Roman combat was accomplished with the short, pointed infantry sword (*gladius*). Tacitus describes how the cohorts of Batavians and Tungrians (1), in particular, were highly trained in close-quarters fighting. Even the shield was used aggressively to batter the enemy, combined with the swift sword thrust, as the auxiliaries advanced, trampling the dead and the dying. Only the wreckage of the Caledonian chariots (2), and the runaway horses, terrified by the close press of bodies, posed a serious obstacle to the inexorable Roman advance.

By contrast, the Caledonian warriors were at a distinct disadvantage. Quite apart from their more individual fighting style, which encouraged un-coordinated attacks, Tacitus notes that they were equipped with short shields and long swords, which were badly suited to combating the auxiliaries' superior protection (3).

Agricola remained with his command group near the Roman camp. Durno, enclosing some 58ha (143 acres) within its ramparts, is the largest camp north of the Forth–Clyde isthmus. The reason for this is unclear, but if it was built on the eve of battle, it perhaps included elements which were not normally found in the average marching camp, providing services that would be required only after hard fighting. While Agricola's army was engaged in combat, the soldiers' servants and camp followers were firing up the ovens to provide a hot meal for the returning heroes.

LEFT
Roman re-enactor equipped as an auxiliary infantryman. The copper alloy scale cuirass was more lightweight than a mail shirt and probably provided a similar level of protection. Officers may have favoured it for its more flamboyant appearance. (© Adrian Wink)

RIGHT
Roman re-enactor equipped as an auxiliary infantryman. With his head-to-knee protection and three-ply wooden shield, this type of soldier in no way constituted 'light infantry'. Our view of the Roman auxiliaries is usually coloured by the depictions on Trajan's Column at Rome, where they are shown wearing a different set of equipment from the legionaries. (© Adrian Wink)

right to be sceptical. Tacitus may well have heard his father-in-law's reminiscence of the speech, but the version that he immortalized must largely have been his own composition. As Plutarch astutely observed when faced with the fulsome battle speeches of previous historians, 'it can be said of the rhetorical wanderings of Ephorus, Theopompus and Anaximenes, which they recite to the end, having armed and drawn up their army: "no one talks such nonsense when there is steel close at hand"' (Plut., *Moral.* 803B).

There is the added implausibility of being able to address 20,000 or so men at once, for it seems impossible for one man to be heard by the entire army. Before the battle of Issus, Alexander the Great allegedly rode along the front of his army, from one end to the other, addressing individuals by name, reminding various units of their past glories, and giving general encouragement to all (Arrian, *Anab.* 2.10; Curt., *Hist. Alex.* 3.10). Agricola could certainly have done the same. In fact, Tacitus' words perhaps imply that he harangued the men as they issued from the camp, for they were 'hardly able to be restrained inside their defences'.

DEPLOYING FOR BATTLE

As soon as Agricola finished speaking, 'the end of the speech was followed by a tremendous outburst of enthusiasm, and they immediately rushed to take up their arms' (Tac., *Agr.* 35.1). We can perhaps envisage lines of men

ROMAN FORCES

1 Auxiliary infantry cohorts
2 Auxiliary cavalry reserve
3 Legionary vexillations

CALEDONIAN FORCES

A Infantry

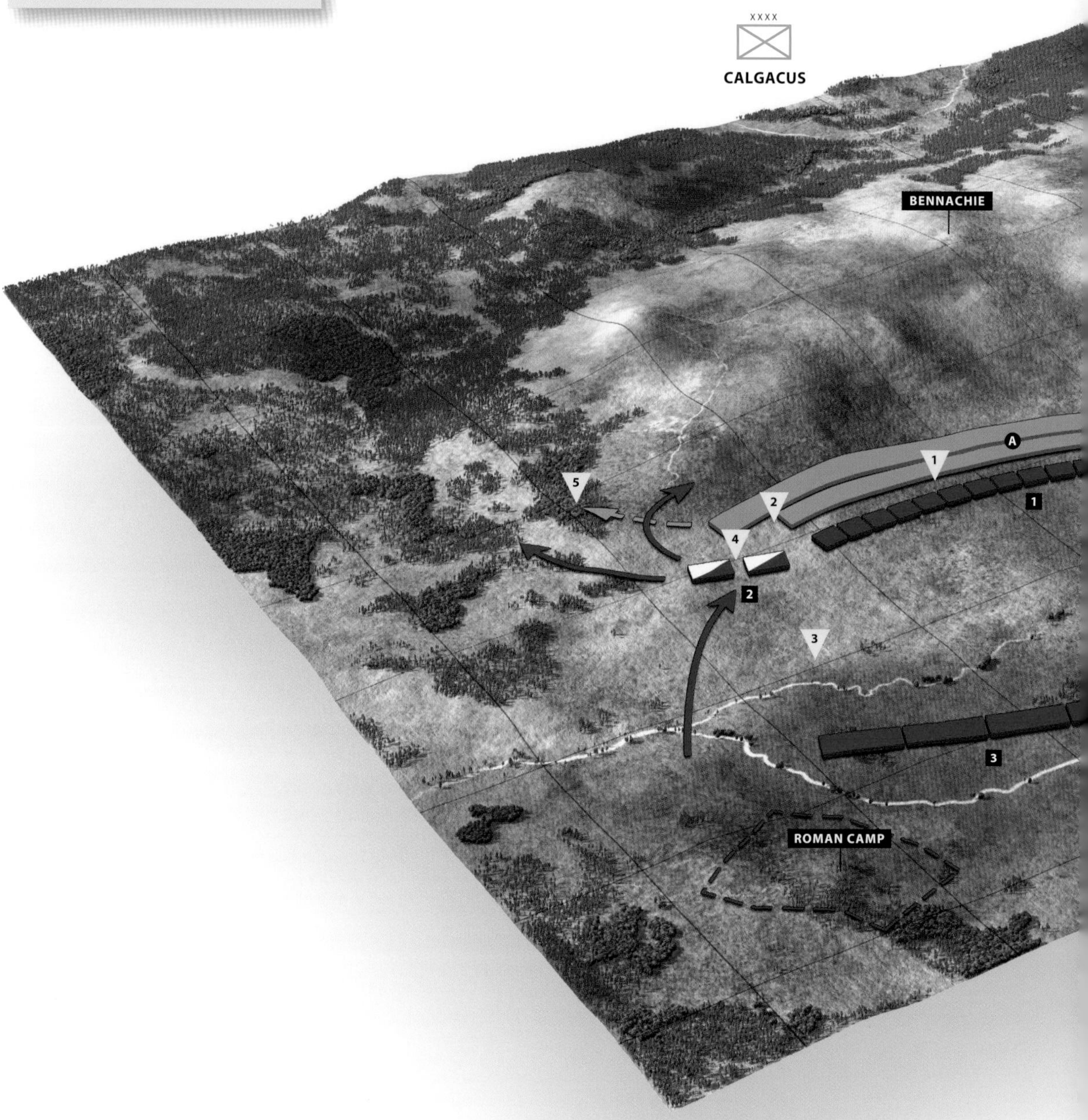
XXXX
CALGACUS
BENNACHIE
A
1
2
4
5
3
ROMAN CAMP

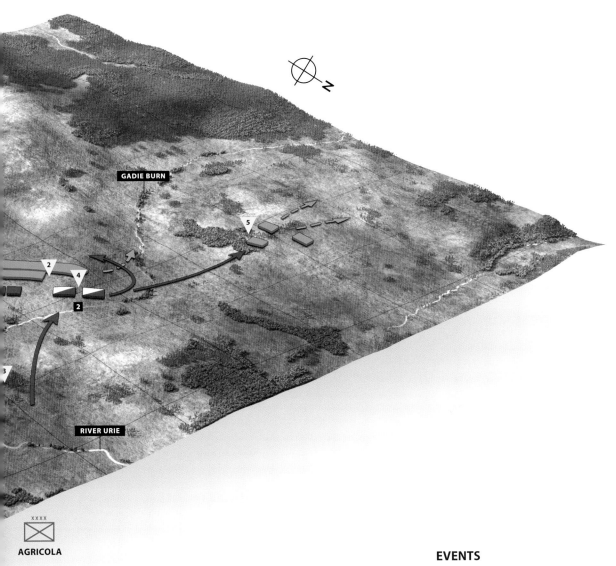

GADIE BURN

RIVER URIE

XXXX

AGRICOLA

EVENTS

1 The Roman auxiliary infantry continues to cut down the Caledonian ranks and steadily advances uphill.

2 The rear ranks of the Caledonian infantry descend to the plain and attempt to outflank the Roman line.

3 Agricola sends the Roman auxiliary cavalry reserve to intercept the Caledonian outflanking manoeuvre.

4 The Roman auxiliary cavalry reserve scatters the Caledonians, and panic sets in.

5 Having been enveloped, the Caledonian force disintegrates and the warbands flee individually. They are hunted down by the Roman cavalry reserve.

MONS GRAUPIUS, SEPTEMBER AD 83: THE CALEDONIAN ROUT.

The Roman infantry steadily crush the front ranks of the Caledonians. In response, their rear ranks attempt an outflanking manoeuvre, but it is foiled and their position collapses.

issuing from the west and south gateways of the Durno camp, and steadily making their way across the river Urie to take up their pre-arranged battle stations. 'While they were fired up and eager to charge, he deployed them like this, so that the auxiliary infantry, which numbered 8,000, made a firm centre to the battle line, while 3,000 cavalry were spread out on the flanks. The legions were stationed in front of the rampart, for it would be a great honour to win a battle without shedding Roman blood, but they were a reserve, if the auxiliaries were driven back' (Tac., *Agr.* 35.2).

The comment about conserving Roman blood was doubtless Tacitus' own interpretation of Agricola's strategy. Nothing in the military history of the times suggests that any Roman general would have thought in this way. The auxiliaries, just like the legionaries, were a valued part of a professional army; both had their particular strengths, and both had their weaknesses. Tacitus was perhaps naively seeking to add to his father-in-law's achievement, but instead he opened a debate that has continued ever since.

Scholars of previous generations were fooled into characterizing the *auxilia* as 'relatively cheap and expendable', the ancient equivalent of 'cannon fodder'. But, apart from Tacitus' comment here, there is no reason to believe that the auxiliary regiments were so undervalued. Previous commentators have been mystified as to why Agricola chose to compose his entire battle line solely from these units. After all, the great battles of the late Republic had been decided by the legions.

The first point, and one that is often missed, is that Agricola clearly could rely upon his auxiliary regiments to acquit themselves well. Indeed, Tacitus later points to their training and long military service (*Agr.* 36.1, quoted below). But, as we noted earlier, each branch of the Roman military service had its own particular strengths. So the second point to make is surely that, somehow, the auxiliaries were more suited to the task at hand.

This, too, has caused great perplexity amongst scholars, who were initially operating under the misapprehension that the *auxilia* were 'light infantry', in contrast to the 'heavy infantry' of the legions. Years of specialized study of the arms and armour of the Roman Army have demonstrated that many auxiliaries were equipped with armour that was equally as 'heavy' as the legionaries'. Certainly, the legions appear to have maintained their own peculiarly distinctive panoply, comprising, by and large, the so-called *lorica segmentata* cuirass, the rectangular, curved shield (*scutum*), and the uniquely designed javelin (*pilum*). But the auxiliary infantry, as depicted, for example, on Trajan's Column, wear the so-called *lorica hamata* mail shirt, which re-enactors agree can weigh half as much again as the segmented cuirass; and they are similarly helmeted and shod, and well-protected behind a flat, oval shield. The auxiliaries at Mons Graupius were not chosen on the grounds of weight.

Tacitus later makes it clear that a large proportion of the battle line, probably 3,000 of the 8,000 infantry, were Batavians, originally recruited from the marshy lands of the Rhine delta, and their Tungrian neighbours. If these regiments had begun recruiting amongst the Britons, they surely maintained the native traditions that made them such staunch warriors. These were the men who had spearheaded Agricola's attack on Anglesey in AD 77 (p. 38, above) by employing their river-crossing abilities. Now, the little river Urie at Durno bears no resemblance to the Menai Straits, so it cannot have been this particular skill that Agricola required. But this is a point to which we shall return.

THE OPENING STAGE

The Caledonians, too, were preparing for battle in a formation that took full advantage of Bennachie's topography, no doubt accompanied by the din of the war horns. 'The Britons' line was posted on high ground, both for show and to strike terror, in such a way that their front ranks were standing on the plain while the rest were rising up along the hill, as if in a curving formation. The charioteers filled the middle of the plain, making a din as they rode around' (Tac., *Agr.* 35.3).

As St Joseph observed, 'the northern face of Bennachie forms a great amphitheatre facing the camp at Durno', with a curving front of 3.5km (2 miles). The Caledonians swarmed over the hillside 'as if in a curving formation' (*acies convexa*), looking down on the plain below, where the scythed chariots rumbled and rattled backwards and forwards, in an attempt to intimidate the Roman lines. There were clearly many dozens of chariots, in order to fill the plain. Each one manoeuvring independently, as its chieftain driver sought to show off his skills, their main tactic was perhaps to run along the front ranks, where one scythed wheel could wreak some damage.

Classicist Stan Wolfson has even noticed a parallel in the poetry of Silius Italicus, who must have witnessed a reading of Tacitus' *Agricola* in Rome, just at the time when he was completing his great epic *Punica*. One of his couplets (quoted above, p. 31) was surely a nod to the battle of Mons Graupius. 'At this point, writes Tacitus, Agricola was anxious that the superior numbers of the enemy might attack his front and flanks at the same time. So he opened out his ranks, although the line would be rather extended and many were urging him to bring up the legions. But, with eager optimism and resolve in the face of difficulties, he sent away his horse and took up his position on foot in front of the standards (*vexilla*)' (Tac., *Agr.* 35.4).

Tacitus makes no explicit mention of how the Caledonian chariots were dealt with, but the fact that Agricola now ordered the ranks to be opened up may hint at his tactics. The use of scythed chariots, of course, recalls Alexander the Great's battle of Gaugamela (331 BC), in which Darius deployed 200 of these machines. The historian Arrian relates how 'the Macedonians had orders, wherever the chariots attacked, to break formation and let them through' (Arr., *Anab.* 3.14; cf. Curt., *Hist. Alex.* 4.15.14–17); once surrounded in this way, they could easily be neutralized.

Far from extending his frontage as a response to the large Caledonian army, it may have been in order to tackle the *covinni*. This, in turn, may have dictated Agricola's choice of auxiliaries for his battle line. The legions were traditionally drawn up in close order, presenting a wall of shields through which the short sword stabs could be delivered. Auxiliaries, on the other hand, were more naturally open-order troops, who could respond flexibly to the special problems posed by scythed chariots.

THE BATTLE IS JOINED

While Agricola took his stand, no doubt with his infantry guard (*pedites singulares*), at the front of the legionary line, his auxiliaries joined battle. In placing himself well to the rear, he was simply following the precepts of Onasander, who wrote a chapter on 'how the general himself should not enter battle' (Onas., *Strat.* 33). 'At its opening, the battle was joined at long range.

Roman cavalry re-enactor, from the Colchester Roman Society. He is shown slashing with the long sword (*spatha*) which was surely designed to give the horseman additional reach. His Connemara pony (aptly named Trajan), with its sturdy frame and characteristic agility, is thought to closely resemble the horses used by the Roman cavalry. (© Nigel Apperley)

With skill and persistence, using their massive swords and short shields, the Britons either parried the missiles of our men or warded them off, while hurling a great barrage of spears themselves' (Tac., *Agr.* 36.1).

While the Romans gradually brought the chariots under control, the battle itself had begun with the traditional shower of missiles. If these were not the auxiliaries' usual sturdy thrusting spears (*hastae*), they were perhaps some of the lighter projectile weapons that archaeologists often turn up on Roman military sites. Javelins of this kind could have been effective at ranges of up to 30m (100ft).

> Then Agricola exhorted the four Batavian and two Tungrian cohorts to fight hand to hand at sword's point. They had trained for this during their long military service, whereas it was awkward for the enemy with their small shields and enormous swords, for the swords of the Britons, having no points, were not designed for grappling and close-quarters fighting. So the Batavians rained blows indiscriminately, struck with their shield-bosses, and stabbed in the face. When they had cut down those posted on the plain, they started to push their battle-line up the hillside. The other cohorts, in eager competition, pressed forward to attack, and cut down the nearest of the enemy. In the haste of victory, a good many were left half-dead or untouched.
> Tac., *Agr.* 36.1–2

Agricola had clearly pinned his hopes on the Batavian and Tungrian soldiers. Whether they had thrown their spears or not, each man now drew his short sword, the classic *gladius*, and stormed into the massed ranks of the Caledonians. Even his plywood shield with its brass edging and iron boss became a weapon, smashing into the face of his opponent. This surge in activity gave encouragement to the other cohorts in the line, and gradually they pressed forwards, clambering over the bodies of the fallen, whether dead or not. It was perhaps during this phase of battle that Aulus Atticus, one of

Roman cavalry re-enactor, from the Colchester Roman Society. He carries the cavalryman's standard equipment of shield and thrusting spear. His cunningly designed saddle allows him to maintain his seat without the use of stirrups. (© Nigel Apperley)

the young prefects, was killed, no doubt relaying orders to his men. Tacitus says only that 'his youthful eagerness and spirited horse had carried him into the enemy's midst' (*Agr.* 37.6).

> Meanwhile, the troops of cavalry fled and the charioteers (*covinnarii*) became embroiled in the infantry battle. But, though they had at first created panic, they began to falter in the crowded ranks of the enemy and the uneven ground. Such fighting was most disadvantageous to our men, maintaining their exhausted battle line for such a long time while being jostled by the horses' flanks. And often, runaway chariots or terrified horses without their driver, as if guided by fear, dashed against them from the side or head on.
> Tac., *Agr.* 36.3 [2]

It is not clear where the Caledonian cavalry had been deployed, but they were presumably on the level ground at the foot of the hill, perhaps even amongst their infantry comrades. They were now routed. Perhaps their lack of a guiding hand made them disorganized. But the reason for their flight is not far to seek, for Agricola had posted 3,000 cavalry on his own flanks. It was presumably these horsemen who outclassed their Caledonian adversaries and led to the rout. That, after all, was the proper business of cavalry.

2. Readers familiar with previous translations of the *Agricola* will notice substantial differences in this passage. I am grateful to the perspicacity of Stan Wolfson for creating intelligible Latin from a manuscript that is badly corrupted at this point.

Meanwhile, the Caledonian chariots, the scythed *covinni*, had badly underperformed. *Covinni* in particular must have required fairly level terrain, to prevent the scythes from fouling in the ground. Unfortunately, the plain beneath Bennachie is by no means level. Equally, in order to employ their main feature to best advantage, the scythed wheels must keep turning. But it is clear that, by this stage in the battle, the Caledonian chariots were largely immobilized, having been swamped by the infantry mêlée. And as the Roman line trudged inexorably forwards, they were buffeted by stray chariot horses and impeded by the wreckage of the machines themselves.

AN OUTFLANKING ATTEMPT

All this time, the Romans had successfully restricted the fighting to the lower slopes of the mountain, drawing the waves of Caledonians down to them, and avoiding the boulder-strewn upper slopes. It was now time for the men stationed on these slopes, with a grandstand view of the battle, to join in. And again, Tacitus' account has a peculiar resonance with the situation at Bennachie, for these forces are said to have been 'stationed on the hilltops', of which Bennachie has, not one, but four.

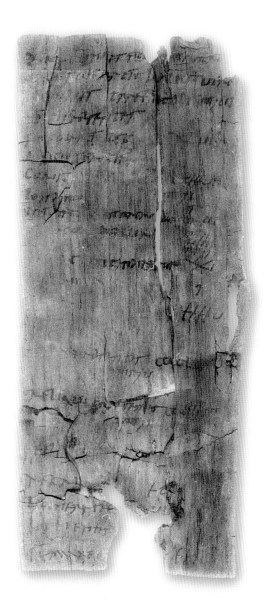

Writing tablet no. 154 from Vindolanda (*AE* 1991, 1162), a strength report of *cohors I Tungrorum*. The writing is faded and difficult to interpret with the untrained eye, but line 5 records the fact that 46 men had been seconded to the governor's bodyguard (*singulares leg(ati) xlvi*). Towards the bottom, the following totals have been deciphered: 'sick, 15; wounded, 6; suffering from eye disease, 10' (*aegri xv | volnerati vi | lippientes x*). (© Vindolanda Trust, by kind permission of Prof. A. R. Birley)

The Britons who had as yet taken no part in the battle because they were stationed on the hilltops, and who being unoccupied were regarding our small numbers with contempt, now began gradually to descend and to work their way round to the rear of the winning side. But Agricola, who had feared this very move, sent four regiments of cavalry, which had been reserved for the emergencies of war, to counter their arrival. And the more ferociously they charged, the more vigorously he repulsed them and dispersed them in flight.
Tac., *Agr.* 37.1

It was for just this kind of eventuality that Agricola had held back a cavalry reserve. These four squadrons were now released for the task of preventing the outflanking manoeuvre. By this time, the flower of the Caledonian forces had probably perished on the battlefield, so that only the lesser folk remained, perhaps poorly armed, almost certainly unarmoured. The nobles and their chariots had been destroyed, the cavalry had long since fled, and the auxiliary battle line continued their butchery, although they must by now have been exhausted.

The new arrivals on the battlefield were no match for galloping horsemen, particularly well-armed and armoured Roman horsemen. From the picture painted by Tacitus, it seems as if the Romans made sport with them, for no sooner had they hunted down and captured some, than they were executed when other victims came into view; and so the process was repeated.

Thus the stratagem of the Britons was turned against them. The cavalry regiments wheeled around from the front of the battle on the general's command and charged the rear ranks of the enemy. Then indeed a vast and grim spectacle filled the open plains: pursuing, cutting down, capturing, and slaughtering as new victims appeared. Each of the enemy acted on his own, as bands of armed men fled before inferior numbers and unarmed individuals wantonly charged and exposed themselves to certain death. Everywhere, there were weapons, bodies, mangled limbs, and blood-soaked earth.

Tac., *Agr.* 37.2–3

MOPPING UP

Once the Britons began to flee, a sure sign that the battle was over, Agricola called for his horse, in order to take an active part in the mopping-up operations. The fate of his Caledonian counterpart, Calgacus, remains unknown. Perhaps as one of the charioteer nobles, he had fallen early in the battle, allowing events to play out in their own way.

> And sometimes even amongst the vanquished there was fury and courage. For when they reached the woods, banding together and knowing the ground, they began to encircle the first incautious pursuers. So that this would not continue, Agricola, rushing everywhere, ordered strong, unencumbered (*expedita*) cohorts to act as a ring of huntsmen; where the forest was dense, some of the cavalry were to dismount, and where it was more open, the remainder were to sweep through, otherwise there might have been casualties from overconfidence.
>
> Tac., *Agr.* 37.4

Members of the Roman Military Research Society, re-enacting as Batavian auxiliaries, are shown rounding up Caledonian warriors using the technique that Tacitus describes as 'in the style of a ring of huntsmen' (*indaginis modo*). Like modern-day grouse beaters, they flushed out any resistance, driving them towards the dismounted cavalry.
(© Jim Bowers)

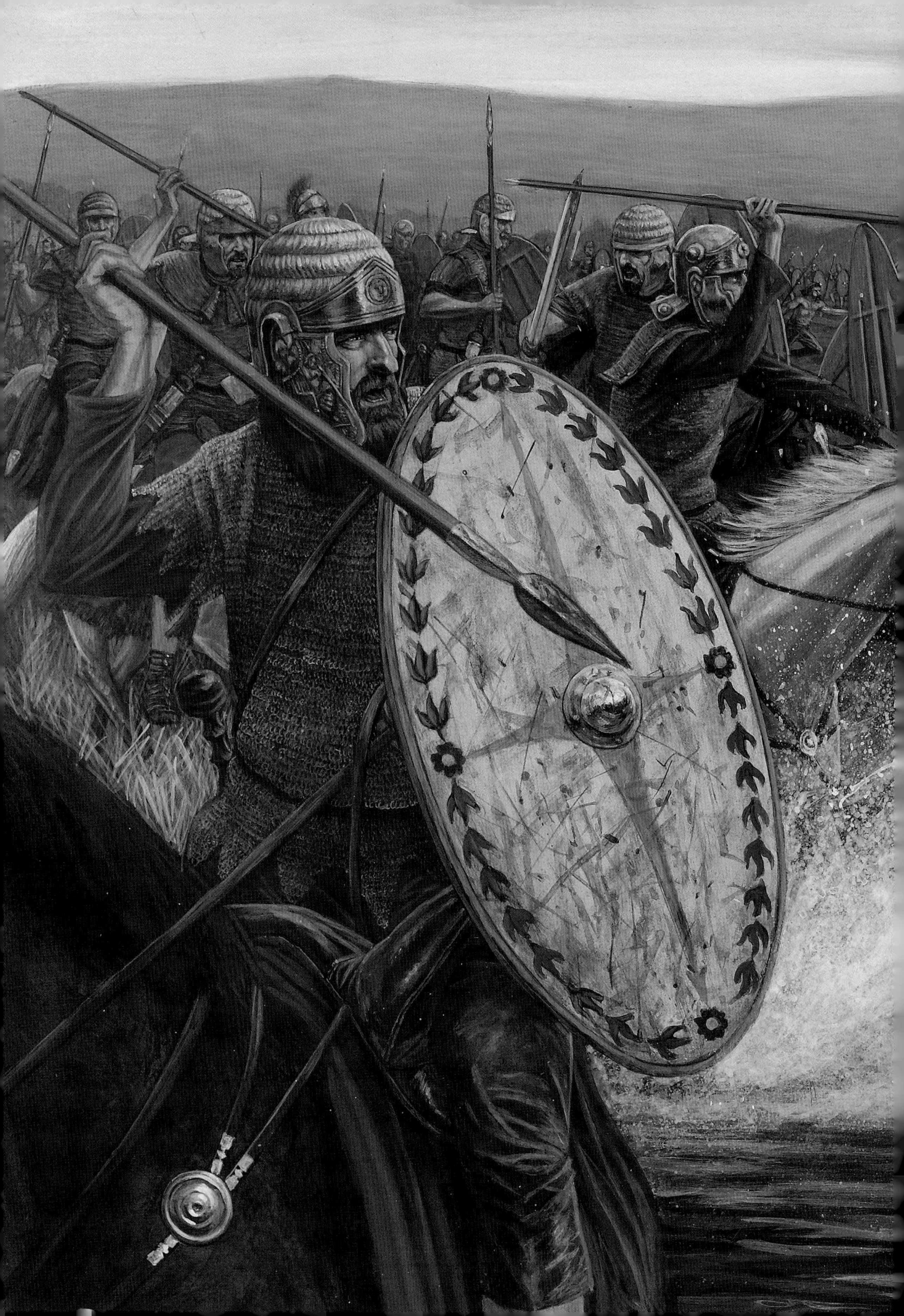

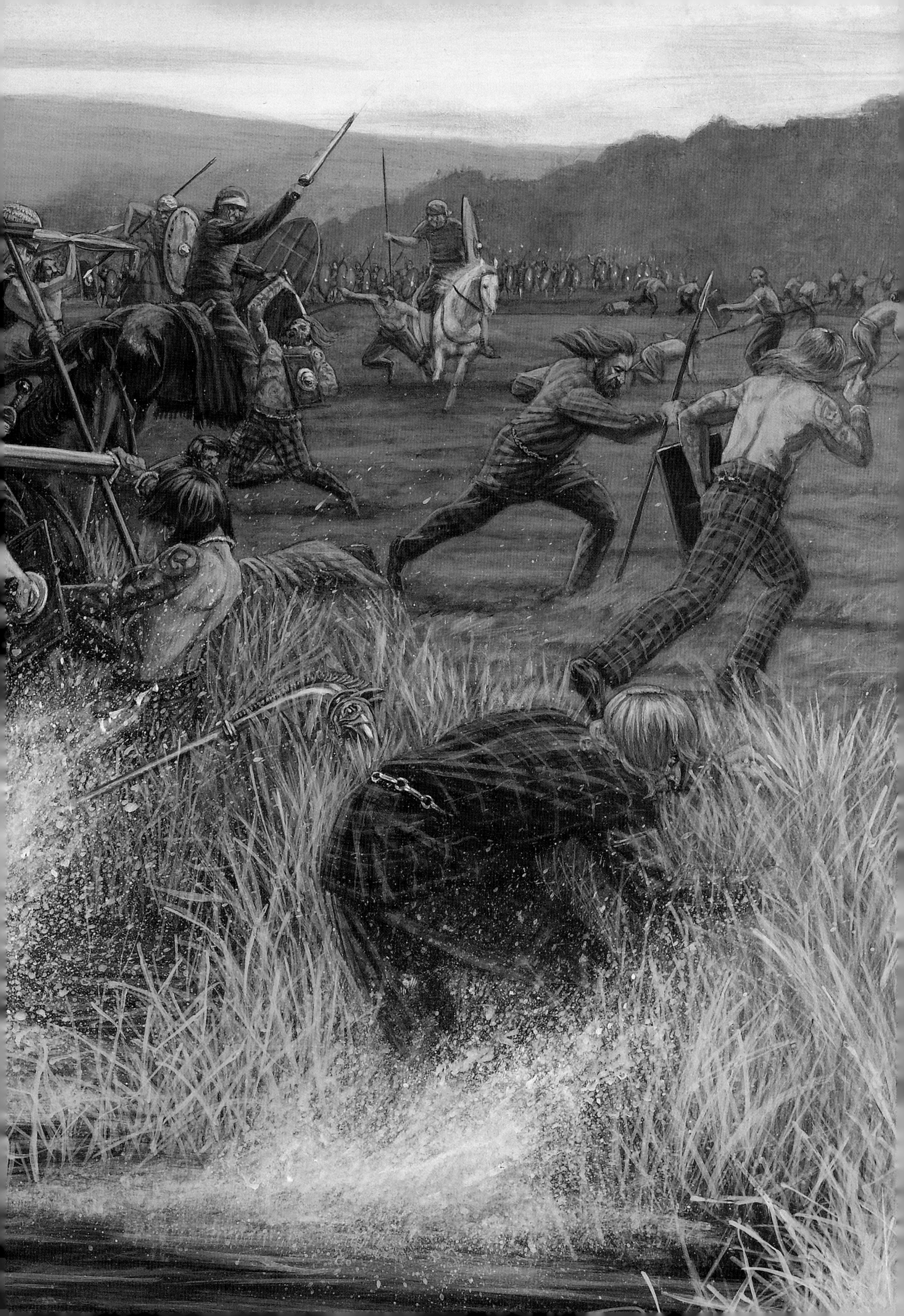

THE ROMAN CAVALRY MOP UP THE REMNANTS OF THE ROUTED CALEDONIANS (pp. 80–81)

The final phase of the battle was a cavalry action, as Agricola released the four squadrons that he had been holding in reserve. Out on the battlefield, the Caledonian cavalry (such as it was) and their chariotry had been defeated. But there was a danger that, with so many foot soldiers on the Caledonian side, successive waves of fresh adversaries would soon overwhelm the Roman auxiliary infantry, who had borne the brunt of the fighting and must, by now, have been nearing exhaustion.

However, the next wave of Caledonians adopted a different tactic. Tacitus believed that they were still contemptuous of the 8,000-strong Roman force, although they had surely been watching as the auxiliaries butchered and trampled over rank upon rank of their compatriots. So, in an evident attempt to turn the tables, fresh Caledonian warbands descended the mountain on the flanks of the battle; they planned to take the Roman line in the rear.

Agricola's cavalry scotched the Caledonian plan by breaking up their warbands and scattering the warriors across the plain. Unable to form up for battle, they fell easy prey to the Roman horsemen **(1)**, whose superior speed and vantage point gave them an enormous advantage over fleeing infantry.

Here, to judge from Tacitus' description, the cavalry made sport with their enemies, pursuing some until they were captured, but quickly dispatching them before riding off in pursuit of others. Even crossing the little Gadie Burn **(2)**, which flows along the valley below Bennachie, could give no protection, and jettisoning any heavy items, such as the carnyx **(3)** seen here, in a desperate attempt to gain speed, was futile in the face of galloping horsemen. Tacitus uses the imagery of the hunt, as a cordon of soldiers was deployed to flush the fleeing Caledonians from the woods where they sought sanctuary. Finally, Tacitus paints a gruesome picture of the field scattered with weapons, bodies and limbs.

Only darkness brought an end to the operations. Untold hundreds had fled without even joining battle. Tacitus claims that 10,000 Britons lay dead, as against only 360 Romans. The disparity seems astonishing. Certainly, it was usual to inflate the numbers of the enemy dead, in order to increase the importance of the victory. But long gone were the days when a Roman general had to slay 5,000 in order to qualify for a triumph; only the emperor now enjoyed such institutionalized adulation. Nevertheless, it does seem that, in ancient warfare, the losers generally suffered disproportionately large casualties, chiefly because of the Roman cavalry's ghastly efficiency in hunting down the fugitives. We may trust that the figure of 360 was reported back to Rome, and could be verified from the exhaustively documented strength returns that each regiment seems to have compiled on a regular basis.

'It was a cheerful night for the victors', writes Tacitus, 'with rejoicing and plunder' (*Agr.* 38.1). Battlefields always provided loot for the winners, but the process of picking over the corpses probably extended over several days. Wherever Roman battlefields have been investigated, they turn up only mundane items in any quantity. Flashy decorations and serviceable weapons will quickly have found new owners. 'The next day revealed the full scale of victory', Tacitus continues. 'Everywhere the silence of desolation, the lonely hills, homesteads smouldering in the distance, nobody spied by the scouts' (*Agr.* 38.2). The conquest was over.

We may well imagine that the camp at Durno was occupied for days or even weeks while the battlefield was cleared and the countryside swept. Its unusual size, surely too large even for Agricola's army, was perhaps to accommodate the special services which would be required only after a battle: a medical area for the care of the wounded; a blacksmithing area for the repair of broken and blunted equipment; a corral for the prisoners, if any survived after the cavalry had had their sport. Traditionally, there was a trophy to be erected, indicating ownership of the battlefield, and decent burial was arranged for the fallen Romans. For them, Tacitus supplies a fitting epitaph, for indeed 'it would not be inglorious to die at the very place where the world and nature end' (Tac., *Agr.* 33.6).

AFTERMATH

The summer was now over. In Roman terms, that meant late September. But, as the army prepared to return to their winter quarters, we encounter another passage of Tacitus that has caused great perplexity over the years; indeed, it has inspired scholars, not only to invent ingenious routes for Agricola's returning army, but also to create a completely new tribe for him to encounter. But here again, as with Tacitus' report of the fifth season (above, p. 46), the Latin text of the *Codex Aesinas* appears to be have been corrupted by earlier miscopying. The mistake has persuaded generations of scholars of the claim that 'Agricola led the army down into the territory of the Boresti', an otherwise unknown tribe.

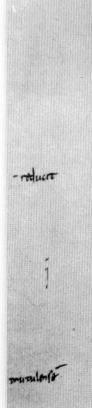

The relevant phrase in the *Codex Aesinas* (folio 63 verso: '*in finis borestorum exercitum deducit*') has only recently been corrected, despite the fact that it makes no sense. Why would Tacitus suddenly mention a new tribe, when up to this point he was content to refer only to 'the inhabitants of Caledonia'? Why did Ptolemy not register the Boresti amongst the many other peoples that he places north of the Forth–Clyde isthmus? Was he not seized by the fascination of the last tribe encountered by the Romans, a people who must have lived on the very edge of the world? Scholars have long complained about the dearth of geographical pointers in the *Agricola*, yet they were willing to add this mystery tribe, whom Ptolemy had unaccountably overlooked.

But some years ago, with an eagle eye for the telltale hints of textual corruption, classicist Stan Wolfson brilliantly emended the Latin to read '*in finis boreos totum exercitum deducit*', consigning the Boresti, in one fell swoop, to oblivion. The new reading makes perfect sense, as Agricola 'led his entire army down into the northern extremities' (*Agr.* 38.2). 'There he took hostages', continues Tacitus, recalling the usual procedure when the Romans had sufficiently overawed a neighbouring people, 'and instructed the prefect of the fleet to sail round Britain' (*Agr.* 38.3). We can well imagine him, making his way down to the Moray Firth and beyond, 'marching unhurriedly so that the courage of the newly conquered peoples was drained by his leisurely progress' (*Agr.* 38.3), and finally settling his men in their forts for the winter. The Carlisle writing tablets show that there were men of *XX Valeria Victrix* at Carlisle in November AD 83 (*AE* 1992, 1139), perhaps having returned from Mons Graupius.

CIRCUMNAVIGATION

We have seen that the poet Statius, writing around a decade after the battle of Mons Graupius, wrote a poem flattering Crispinus, the son of Vettius Bolanus (above, p. 11). In it, he claims that the young man's father, 'carrying out his orders, reached Thule that bars the western waves, where Hyperion is ever weary' (*Silv.* 5.2.53-56). The basis of this claim is difficult to discern, as it is highly unlikely that Bolanus ever had the opportunity to explore the northern waters. But Statius is fond of maritime images, and clearly, the idea of this northernmost island, *ultima Thule* (which is surely to be located amongst the Shetland Isles), was current at Rome at the very time that Tacitus was composing the *Agricola*.

If Statius, as an epic poet, may be forgiven for his hyperbole, it may well have spurred Tacitus to set down in writing his own version of events. For it seems that the voyage of the *classis Britannica* ('British fleet') to Shetland properly belonged, not to Bolanus, but to Agricola. 'It was then, for the first time', Tacitus emphasizes, 'that a Roman fleet, circumnavigating this coast of the remotest sea, established that Britain was an island' (*Agr.* 10.4). Having subjugated the Orkneys, Agricola's fleet sailed on. 'And Thule was closely examined because they had been commanded to go this far, but winter was approaching' (Tac., *Agr.* 10.4). At any rate, the historian Cassius Dio knew that Britain had been proven to be an island during the governorship, not of Bolanus, but of Agricola (Cass. Dio 39.50.4).

The voyage was apparently shared by a certain Demetrius, a grammarian (*grammaticus*) from Tarsus, who observed that there were many uninhabited islands and one which supported a religious community (Plut., *Moral.* 410A, 419E). He set up a pair of silvered bronze plates at York, one of them dedicated, appropriately, 'To Ocean and Tethys' (*RIB* 663). It has been observed that Alexander the Great worshipped the same deities on the Indus in 325 BC (Diod. Sic. 17.104), at the eastern edge of the world. How appropriate that they should likewise be invoked at its northern edge.

Having dispensed with the imaginary Boresti, we must now excise one last geographical fiction from the story of Mons Graupius, for scholars have long laboured under the misapprehension that Agricola's fleet wintered in the 'Trucculensian harbour' (*portus Trucculensis*), an otherwise unknown location. Scholars have searched far and wide for a suitable harbour, without success. But again, as we have now seen twice before, the text of the *Codex Aesinas* is at fault.

Our received text reads '*trucculensem portum tenuit*' (*Codex Aesinas*, folio 63 verso), but again, as in the case of Cogidubnus (illustration on p. 10), the 9th-century copyist has made a marginal note. It seems that he had found an alternative, even preferable, reading for the first word: '*trutulensem*'. Stan Wolfson has ingeniously improved the Latin even further, suggesting

OPPOSITE
Extract from the *Codex Aesinas*, folio 63 verso (left-hand column). On lines 8–9 can be seen the spurious reference to the Boresti (*in finis bores totum* can be read, leading to the explanation suggested in the main text). Further down (lines 18–19) can be seen the equally spurious reference to the Trucculensian harbour, but here the scribe has suggested his own correction in the margin, writing *trutulensem* (and leading to the explanation in the main text). (Author's collection)

that it ought to read '*trux Thulensem portum tenuit*', thus incorporating a reference to Thule. (The adjective *trux* must here refer to the Roman fleet's 'ruthless' reputation.)

So, instead of Agricola's fleet reaching an unheard-of port, which would have meant nothing to Tacitus' audience at Rome, 'the fleet, with its ruthlessness enhanced by rumour and favourable weather, reached Shetland harbour' (*Agr.* 38.5). Now, at last, Roman arms had truly reached the furthest edge of the world.

EVENTS AT ROME

Some time in the summer of AD 83, certainly by September, Domitian added the name *Germanicus* ('conqueror of Germany') to his collection of titles, advertising his conquest of the Chatti. This was probably also the occasion of his fourth imperatorial acclamation, although by a quirk of fate *IMP IV* is not recorded on any known inscriptions. (Sooner or later, a diploma will turn up confirming Domitian's precise list of titles in the summer of AD 83.)

Tacitus took a very dim view of Domitian's Chattan war and his subsequent triumph. In later years, he wrote that 'the Germans were more triumphed over than conquered' (*Germ.* 37), an opinion apparently shared by Cassius Dio, who wrote that 'he made a campaign into Germany and returned without having so much as seen any hostilities anywhere' (Dio 67.4.1), and Tacitus' friend Pliny made a similar allusion in his Panegyric addressed to the Emperor Trajan, by contrasting the new emperor's well-deserved triumph with previous 'images of a sham victory' (Plin., *Pan.* 16).

News of Agricola's victory at Mons Graupius must have travelled to Rome during the winter of AD 83, no doubt by laurelled dispatch (*laureata*). Meanwhile, determined to outdo his father and illustrious brother, Domitian took a fifth, sixth and seventh imperatorial acclamation during AD 84, one of which must surely relate to Mons Graupius. In the following years, the acclamations came thick and fast, so that Domitian entered AD 87 as *IMP XIV*, and by the time of his death on 18 September AD 96, he was *IMP XXII*.

Although only the emperor could celebrate a triumph, Agricola was awarded 'triumphal decorations' (*ornamenta triumphalia*) and the honour of a public statue (Tac., *Agr.* 40.1). For many men, this would have been their crowning achievement. But Tacitus expected his father-in-law to secure further employment, perhaps as governor of Syria, a consular province like Britain. In fact, it was highly unusual for men to hold more than one such command. One of the very few who did so, Titus Atilius Rufus, had just died in office governing Syria, so this may have been preying on Tacitus' mind. He hoped also for the proconsulship of Africa or Asia, the two plum senatorial provinces, governed for one year at a time. But competition for these was fierce, and many were well into their 50s before securing election to one or the other.

Agricola was dead by the age of 53, perhaps through illness. His British conquests were never consolidated, as troops were increasingly siphoned off to the troubled Danube frontier. At around this time, a trooper of the *ala Tampiana*, for example, died at Carnuntum, the great military base on the Danube; he was serving in a *vexillatio Britannica* ('British detachment') that was no doubt involved in Domitian's Sarmatian war. All of *II Adiutrix* had been withdrawn, too. Britain was now a low priority. By AD 90 at the latest, Caledonia had been left to the Caledonians.

THE HISTORICAL TRUTH

When he published his commentary to the *Agricola* in 1967, Ogilvie was in no doubt that 'the details of the battle are authentic. It is in no sense an imaginary battle modelled on a famous earlier engagement such as Pharsalus', as one sceptic had claimed. However, academic study is often cyclical: old theories fall out of favour, and new ones become popular, before being discarded in turn. Lately, it has become fashionable to doubt the veracity of Tacitus' account. Indeed, Martin Henig, a specialist in ancient art, has gone so far as to doubt whether the battle of Mons Graupius ever occurred. He claims that 'the notion of a pitched battle in mountainous terrain seems inherently implausible' (*British Archaeology* 37, 1998). But, of course, Tacitus tells us that the battle took place 'on the flat ground' (*Agr.* 35.3) at the foot of the mountain; there is nothing implausible about that.

Then, having claimed that 'no such battle ever took place', he absurdly accuses Agricola of embroidering the details of the fighting, on the grounds that 'a battle in such a place has few witnesses'. But, of course, he is wrong. On the Roman side, unfortunately the only side in a position to pass judgement on Tacitus' description, there were thousands of witnesses. Furthermore, we have seen that the emperor was usually kept well informed of events on the frontiers, even in distant Britain. And, although Agricola would have filed an official report at the close of the campaign, he was not the emperor's only representative in the province. In AD 61, for example, when Nero's general Suetonius Paullinus was crushing the Boudiccan revolt with fire and steel, the equestrian procurator, Julius Classicianus, saw fit to send an unfavourable report to Nero (Tac., *Ann.* 14.38). Agricola had his own equestrian procurator with the power to make or break his career.

In the field of foreign affairs, it seems there were always plenty of witnesses. Fifteen years after the battle of Mons Graupius, when Tacitus aired his version of events, many of Agricola's senatorial officers would have been important men in Rome. For example, Roscius Aelianus, who served as a tribune in Agricola's army, was destined to hold the consulship in AD 100; the other tribunes, whose names we do not know, will have seen their careers progress in a similar way. By the same token, Agricola's legionary legates will have progressed to other official positions. Gaius Caristanius Fronto, who commanded *VIIII Hispana* in the early years of Agricola's governorship, went on to hold the consulship in AD 90 (*ILS* 9485); he and his colleagues in command of the other legions could certainly testify to Agricola's character, and their successors, whose names remain unknown to us, would have witnessed the battle of Mons Graupius.

Are we to suppose that such men colluded in Tacitus' falsification of history? The idea seems preposterous. Henig rests his case on the lack of material evidence, but few other ancient battles are known archaeologically, and it is a fundamental maxim that absence of evidence does not constitute evidence of absence. Simply because archaeologists have not yet found evidence on the ground, the mass grave of the Caledonian dead, the scatter of discarded and broken equipment, this does not mean that such evidence is not waiting to be found one day.

Henig subsequently recanted his denial of Mons Graupius, conceding that there was 'a skirmish in the hills' (*British Archaeology* 41, 1999). But there are others who contend that Tacitus wrote fiction. This is far too simplistic a verdict on the *Agricola*. It is true that Tacitus' purpose was to eulogize his father-in-law,

Roman Scotland, *c.* AD 86

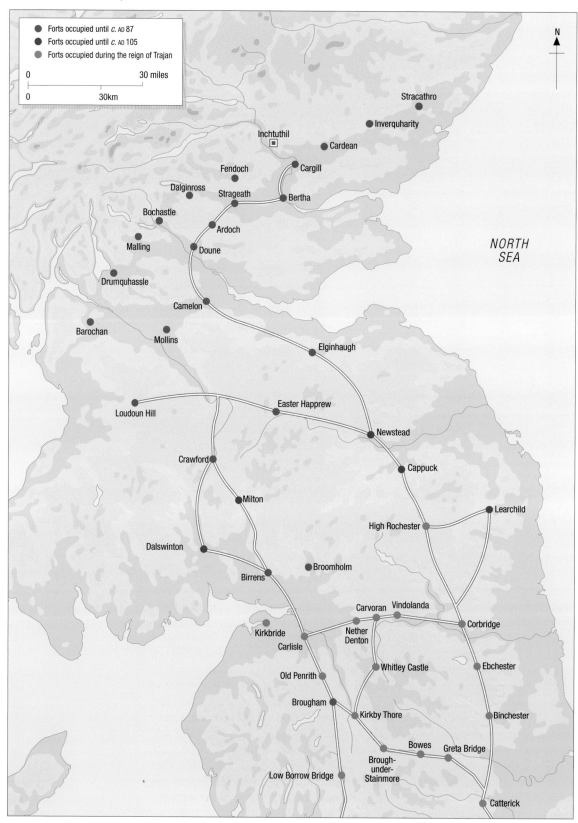

Forts occupied until *c.* AD 87
Forts occupied until *c.* AD 105
Forts occupied during the reign of Trajan

0 ——————————— 30 miles
0 ——————————— 30km

N

NORTH
SEA

Stracathro
Inverquharity
Inchtuthil
Cardean
Fendoch
Cargill
Dalginross
Strageath
Bertha
Bochastle
Ardoch
Malling
Doune
Drumquhassle
Camelon
Barochan
Mollins
Elginhaugh
Easter Happrew
Loudoun Hill
Newstead
Crawford
Cappuck
Milton
Learchild
High Rochester
Dalswinton
Broomholm
Birrens
Carvoran
Vindolanda
Corbridge
Kirkbride
Nether
Denton
Carlisle
Whitley Castle
Ebchester
Old Penrith
Brougham
Kirkby Thore
Binchester
Bowes
Greta Bridge
Brough-
under-
Stainmore
Low Borrow Bridge
Catterick

Outer face of a diploma (*CIL* 16, 30 = *ILS* 1997) found at Carnuntum. It was issued to a veteran of the Pannonian army on 3 September AD 84 (the formula *a(nte) d(iem) III Nonas Sept(embres) C(aio) Tullio Capitone Pomponiano Firmo C(aio) Cornelio Gallicano co(n)s(ulibus)* gives the date), and is the first official document to name the Emperor Domitian as *Germanicus* ('Conqueror of Germany'). (© Hungarian National Museum, Budapest. Photo: A. Dabasi)

not to record bare facts. Professor J. G. C. Anderson, an Oxford classicist and Tacitus scholar of the 1920s, was well aware that 'everything, or nearly everything, serves in one way or another to set in relief the hero's character and achievements'. But, as another Tacitean scholar, M. P. Charlesworth, long ago observed, 'his accuracy, though severely probed by modern criticism, can rarely be impugned'.

It is foolish, for example, to brand the primary historian of the early empire a liar, simply on the say-so of the Christian apologist Tertullian. Writing a century after Tacitus, Tertullian condemned his predecessor's vague knowledge of the early Christian church, calling him 'that blurter of falsehoods' (*Apol.* 16.1) for claiming that the Jews worshipped an ass's head (Tac., *Hist.* 5.3). Quite apart from the fact that Tacitus' ignorance of a minority eastern religion in a province that he never visited has absolutely no relevance to his knowledge of contemporary affairs in Britain, he was simply following the received wisdom of the day, in repeating a story also found in Plutarch and others.

And, as Ogilvie himself realized, the fact that Tacitus' style has echoes of earlier authors does not mean that his content is lifted from their work. It is one thing to identify literary borrowings from earlier writers (as, for example, when he describes the older Caledonian warriors, whose 'old age was still fresh and green', a quotation from the poet Vergil). Or to suggest that he has exaggerated Agricola's achievements (as, for example, when he claims that 'no fort established by Agricola was ever taken by enemy assault'). But it is quite another thing to accuse him of wholesale mendacity.

We have seen that Tacitus might even have had first-hand experience of the army in Britain during the years AD 77–79. If so, it is at least possible that the historian accompanied his father-in-law as far as the river Tay, and heard with his own ears the veterans who 'commented that no other general selected suitable sites more wisely' (Tac., *Agr.* 22.2). If, as seems likely, his absence from Rome in the years running up to AD 93 was on account of his service as a legionary legate, we may further speculate that his legion lay on the Rhine. It is interesting to note that the governor of Upper Germany during these years was Lucius Javolenus Priscus, who had served as *iuridicus* in Britain around AD 84, some years after Salvius Liberalis. If we have correctly located Tacitus in the early AD 90s, he would have been ideally placed to gather more detailed information on Britain.

THE BATTLEFIELD TODAY

Despite these arguments, there may still be some who believe that the battle of Mons Graupius existed only in the mind of Tacitus, or at least only in the mind of Agricola. Even so, it would still be a valuable exercise to study Tacitus' description, as it would have needed to convince his Roman readers and, as such, may be held up as an authentic reconstruction of Roman combat.

However, there are rather more who believe that there is a Roman battlefield waiting to be discovered somewhere in Scotland. Throughout this book, I have assumed that the battle took place on the slopes of Bennachie, near Inverurie in Aberdeenshire. In this, I have followed the interpretation of the late Professor Kenneth St Joseph, who believed that the site satisfied two out of three necessary conditions: firstly, that there should be a suitable gathering ground for the Caledonian host; secondly, that there should be a Roman camp whose size and position did not conflict with Tacitus' narrative; and thirdly, that there should be some evidence that a battle actually took place.

The entrance to the Archaeolink Prehistory Park, near Inverurie (Aberdeenshire). The mountain of Bennachie can be seen in the background. (Author's collection)

Critics may carp that St Joseph's third criterion has not been met, and no material evidence of the battle has ever been found. There are none of the hobnails or sling bullets that turn up in large quantities, for example, at Andagoste and Baecula (Spain); nor are there any of the bent and blunted weapons familiar, for example, from Alesia (France). But no material evidence of the battle has ever been sought, either. And it should be remembered that none of the other candidates (conveniently listed by Gordon Maxwell in *A Battle Lost*) can show this kind of evidence either. It is as true today as it was 30 years ago, when St Joseph himself wrote:

> Readers will form their own judgement on the identification of this elusive hill. A camp of unique size, in significant juxtaposition to a highly distinctive mountain that it partly outflanks; ample space afforded for the massing of large native forces; ground suited to the tactics of the battle; such details of terrain as the concave hill-slopes and the mountain mass with its distinct peaks; interruption of the normal spacing of the large Roman camps by the position at Durno;... these considerations, taken individually, might be judged of little account, but the chances are overwhelmingly against there being in some other locality the significant association which is so evident at Durno-Bennachie.
> J. K. St Joseph, *Britannia* 9, 1978, pp. 286–877

The ideal spot for readers to begin making their own judgement is at the Archaeolink Prehistory Park, near the village of Oyne, just off the A96 Inverurie–Huntly road. (Rail travellers can alight at Insch and take the connecting bus to Oyne. Full information can be accessed from the official web site: http://www.archaeolink.co.uk) Besides its location between Bennachie and Durno, this living history park has its own visitor attractions, including a reconstructed Iron Age roundhouse and a section of Roman rampart and ditch.

BIBLIOGRAPHY

Birley, A. R., Tacitus, *Agricola and Germany* Oxford University Press: Oxford, 1999

——, 'Britain 71–105: Advance and retrenchment', L. De Ligt, E. A. Hemelrijk, and H.W. Singor (eds.), *Roman Rule and Civic Life: Local and Regional Perspectives* Gieben: Amsterdam, 2004

Burn, A. R., *Agricola and Roman Britain* English Universities Press: London, 1953

Breeze, A., 'Philology on Tacitus's Graupian Hill and Trucculan Harbour', *Proceedings of the Society of Antiquaries of Scotland* 132 (2002), 305–11

Campbell, D. B., 'The consulship of Agricola', *Zeitschrift für Papyrologie und Epigraphik* 63 (1986), 197–200

Maxwell, G. S., *The Romans in Scotland* Mercat Press: Edinburgh, 1989

——, *A Battle Lost. Romans and Caledonians at Mons Graupius* Edinburgh University Press: Edinburgh, 1990

Ogilvie, R. M., and Richmond, I. A. (eds.), *Cornelii Taciti De Vita Agricolae* Clarendon Press: Oxford, 1967

Raepsaet-Charlier, M.-T., 'Cn. Iulius Agricola: mise au point prosopographique', *Aufstieg und Niedergang der römischen Welt* II.33.3 (1991), 1807–57

St Joseph, J. K., 'The camp at Durno, Aberdeenshire, and the site of Mons Graupius', *Britannia* 9 (1978), 271–87

Strobel, K., 'Nochmals zur Datierung der Schlacht am Mons Graupius', *Historia* 36 (1987), 198–212

Wolfson, S., Tacitus, Thule and Caledonia (2002: http://myweb.tiscali.co.uk/fartherlands)

ABBREVIATIONS

AE	*L'Année épigraphique* (http://www.anneeepigraphique.msh-paris.fr)
CIL	*Corpus Inscriptionum Latinarum* (http://cil.bbaw.de)
ILS	H. Dessau (ed.), *Inscriptiones Latinae Selectae* (Berlin, 1892–1916)
RGDA	*Res Gestae Divi Augusti* (*Achievements of the Divine Augustus*)
RIB	R. G. Collingwood & R. P. Wright (eds.), *The Roman Inscriptions of Britain* (Oxford, 1965)
Tab. Luguval.	*Tabulae Luguvalienses* (*The Carlisle writing tablets*), published n *Britannia* 29 (1998), 31–84
Tab. Vindol.	*Tabulae Vindolandenses* (*The Vindolanda writing tablets*), published in: A. K. Bowman & J. D. Thomas, *The Vindolanda Writing Tablets* (London, 1994)
Arrian, *Anab.*	Arrian, *Anabasis Alexandri* (*The campaigns of Alexander*)
Caes., *BCiv.*	Caesar, *Bellum civile* (*The Civil War*)
Caes., *BGall.*	Caesar, *Bellum Gallicum* (*The Gallic War*)
Cic., *Epist. ad Att.*	Cicero, *Epistulae ad Atticum* (*Letters to Atticus*)
Cic., *Epist. ad fam.*	Cicero, *Epistulae ad familiares* (*Letters to his friends*)
Curt., *Hist. Alex.*	Quintus Curtius Rufus, *Historiae Alexandri* (*The history of Alexander*)
Cass. Dio	Cassius Dio (*Roman History*)
Diod. Sic., *Bibl. hist.*	Diodorus Siculus, *Bibliotheca historica* (*Universal history*)
Frontin., *Strat.*	Frontinus, *Strategemata* (*Stratagems*)
Hyg., *De mun. castr.*	Hyginus, *De munitionibus castrorum* (*On fortifying a camp*)
Jos., *Bell. Jud.*	Josephus, *Bellum Judaicum* (*The Jewish War*)
Luc., *BCiv.*	Lucan, *Bellum civile* (*The Civil War*, also known as *Pharsalia*)
Mart., *Epig.*	Martial, *Epigrammata* (*Epigrams*)
Mela	Pomponius Mela, *De situ orbis libri III* (*Description of the world*)
Onas., *Strat.*	Onasander, *Strategikos* (*The General*)
Ovid, *Fast.*	Ovid, *Fasti* (*Festivals*)
Plb.	Polybius (*Histories*)
Plin., *Nat. Hist.*	Pliny (the elder), *Naturalis historia* (*Natural History*)
Plin., *Pan.*	Pliny (the younger), *Panegyricus Traiani* (*In praise of Trajan*)
Plut., *Moral.*	Plutarch, *Moralia* (*Morals*)
Ptol., *Geog.*	Ptolemy, *Geographia* (*The Geography*)
Sen., *Apoc.*	Seneca (the younger), *Apocolocyntosis* (*The pumpkinification of the emperor Claudius*)
Sil. Ital., *Pun.*	Silius Italicus, *Punica* (*The Punic War*)
Stat., *Silv.*	Statius, *Silvae* (*Woodlands*)
Strabo, *Geog.*	Strabo, *Geographia* (*The Geography*)
Suet., *Calig.*	Suetonius, *Caligula* ('Caligula' from the *Twelve Caesars*)
Suet., *Div. Claud.*	Suetonius, *Divus Claudius* ('The deified Claudius' from the *Twelve Caesars*)
Suet., *Div. Vesp.*	Suetonius, *Divus Vespasianus* ('The deified Vespasian' from the *Twelve Caesars*)
Tac., *Ann.*	Tacitus, *Annales* (*The Annals*)
Tac., *Agr.*	Tacitus, *De vita Iulii Agricolae* (*The Agricola*)
Tac., *Germ.*	Tacitus, *Germania* (*On Germany*)
Tac., *Hist.*	Tacitus, *Historiae* (*The Histories*)
Tert., *Apol.*	Tertullian, *Apologeticus* (*Apology for the Christians*)
Veg., *De re mil.*	Vegetius, *De re militari* (*On military matters*, also known as *Epitoma rei militaris*)

INDEX

Numbers in **bold** refer to plates, maps and illustrations.